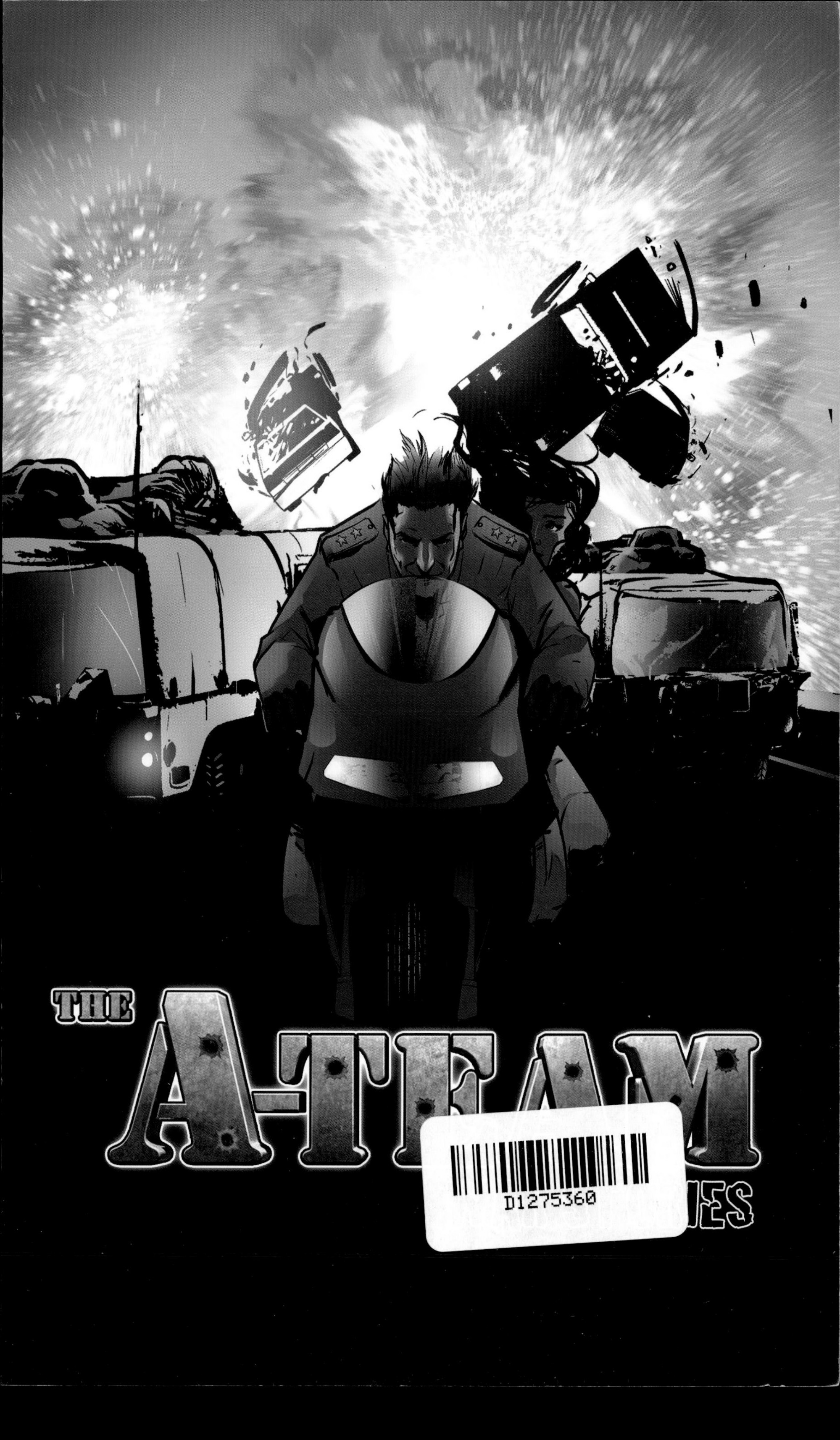
THE
A-TEAM

THE A-TEAM
WAR STORIES

All stories written by

CHUCK DIXON AND ERIK BURNHAM

HANNIBAL
Art by
HUGO PETRUS
Colors by
GERMAN TORRES

B.A.
Art by
CASEY MALONEY
Colors by
JOSH PEREZ

FACE
Art by
ALBERTO MURIEL
Colors by
GERRY KISSELL

MURDOCK
Art by
GUIU VILANOVA
Colors by
RUBEN CUBILES

Lettering and Collection design by
NEIL UYETAKE
Original series edits by
TOM WALTZ
Collection edits by
JUSTIN EISINGER AND MARIAH HUEHNER
Covert art by
MICHAEL GAYDOS

 Special thanks to Debbie Olshan and Nicole Spiegel for their invaluable assistance.
www.IDWpublishing.com   ISBN: 978-1-60010-727-6   13 12 11 10   1 2 3 4

Operations: Ted Adams, Chief Executive Officer • Greg Goldstein, Chief Operating Officer • Matthew Ruzicka, CPA, Chief Financial Officer • Alan Payne, VP of Sales • Lorelei Bunjes, Dir. of Digital Services • AnnaMaria White, Marketing & PR Manager • Marci Hubbard, Executive Assistant • Alonzo Simon, Shipping Manager • Angela Loggins, Staff Accountant • Editorial: Chris Ryall, Publisher/Editor-in-Chief • Scott Dunbier, Editor, Special Projects • Andy Schmidt, Senior Editor • Bob Schreck, Senior Editor • Justin Eisinger, Editor • Kris Oprisko, Editor/Foreign Lic. • Denton J. Tipton, Editor • Tom Waltz, Editor • Mariah Huehner, Associate Editor • Carlos Guzman, Editorial Assistant • Design: Robbie Robbins, EVP/Sr. Graphic Artist • Neil Uyetake, Art Director • Chris Mowry, Graphic Artist • Amauri Osorio, Graphic Artist • Gilberto Lazcano, Production Assistant • Shawn Lee, Production Assistant

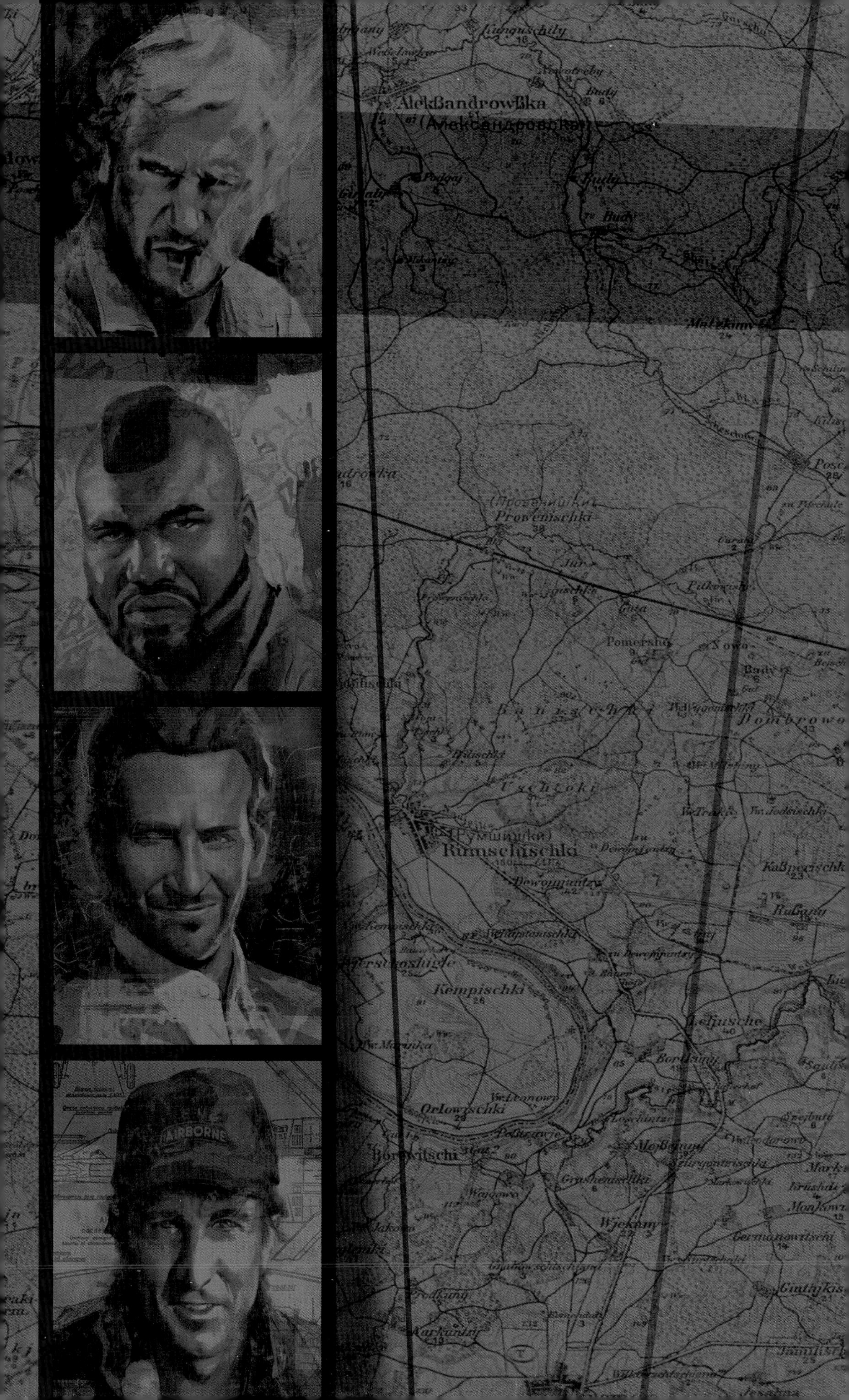

Alekßandrowßka
Prowenischki
Pomerschu
Nowo
Budy
Dombrowo
Rumschischki
Kempischki
Orlowschki
Borowitschi
Germanowitschi
AIRBORNE

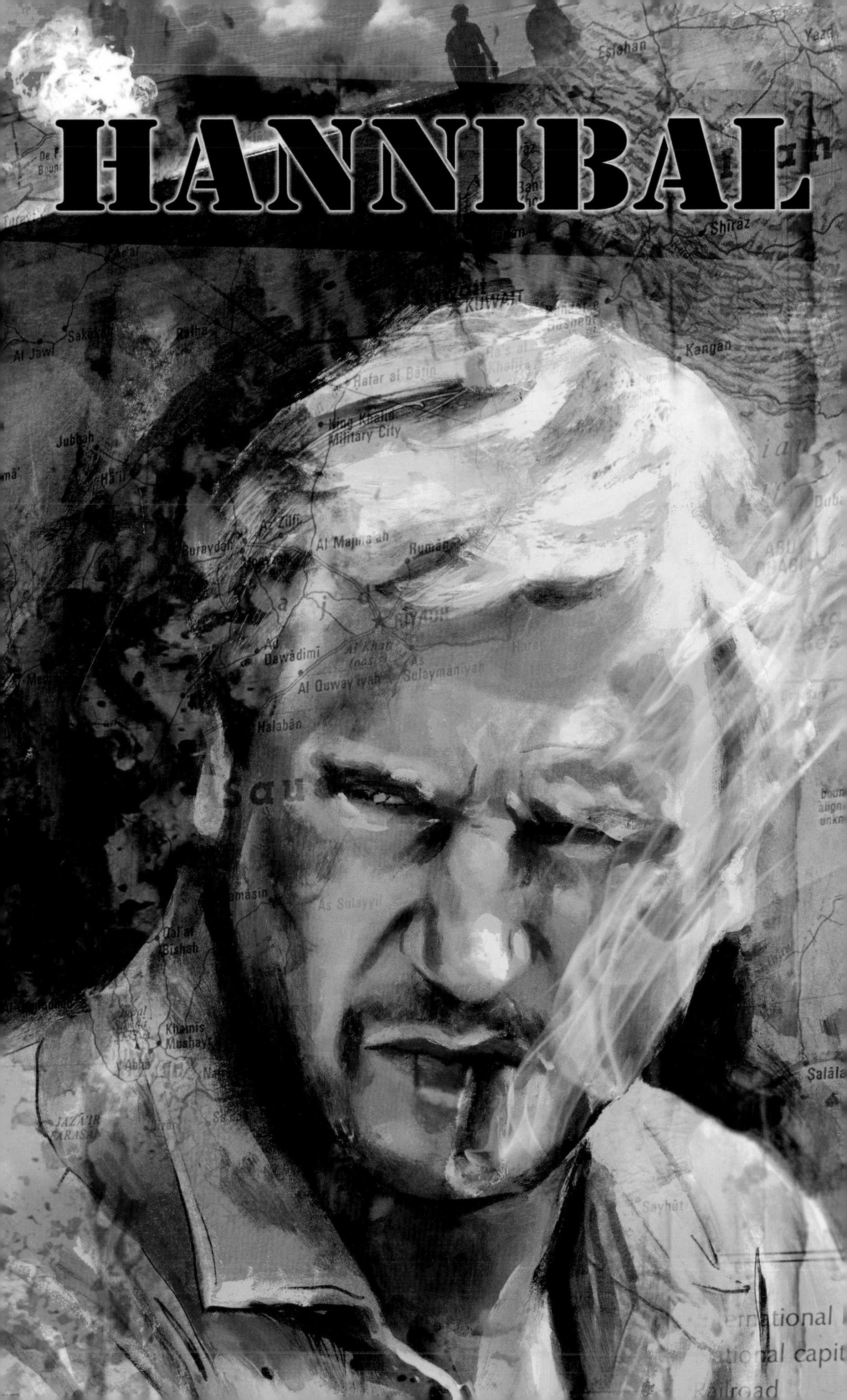

HANNIBAL
Esfahan
Yazd
Shiraz
Kangan
Sakakah
Rafha
Al Jawf
Hafar al Batin
King Khalid Military City
Jubbah
Ha'il
Buraydah
Al Majma'ah
Rumah
Ad Dawadimi
Al Quway'iyah
As Sulaymaniyah
Halaban
As Sulayyil
Qal'at Bishah
Khamis Mushayt
Abha
Salalah
Sayhut

JANUARY 30TH, 1991.
AND NOW WE'RE GOING TO SHOW A PICTURE OF THE LUCKIEST MAN IN IRAQ ON THIS PARTICULAR DAY.
KEEP YOUR EYES ON THE CROSSHAIRS RIGHT THERE.
AND IN HIS REARVIEW MIRROR...

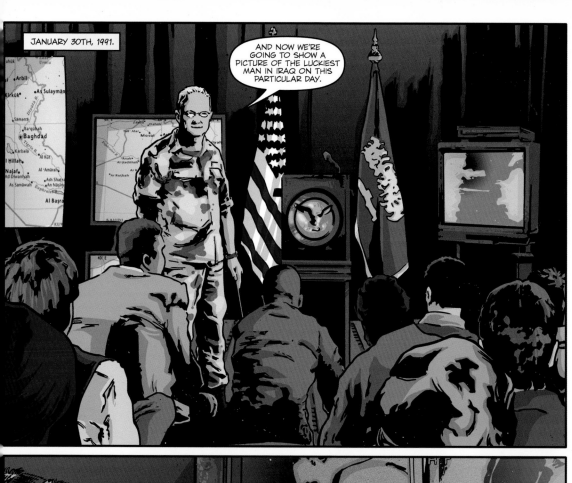

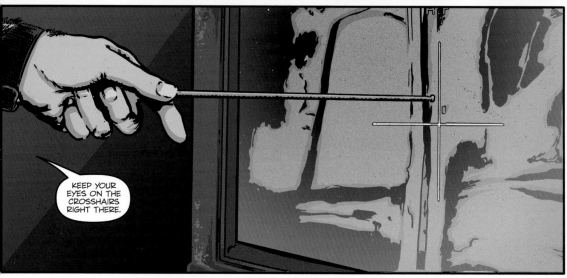

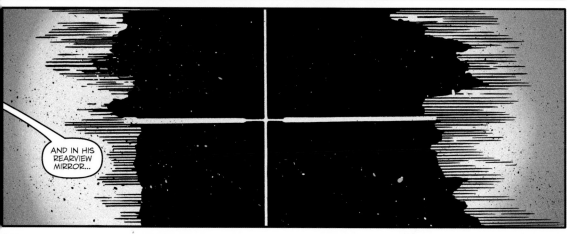

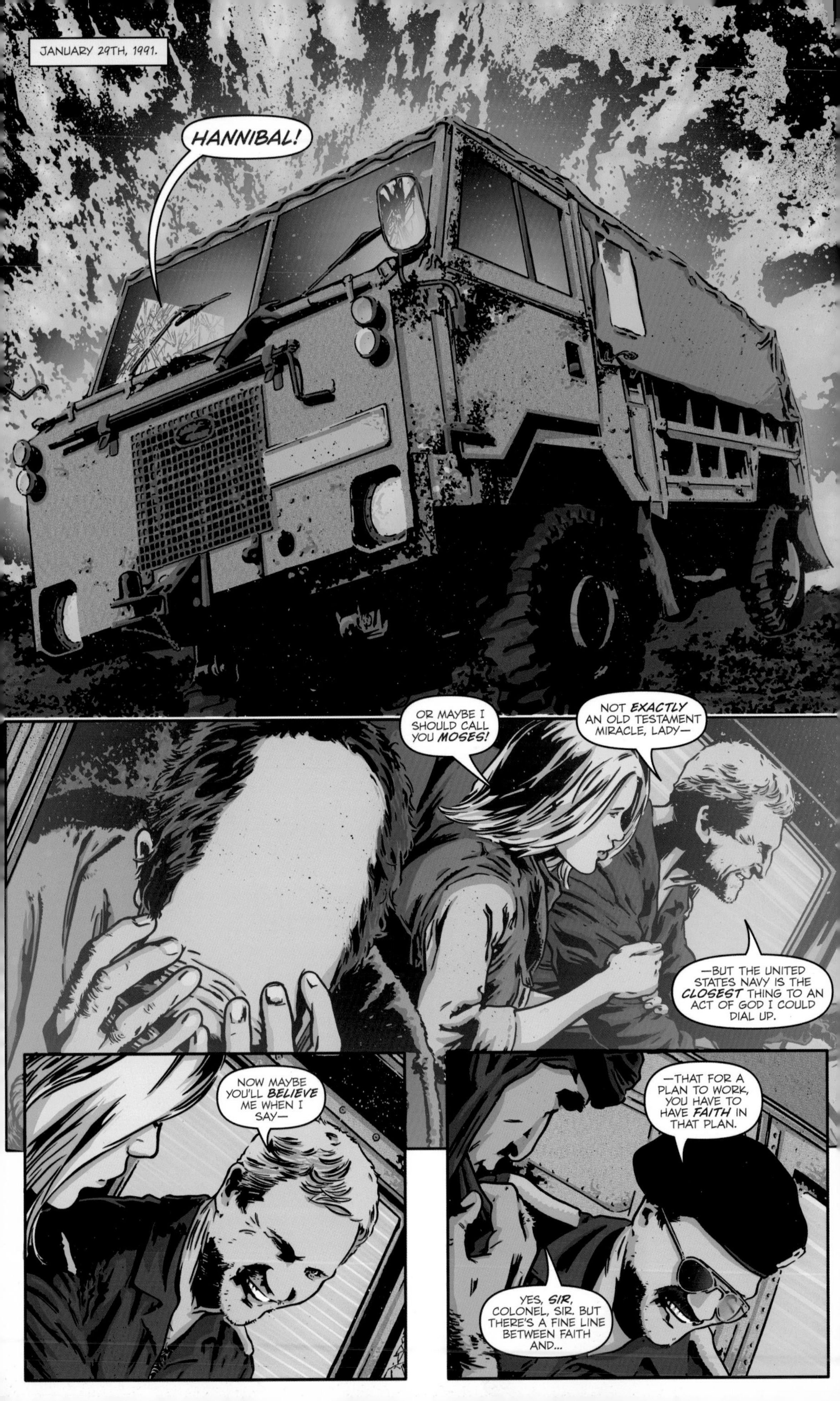
JANUARY 29TH, 1991.
HANNIBAL!
OR MAYBE I SHOULD CALL YOU MOSES!
NOT EXACTLY AN OLD TESTAMENT MIRACLE, LADY—
—BUT THE UNITED STATES NAVY IS THE CLOSEST THING TO AN ACT OF GOD I COULD DIAL UP.
NOW MAYBE YOU'LL BELIEVE ME WHEN I SAY—
—THAT FOR A PLAN TO WORK, YOU HAVE TO HAVE FAITH IN THAT PLAN.
YES, SIR, COLONEL, SIR. BUT THERE'S A FINE LINE BETWEEN FAITH AND...

JANUARY 27TH, 1991.
JUST FOLLOW MY LEAD AND STAY IN CHARACTER, SOLDIER.
...A SECTION EIGHT.
YOU HAVE TO BE NUTS TO CONSIDER CHOPPERING IN COUNTRY AND LANDING ON THE ROOF OF ONE OF SADDAM'S PALACES.
SIR.
"THE LUCKIEST MAN IN IRAQ"

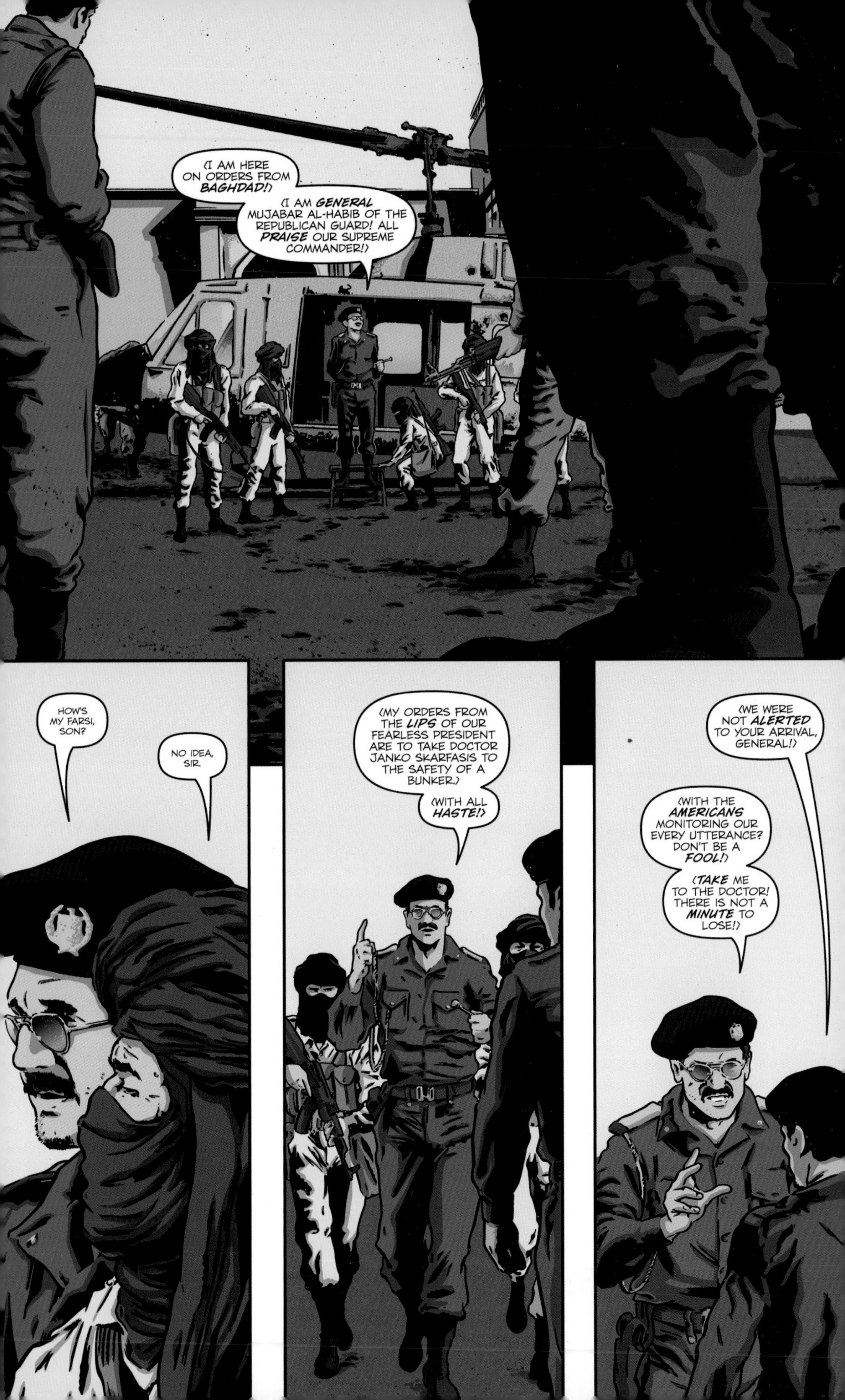

‹I AM HERE ON ORDERS FROM BAGHDAD!›
‹I AM GENERAL MUJABAR AL-HABIB OF THE REPUBLICAN GUARD! ALL PRAISE OUR SUPREME COMMANDER!›
HOW'S MY FARSI, SON?
NO IDEA, SIR.
‹MY ORDERS FROM THE LIPS OF OUR FEARLESS PRESIDENT ARE TO TAKE DOCTOR JANKO SKARFASIS TO THE SAFETY OF A BUNKER.›
‹WITH ALL HASTE!›
‹WE WERE NOT ALERTED TO YOUR ARRIVAL, GENERAL!›
‹WITH THE AMERICANS MONITORING OUR EVERY UTTERANCE? DON'T BE A FOOL!›
‹TAKE ME TO THE DOCTOR! THERE IS NOT A MINUTE TO LOSE!›

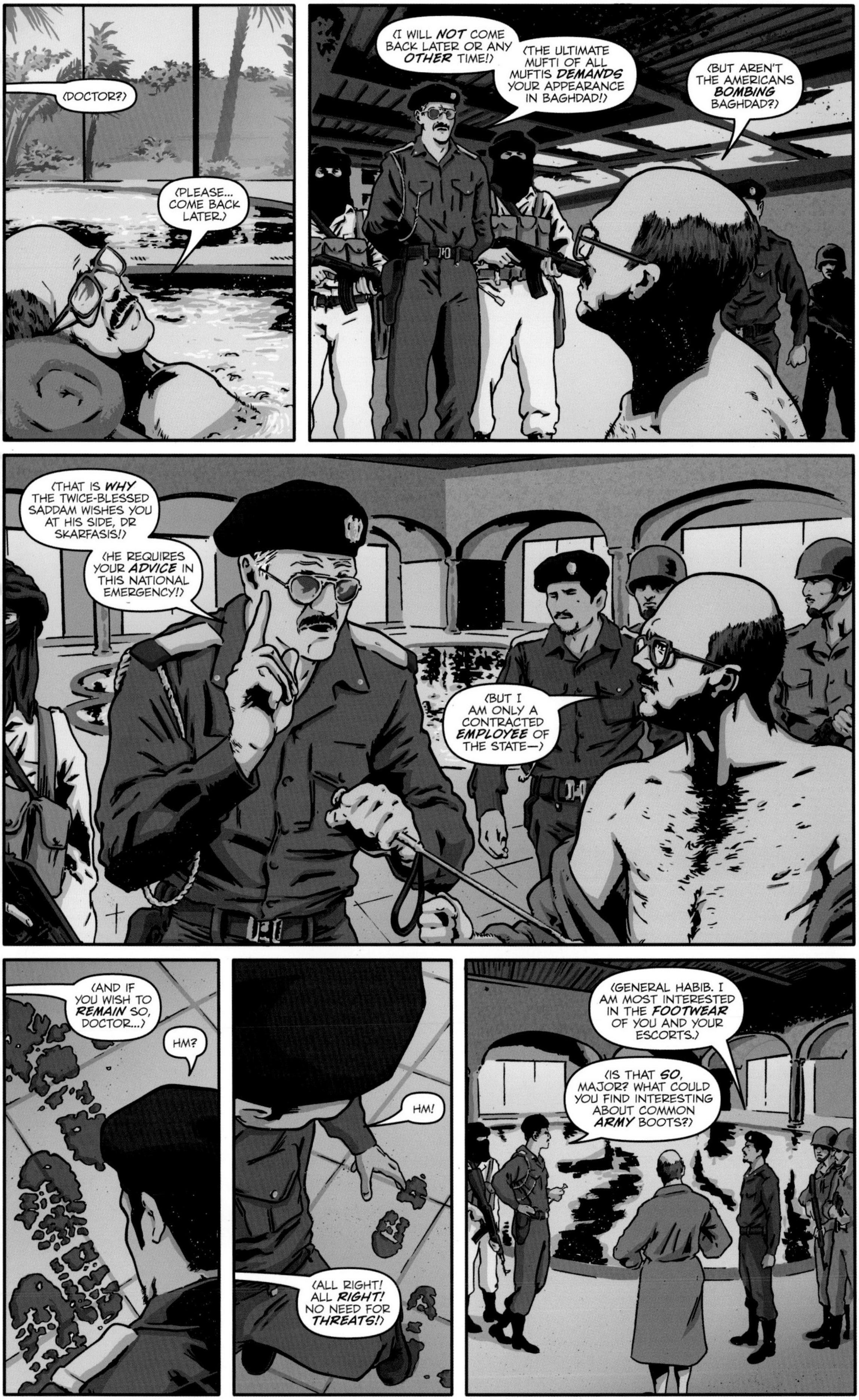
(DOCTOR?)
(PLEASE... COME BACK LATER.)
(I WILL NOT COME BACK LATER OR ANY OTHER TIME!)
(THE ULTIMATE MUFTI OF ALL MUFTIS DEMANDS YOUR APPEARANCE IN BAGHDAD!)
(BUT AREN'T THE AMERICANS BOMBING BAGHDAD?)
(THAT IS WHY THE TWICE-BLESSED SADDAM WISHES YOU AT HIS SIDE, DR SKARFASIS!)
(HE REQUIRES YOUR ADVICE IN THIS NATIONAL EMERGENCY!)
(BUT I AM ONLY A CONTRACTED EMPLOYEE OF THE STATE—)
(AND IF YOU WISH TO REMAIN SO, DOCTOR...)
HM?
HM!
(ALL RIGHT! ALL RIGHT! NO NEED FOR THREATS!)
(GENERAL HABIB. I AM MOST INTERESTED IN THE FOOTWEAR OF YOU AND YOUR ESCORTS.)
(IS THAT SO, MAJOR? WHAT COULD YOU FIND INTERESTING ABOUT COMMON ARMY BOOTS?)

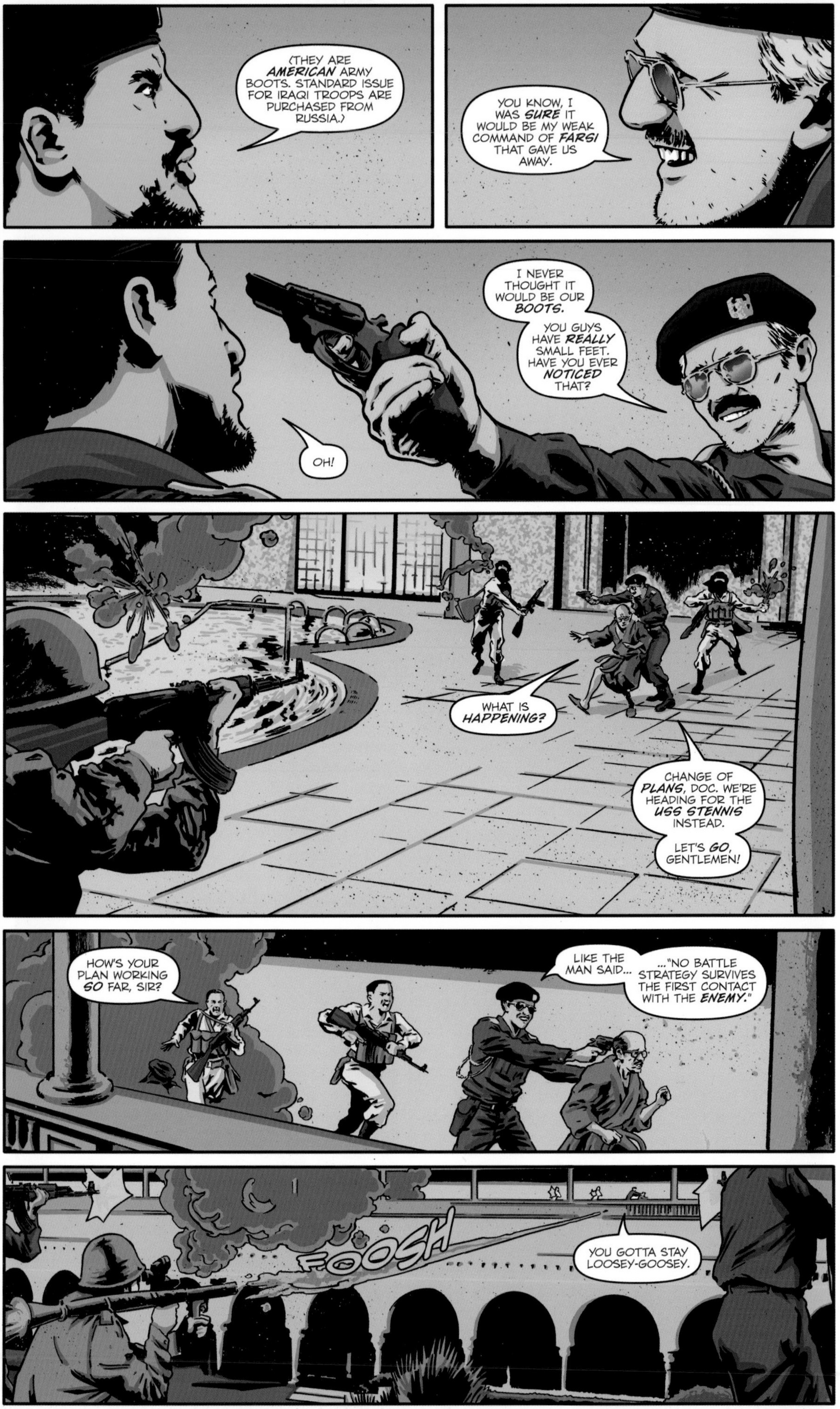

(THEY ARE AMERICAN ARMY BOOTS. STANDARD ISSUE FOR IRAQI TROOPS ARE PURCHASED FROM RUSSIA.)
YOU KNOW, I WAS SURE IT WOULD BE MY WEAK COMMAND OF FARSI THAT GAVE US AWAY.
I NEVER THOUGHT IT WOULD BE OUR BOOTS.
YOU GUYS HAVE REALLY SMALL FEET. HAVE YOU EVER NOTICED THAT?
OH!
WHAT IS HAPPENING?
CHANGE OF PLANS, DOC. WE'RE HEADING FOR THE USS STENNIS INSTEAD.
LET'S GO, GENTLEMEN!
HOW'S YOUR PLAN WORKING SO FAR, SIR?
LIKE THE MAN SAID...
..."NO BATTLE STRATEGY SURVIVES THE FIRST CONTACT WITH THE ENEMY."
FOOSH
YOU GOTTA STAY LOOSEY-GOOSEY.

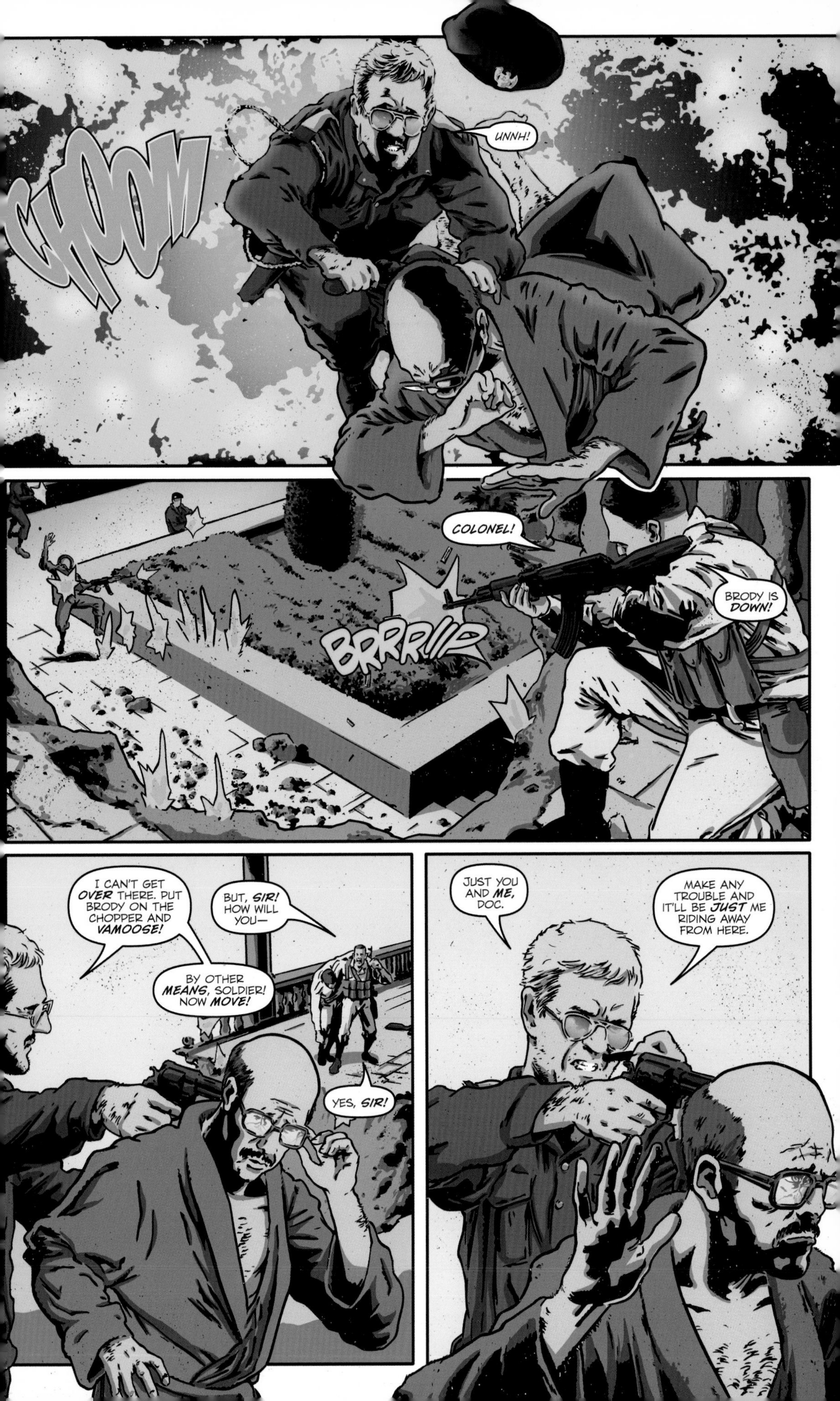
CHOOM
UNNH!
COLONEL!
BRRRIIP
BRODY IS DOWN!
I CAN'T GET OVER THERE. PUT BRODY ON THE CHOPPER AND VAMOOSE!
BUT, SIR! HOW WILL YOU—
BY OTHER MEANS, SOLDIER! NOW MOVE!
YES, SIR!
JUST YOU AND ME, DOC.
MAKE ANY TROUBLE AND IT'LL BE JUST ME RIDING AWAY FROM HERE.

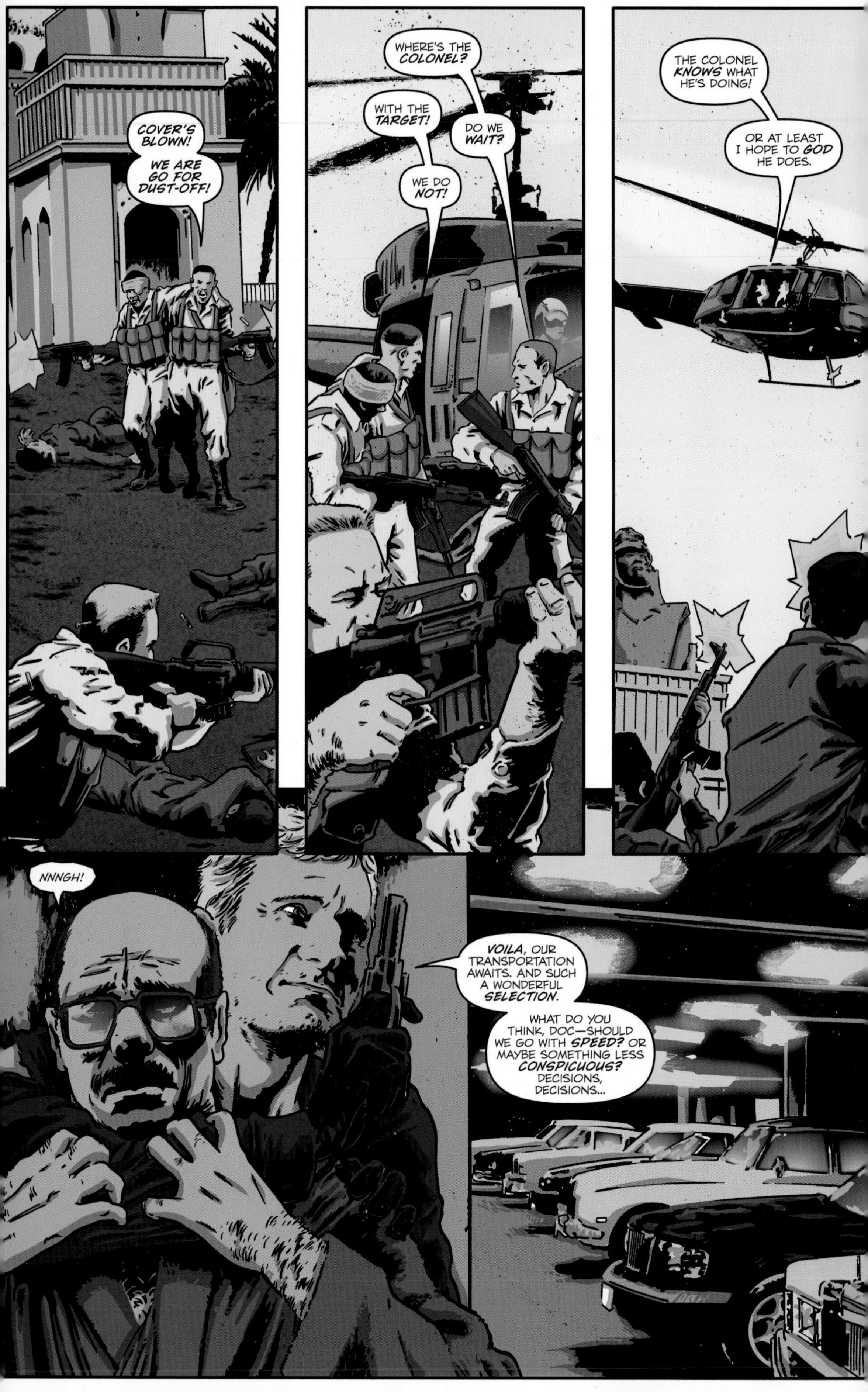
COVER'S BLOWN!
WE ARE GO FOR DUST-OFF!
WHERE'S THE COLONEL?
WITH THE TARGET!
DO WE WAIT?
WE DO NOT!
THE COLONEL KNOWS WHAT HE'S DOING!
OR AT LEAST I HOPE TO GOD HE DOES.
NNNGH!
VOILA, OUR TRANSPORTATION AWAITS. AND SUCH A WONDERFUL SELECTION.
WHAT DO YOU THINK, DOC—SHOULD WE GO WITH SPEED? OR MAYBE SOMETHING LESS CONSPICUOUS? DECISIONS, DECISIONS...

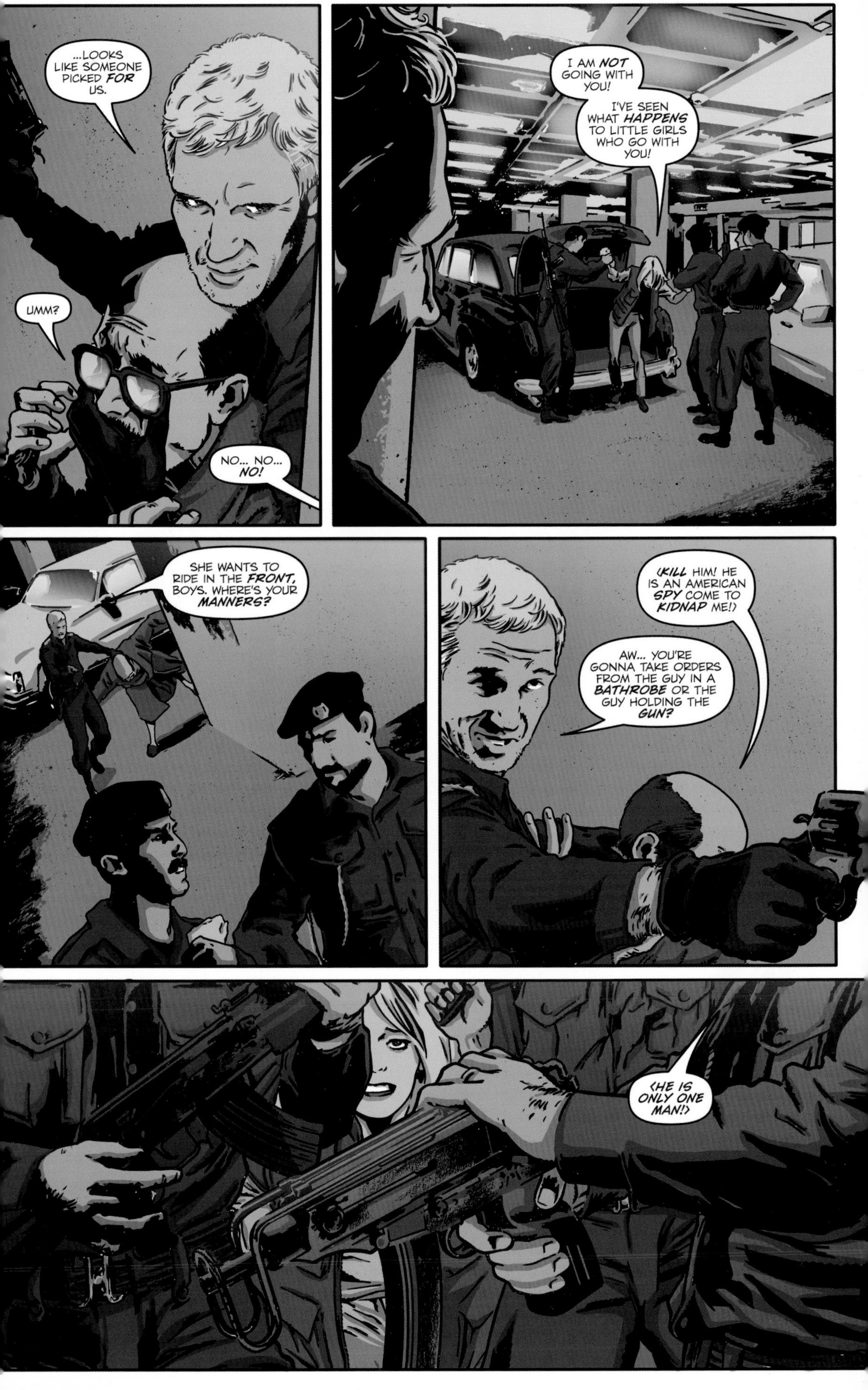
...LOOKS LIKE SOMEONE PICKED FOR US.
UMM?
NO... NO... NO!
I AM NOT GOING WITH YOU!
I'VE SEEN WHAT HAPPENS TO LITTLE GIRLS WHO GO WITH YOU!
SHE WANTS TO RIDE IN THE FRONT, BOYS. WHERE'S YOUR MANNERS?
<KILL HIM! HE IS AN AMERICAN SPY COME TO KIDNAP ME!>
AW... YOU'RE GONNA TAKE ORDERS FROM THE GUY IN A BATHROBE OR THE GUY HOLDING THE GUN?
<HE IS ONLY ONE MAN!>

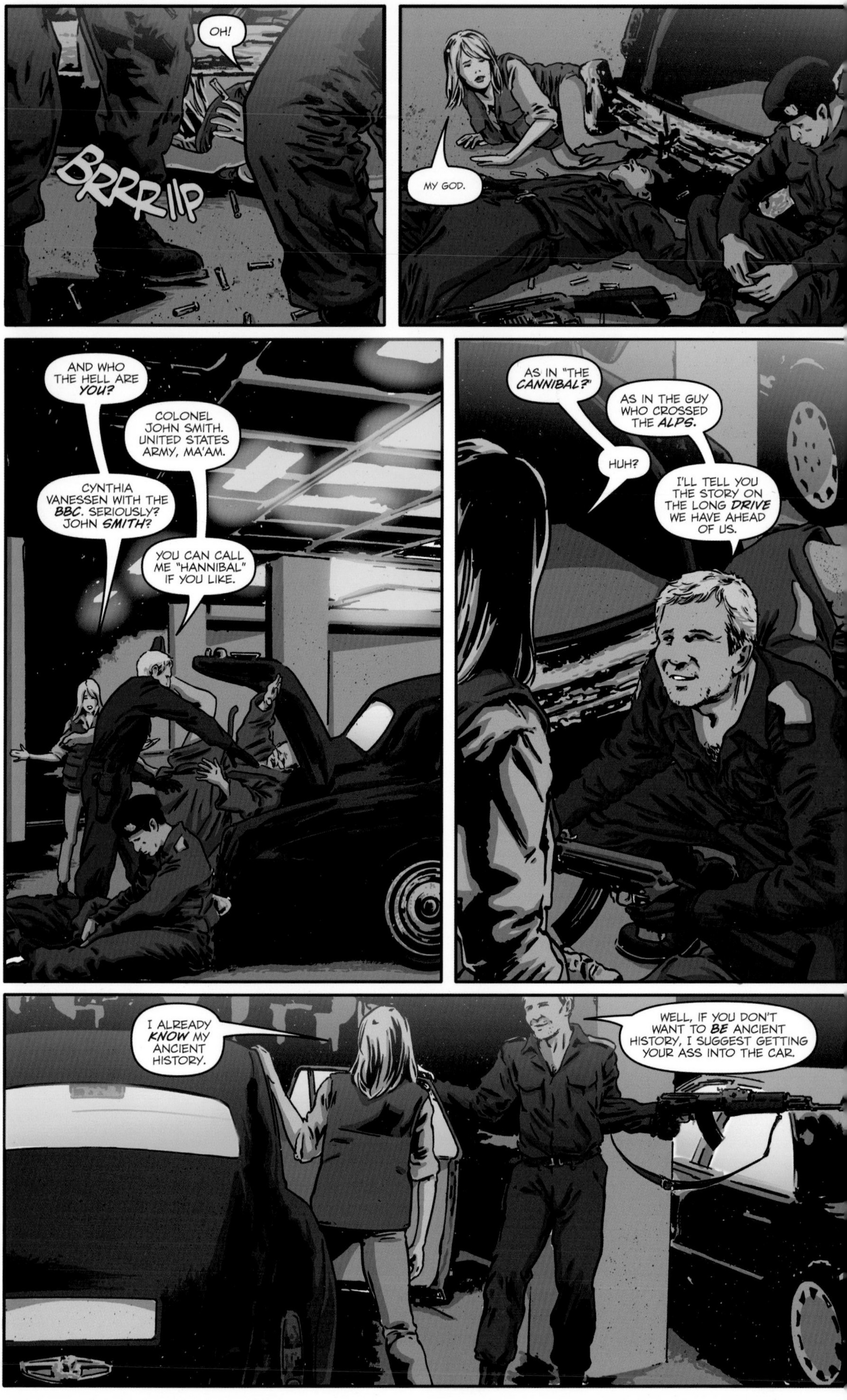
OH!
BRRRIIP
MY GOD.
AND WHO THE HELL ARE *YOU?*
COLONEL JOHN SMITH. UNITED STATES ARMY, MA'AM.
CYNTHIA VANESSEN WITH THE *BBC*. SERIOUSLY? JOHN *SMITH?*
YOU CAN CALL ME "HANNIBAL" IF YOU LIKE.
AS IN "THE *CANNIBAL?*"
AS IN THE GUY WHO CROSSED THE *ALPS.*
HUH?
I'LL TELL YOU THE STORY ON THE LONG *DRIVE* WE HAVE AHEAD OF US.
I ALREADY *KNOW* MY ANCIENT HISTORY.
WELL, IF YOU DON'T WANT TO *BE* ANCIENT HISTORY, I SUGGEST GETTING YOUR ASS INTO THE CAR.

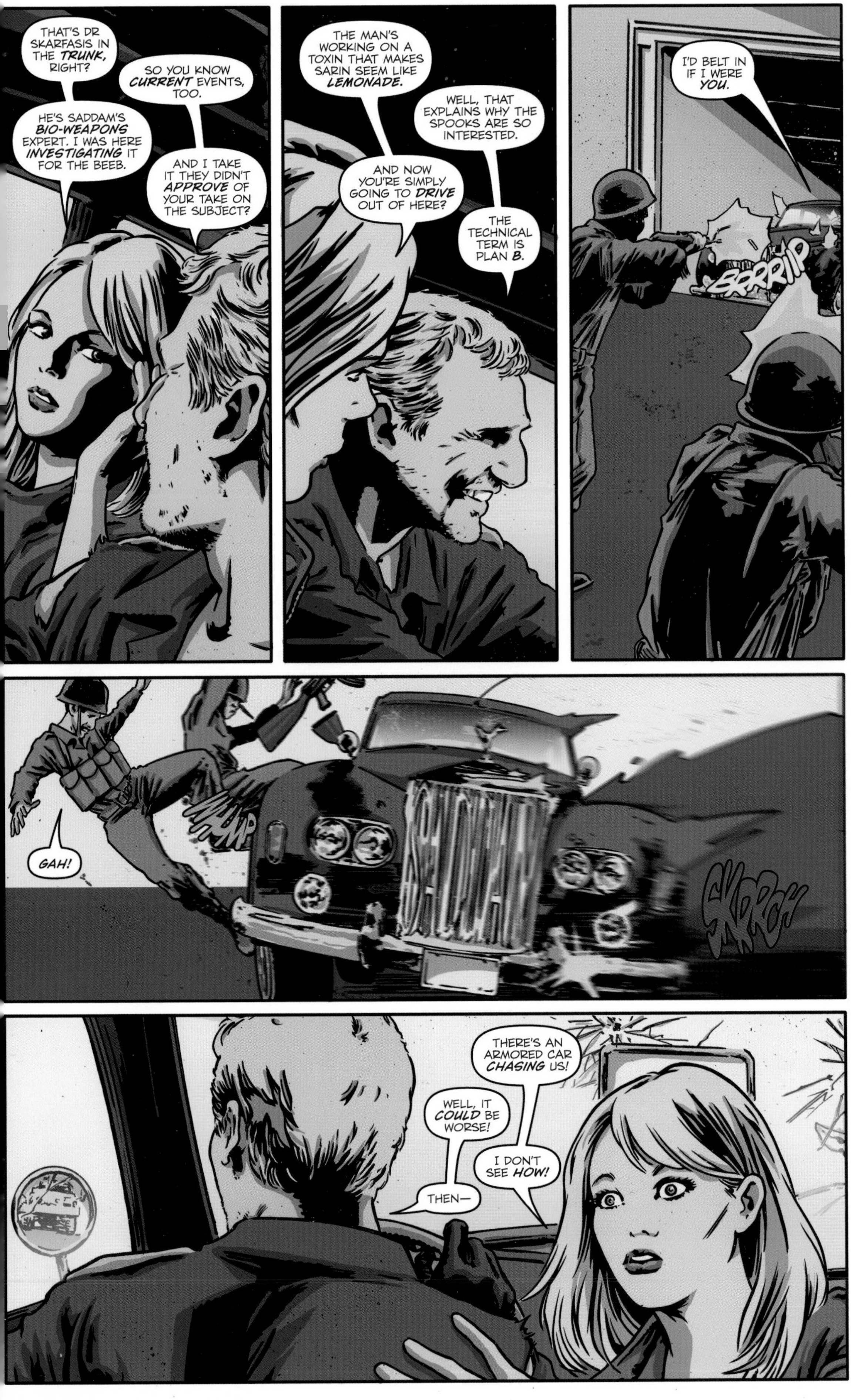
THAT'S DR SKARFASIS IN THE TRUNK, RIGHT?
HE'S SADDAM'S BIO-WEAPONS EXPERT. I WAS HERE INVESTIGATING IT FOR THE BEEB.
SO YOU KNOW CURRENT EVENTS, TOO.
AND I TAKE IT THEY DIDN'T APPROVE OF YOUR TAKE ON THE SUBJECT?
THE MAN'S WORKING ON A TOXIN THAT MAKES SARIN SEEM LIKE LEMONADE.
WELL, THAT EXPLAINS WHY THE SPOOKS ARE SO INTERESTED.
AND NOW YOU'RE SIMPLY GOING TO DRIVE OUT OF HERE?
THE TECHNICAL TERM IS PLAN B.
I'D BELT IN IF I WERE YOU.
BRRRIIP
GAH!
SKRRCH
THERE'S AN ARMORED CAR CHASING US!
WELL, IT COULD BE WORSE!
I DON'T SEE HOW!
THEN—

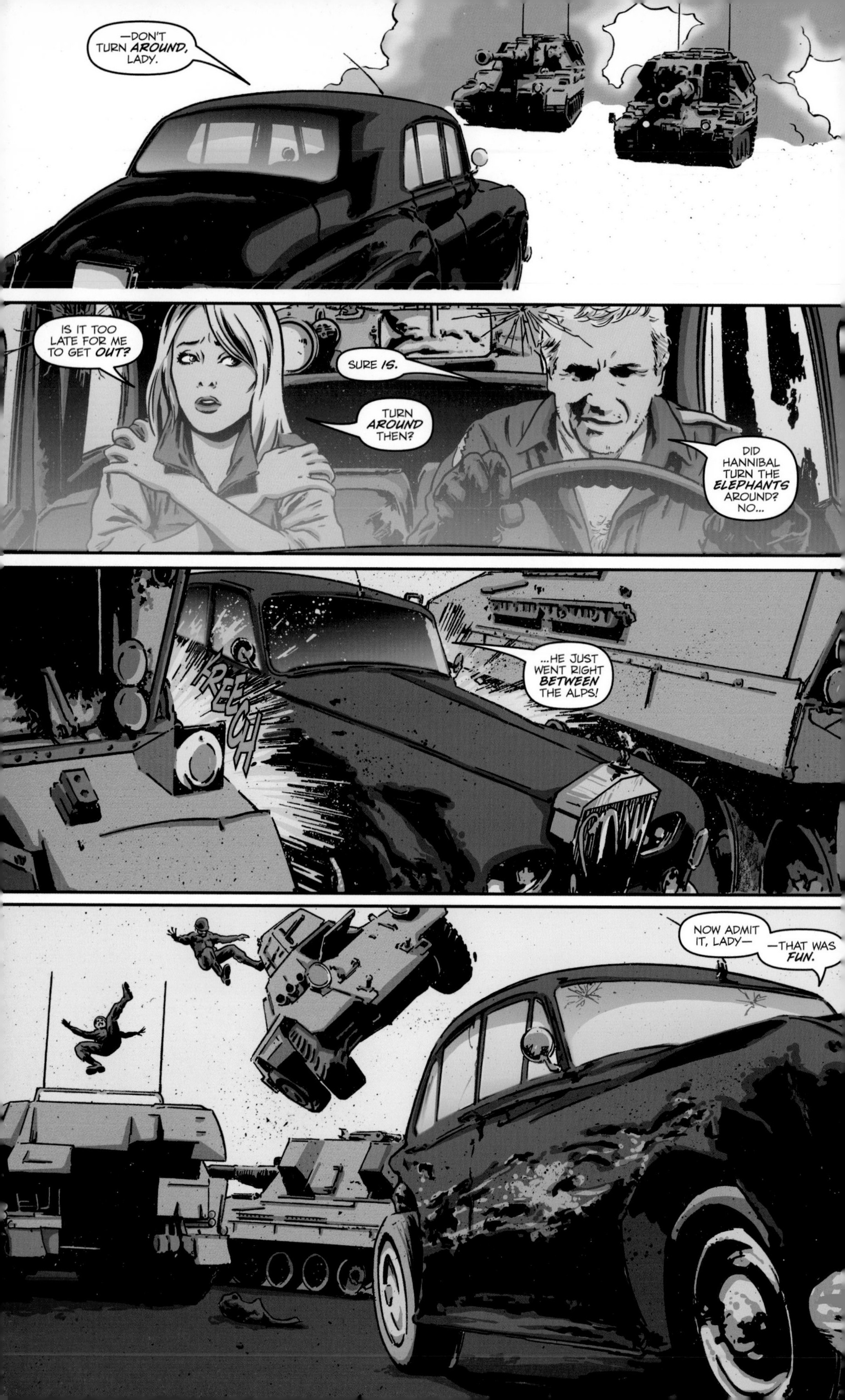
—DON'T TURN *AROUND,* LADY.
IS IT TOO LATE FOR ME TO GET *OUT?*
SURE *IS.*
TURN *AROUND* THEN?
DID HANNIBAL TURN THE *ELEPHANTS* AROUND? NO...
SKREECH
...HE JUST WENT RIGHT *BETWEEN* THE ALPS!
NOW ADMIT IT, LADY—
—THAT WAS *FUN.*

FUN?!

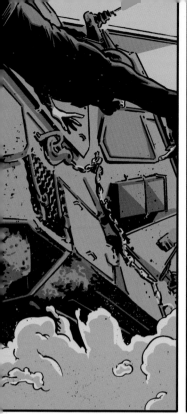

HA HA HA HA HA!

YOU'RE *LAUGHING?* WE'RE GOING TO DIE AND *YOU'RE* HAVING A LAUGH?

WHY DIE *GLOOMY?*

NO ONE *SANE* COULD THINK THIS IS FUNNY!

BESIDES *YOU?*

NO ONE!

(PLEASE, GOD... I HAVE STARTED BELIEVING IN YOU AGAIN...)

YOU KNOW... THIS *MIGHT* JUST WORK.

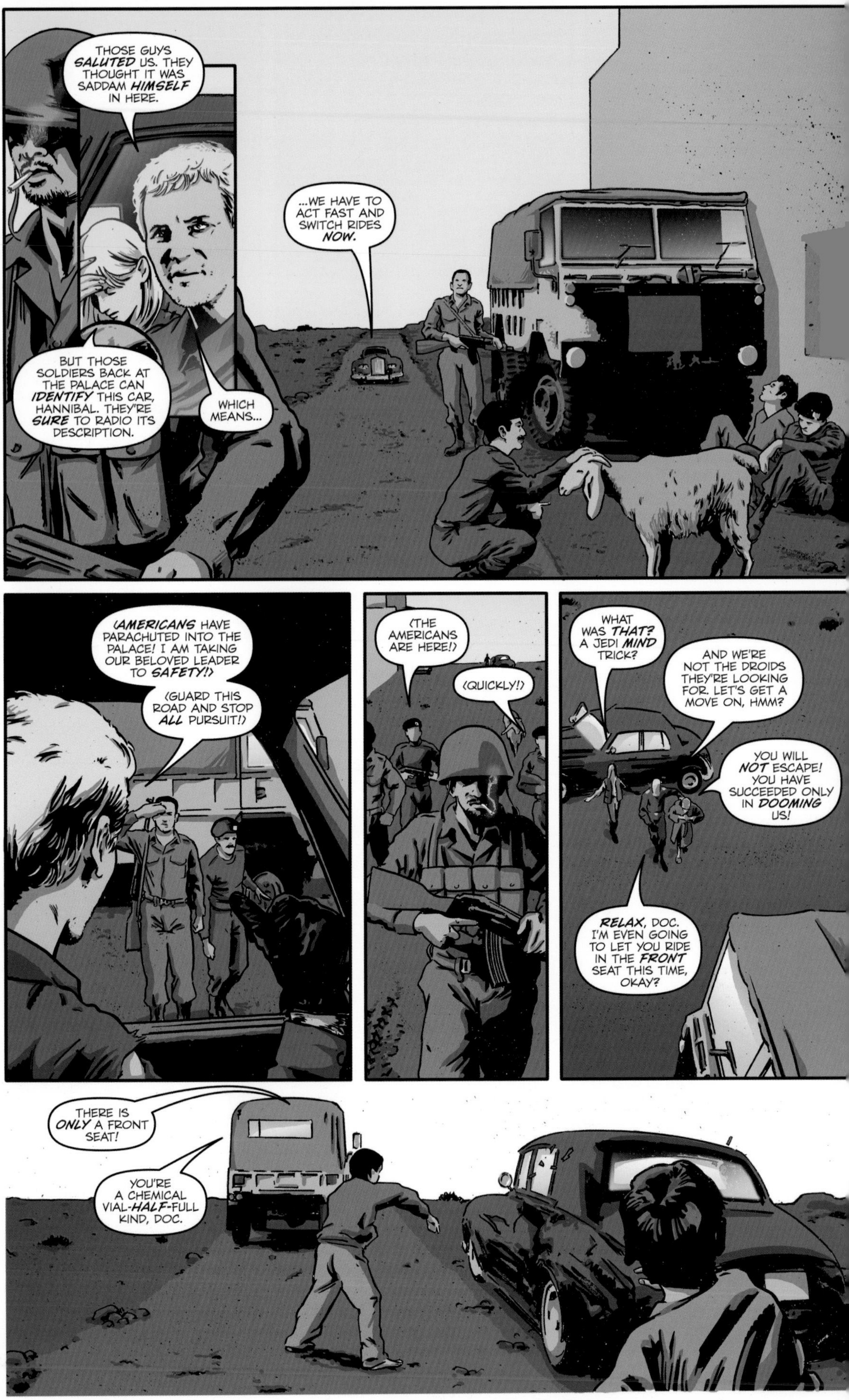
THOSE GUYS SALUTED US. THEY THOUGHT IT WAS SADDAM HIMSELF IN HERE.
BUT THOSE SOLDIERS BACK AT THE PALACE CAN IDENTIFY THIS CAR, HANNIBAL. THEY'RE SURE TO RADIO ITS DESCRIPTION.
WHICH MEANS...
...WE HAVE TO ACT FAST AND SWITCH RIDES NOW.
(AMERICANS HAVE PARACHUTED INTO THE PALACE! I AM TAKING OUR BELOVED LEADER TO SAFETY!)
(GUARD THIS ROAD AND STOP ALL PURSUIT!)
(THE AMERICANS ARE HERE!)
(QUICKLY!)
WHAT WAS THAT? A JEDI MIND TRICK?
AND WE'RE NOT THE DROIDS THEY'RE LOOKING FOR. LET'S GET A MOVE ON, HMM?
YOU WILL NOT ESCAPE! YOU HAVE SUCCEEDED ONLY IN DOOMING US!
RELAX, DOC. I'M EVEN GOING TO LET YOU RIDE IN THE FRONT SEAT THIS TIME, OKAY?
THERE IS ONLY A FRONT SEAT!
YOU'RE A CHEMICAL VIAL-HALF-FULL KIND, DOC.

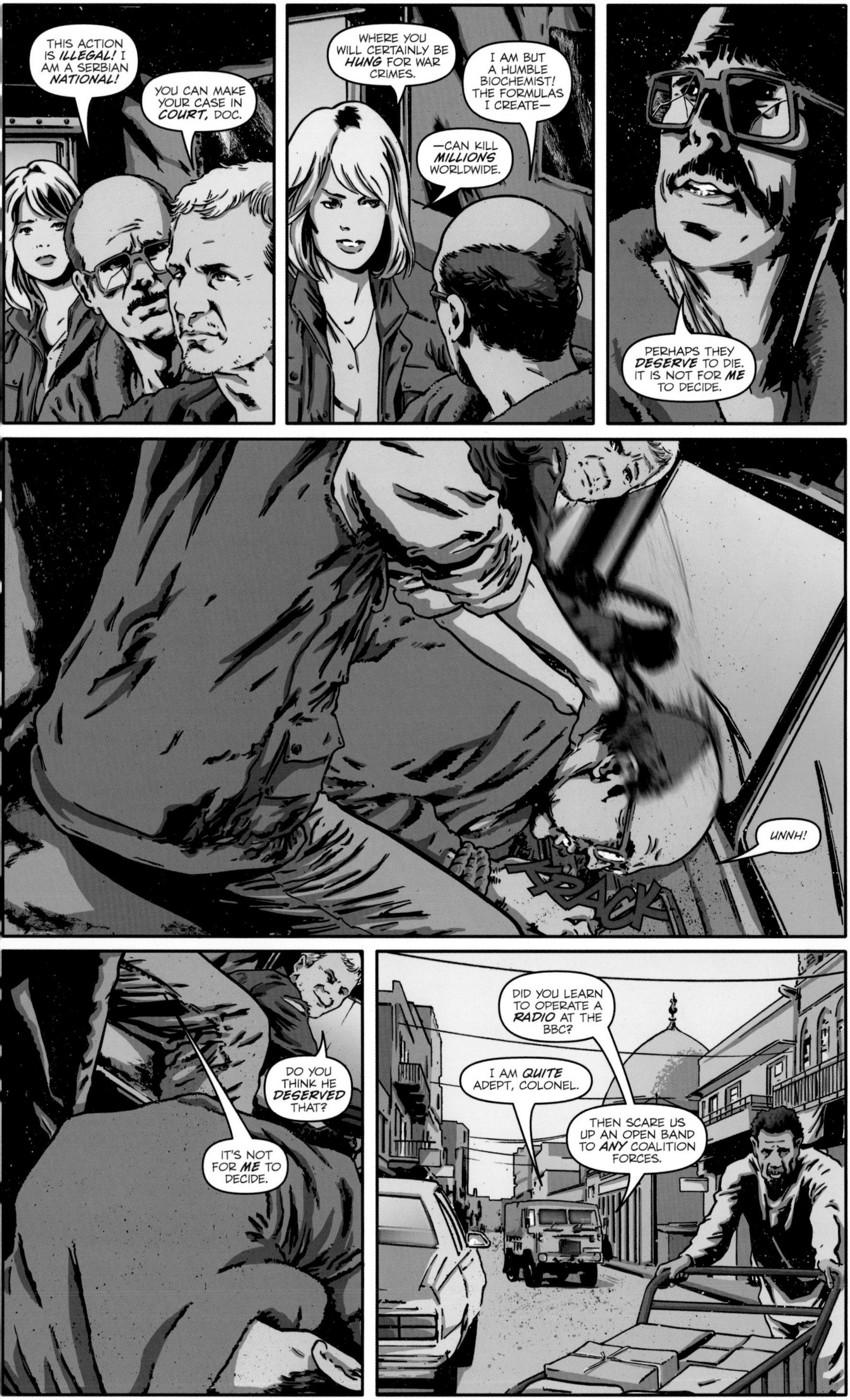
THIS ACTION IS *ILLEGAL!* I AM A SERBIAN *NATIONAL!*
YOU CAN MAKE YOUR CASE IN *COURT,* DOC.
WHERE YOU WILL CERTAINLY BE *HUNG* FOR WAR CRIMES.
I AM BUT A HUMBLE BIOCHEMIST! THE FORMULAS I CREATE—
—CAN KILL *MILLIONS* WORLDWIDE.
PERHAPS THEY *DESERVE* TO DIE. IT IS NOT FOR *ME* TO DECIDE.
KRACK
UNNH!
DO YOU THINK HE *DESERVED* THAT?
IT'S NOT FOR *ME* TO DECIDE.
DID YOU LEARN TO OPERATE A *RADIO* AT THE BBC?
I AM *QUITE* ADEPT, COLONEL.
THEN SCARE US UP AN OPEN BAND TO *ANY* COALITION FORCES.

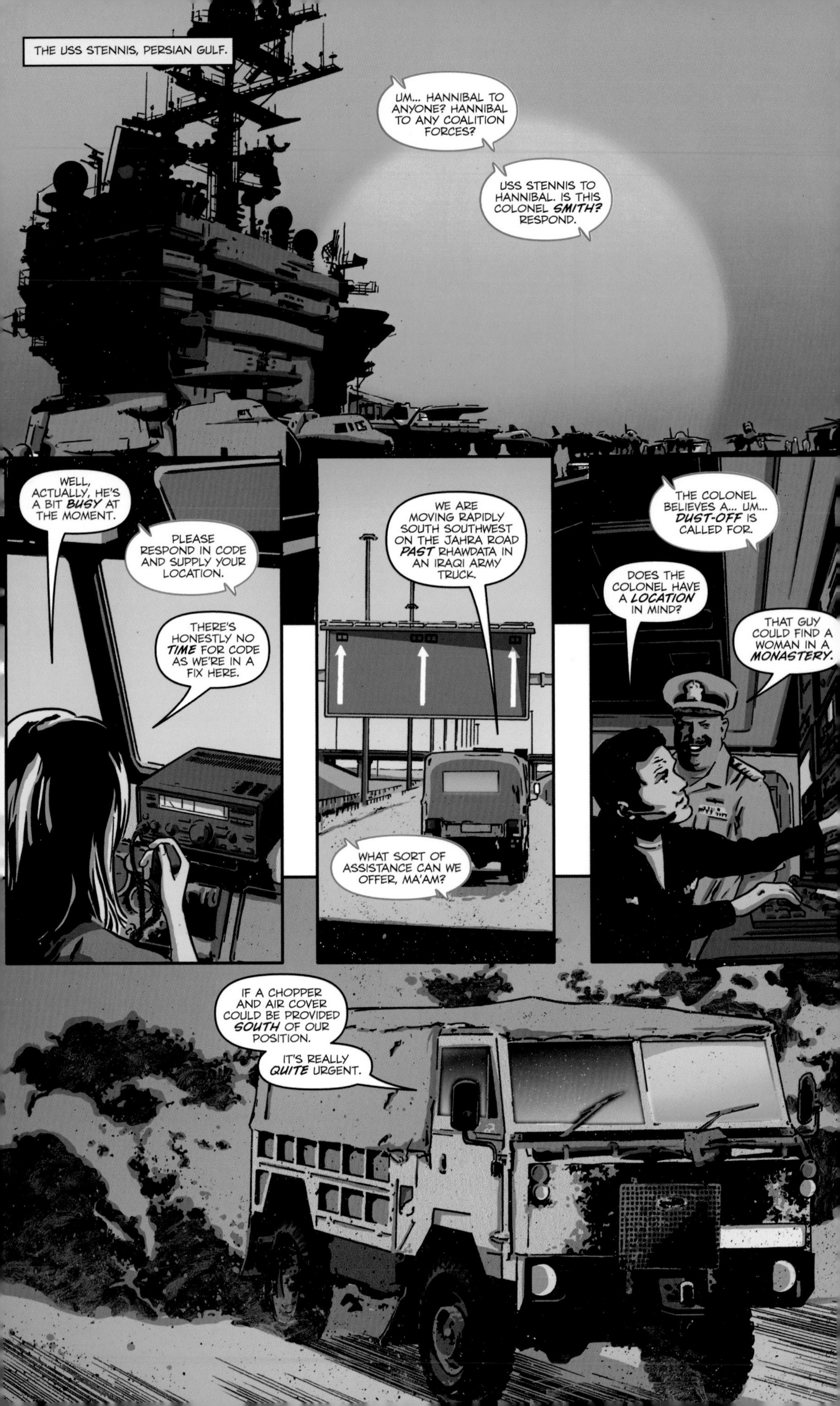
THE USS STENNIS, PERSIAN GULF.
UM... HANNIBAL TO ANYONE? HANNIBAL TO ANY COALITION FORCES?
USS STENNIS TO HANNIBAL. IS THIS COLONEL SMITH? RESPOND.
WELL, ACTUALLY, HE'S A BIT BUSY AT THE MOMENT.
PLEASE RESPOND IN CODE AND SUPPLY YOUR LOCATION.
THERE'S HONESTLY NO TIME FOR CODE AS WE'RE IN A FIX HERE.
WE ARE MOVING RAPIDLY SOUTH SOUTHWEST ON THE JAHRA ROAD PAST RHAWDATA IN AN IRAQI ARMY TRUCK.
WHAT SORT OF ASSISTANCE CAN WE OFFER, MA'AM?
THE COLONEL BELIEVES A... UM... DUST-OFF IS CALLED FOR.
DOES THE COLONEL HAVE A LOCATION IN MIND?
THAT GUY COULD FIND A WOMAN IN A MONASTERY.
IF A CHOPPER AND AIR COVER COULD BE PROVIDED SOUTH OF OUR POSITION.
IT'S REALLY QUITE URGENT.

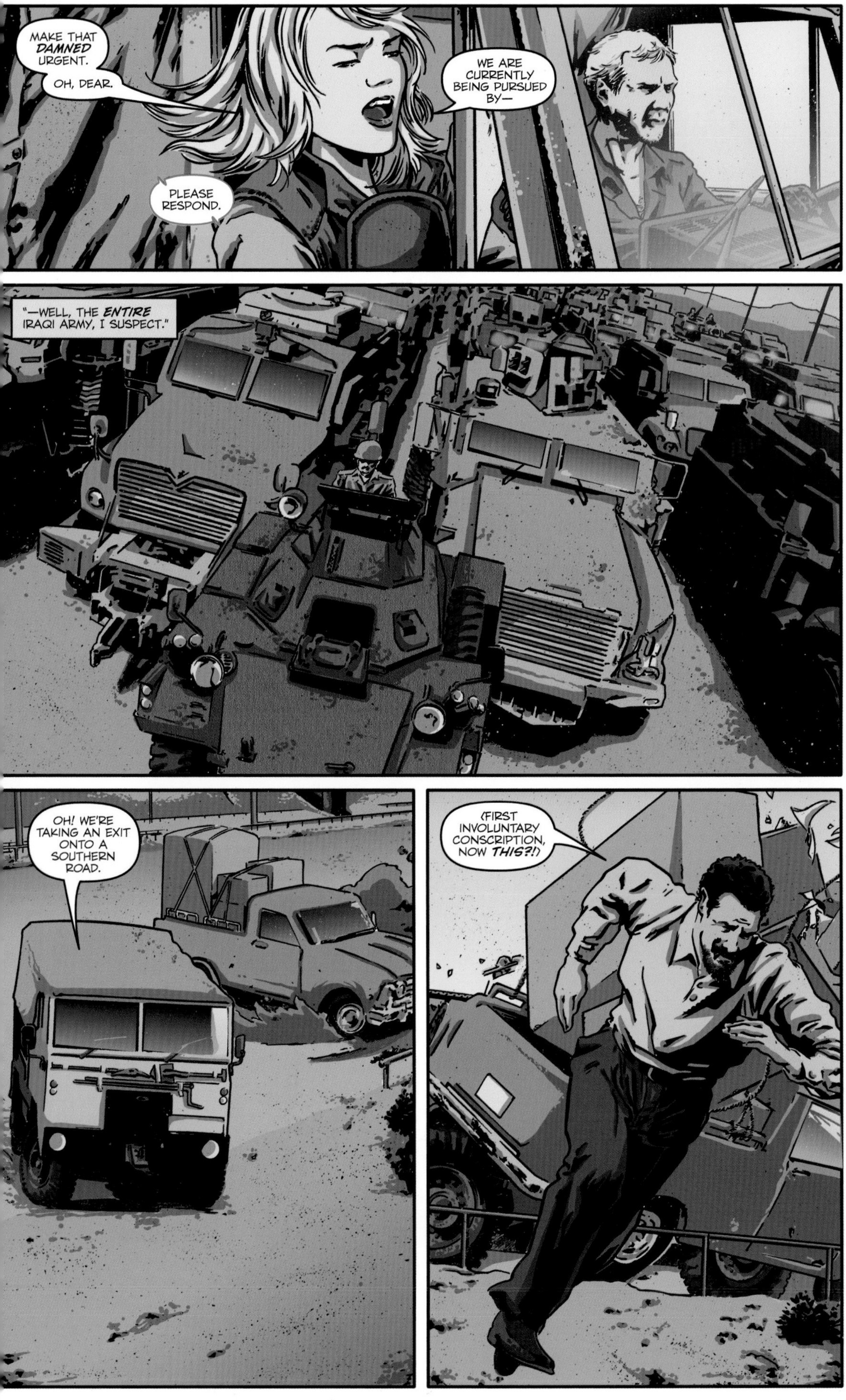
MAKE THAT *DAMNED* URGENT.
OH, DEAR.
WE ARE CURRENTLY BEING PURSUED BY—
PLEASE RESPOND.
"—WELL, THE *ENTIRE* IRAQI ARMY, I SUSPECT."
OH! WE'RE TAKING AN EXIT ONTO A SOUTHERN ROAD.
‹FIRST INVOLUNTARY CONSCRIPTION, NOW *THIS?!*›

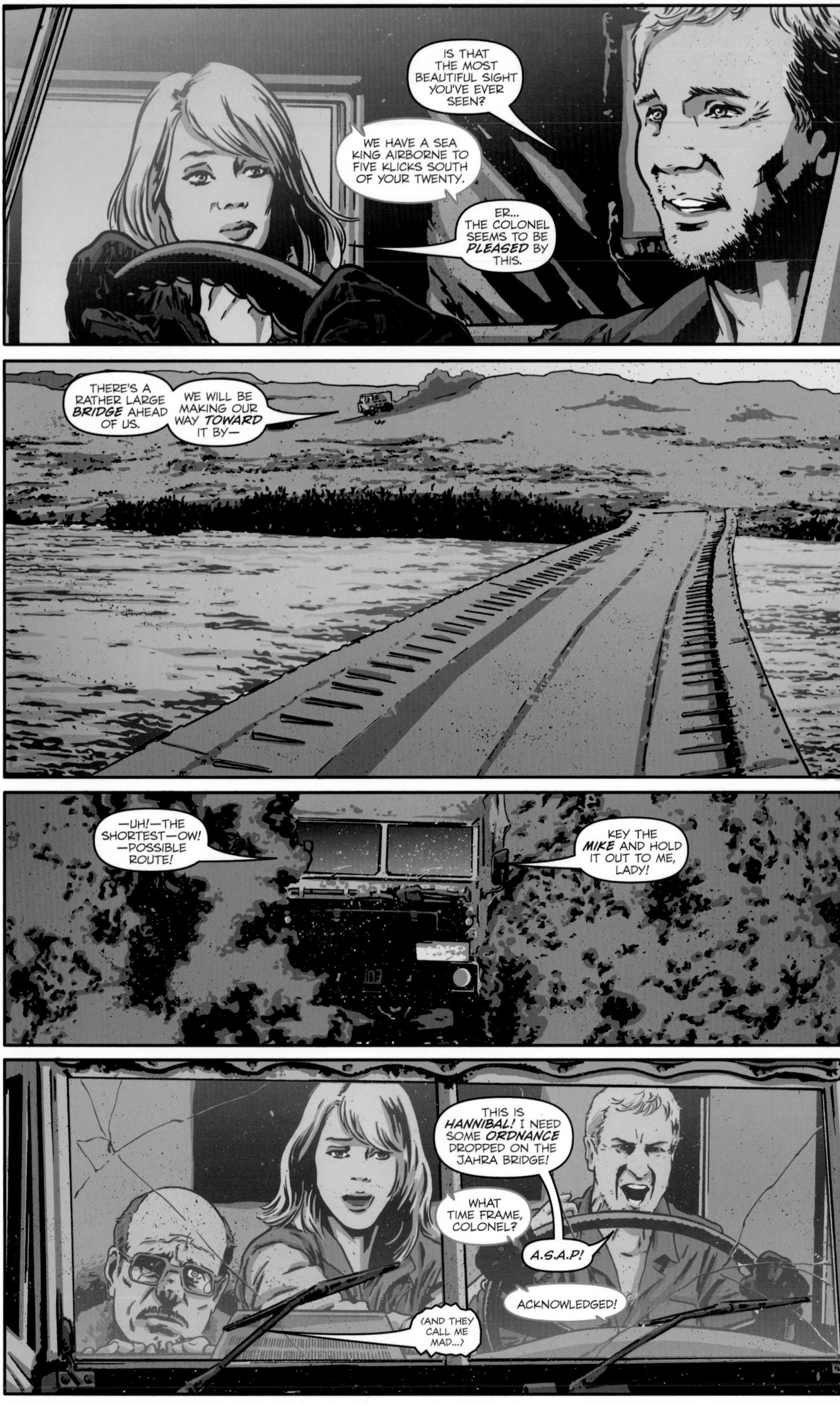
IS THAT THE MOST BEAUTIFUL SIGHT YOU'VE EVER SEEN?
WE HAVE A SEA KING AIRBORNE TO FIVE KLICKS SOUTH OF YOUR TWENTY.
ER... THE COLONEL SEEMS TO BE PLEASED BY THIS.
THERE'S A RATHER LARGE BRIDGE AHEAD OF US.
WE WILL BE MAKING OUR WAY TOWARD IT BY—
—UH!—THE SHORTEST—OW! —POSSIBLE ROUTE!
KEY THE MIKE AND HOLD IT OUT TO ME, LADY!
THIS IS HANNIBAL! I NEED SOME ORDNANCE DROPPED ON THE JAHRA BRIDGE!
WHAT TIME FRAME, COLONEL?
A.S.A.P!
ACKNOWLEDGED!
(AND THEY CALL ME MAD...)

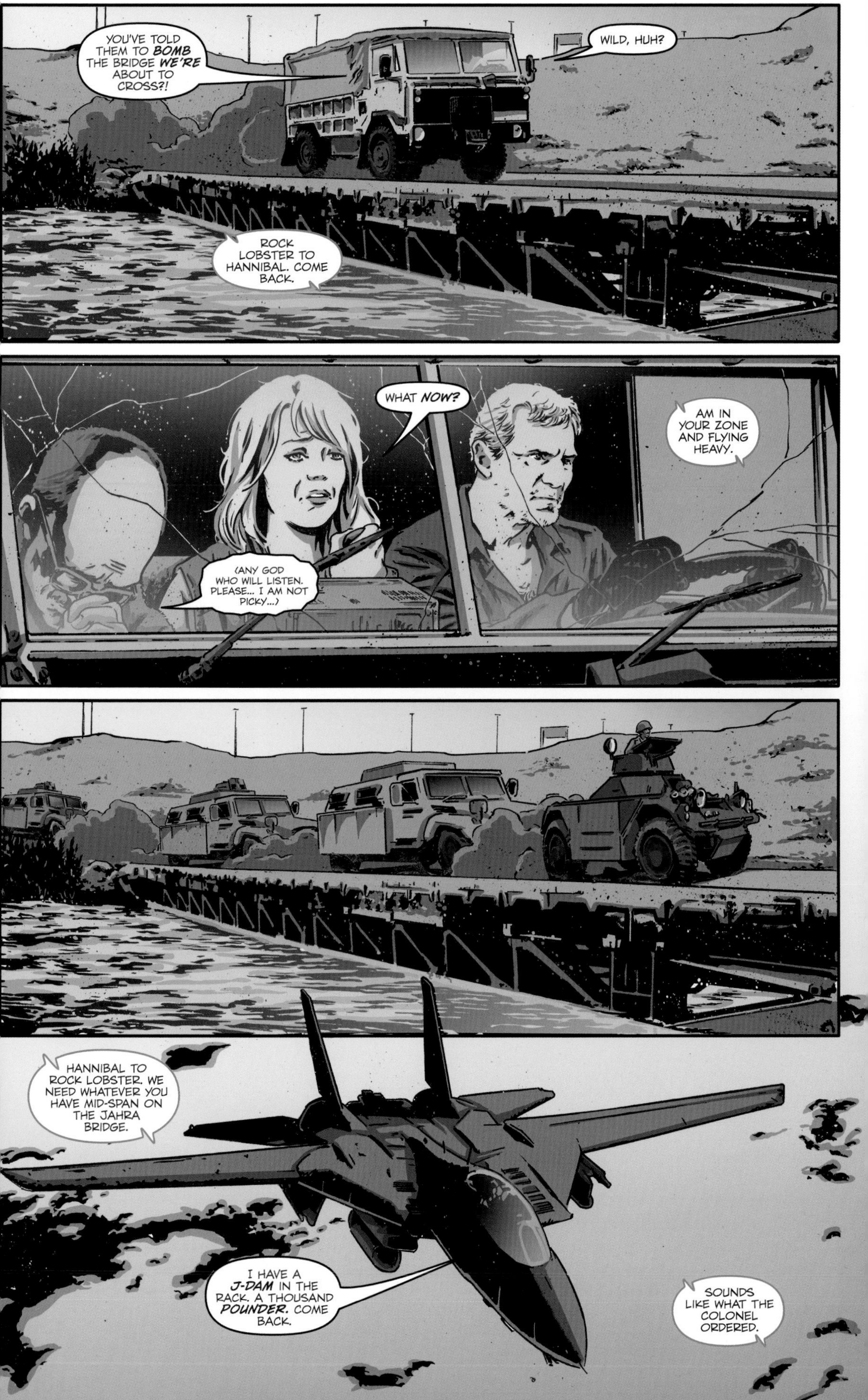
YOU'VE TOLD THEM TO BOMB THE BRIDGE WE'RE ABOUT TO CROSS?!
WILD, HUH?
ROCK LOBSTER TO HANNIBAL. COME BACK.
WHAT NOW?
AM IN YOUR ZONE AND FLYING HEAVY.
(ANY GOD WHO WILL LISTEN. PLEASE... I AM NOT PICKY...)
HANNIBAL TO ROCK LOBSTER. WE NEED WHATEVER YOU HAVE MID-SPAN ON THE JAHRA BRIDGE.
I HAVE A J-DAM IN THE RACK. A THOUSAND POUNDER. COME BACK.
SOUNDS LIKE WHAT THE COLONEL ORDERED.

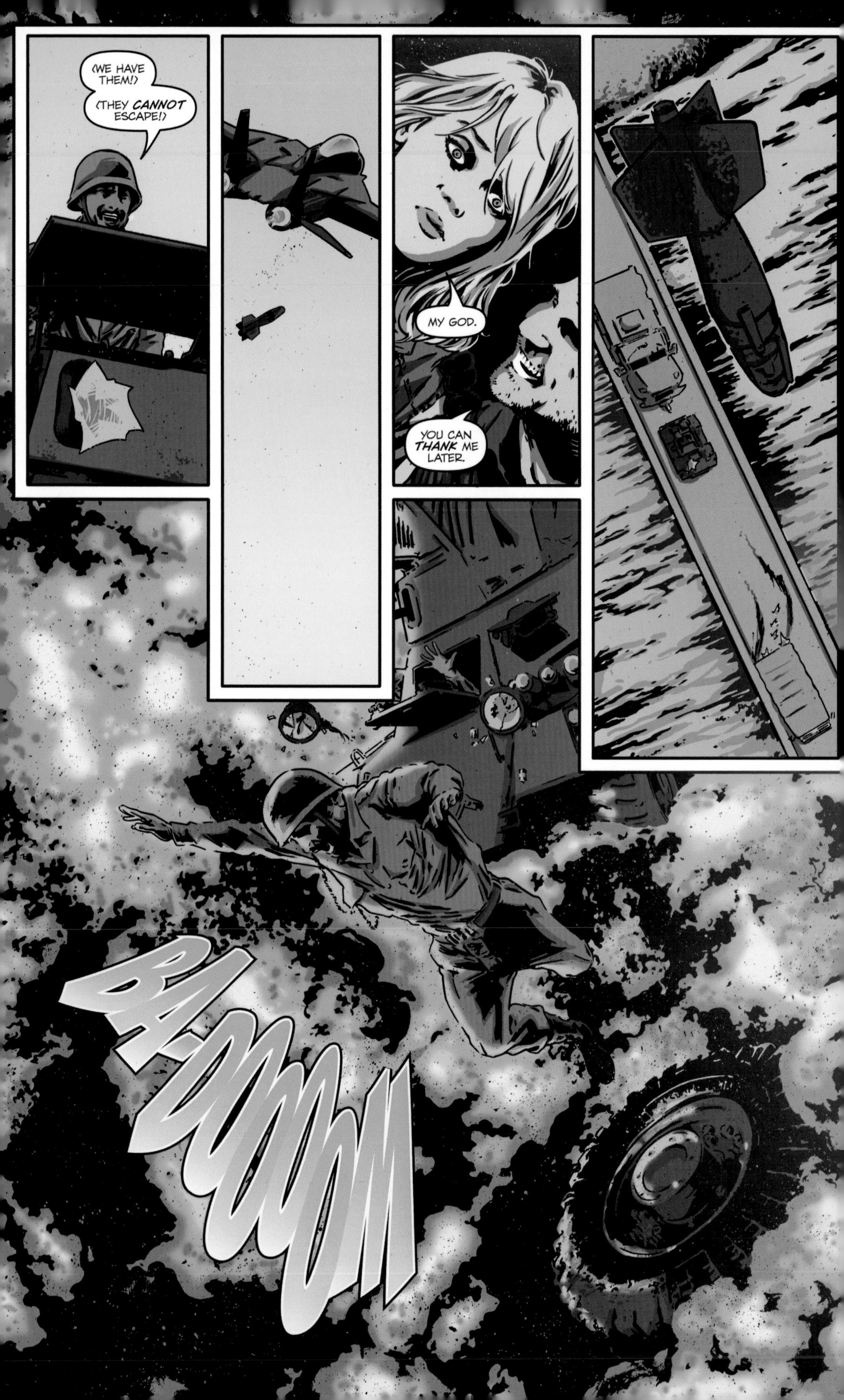
‹WE HAVE THEM!›
‹THEY CANNOT ESCAPE!›
MY GOD.
YOU CAN THANK ME LATER.
BA-OOOOOM

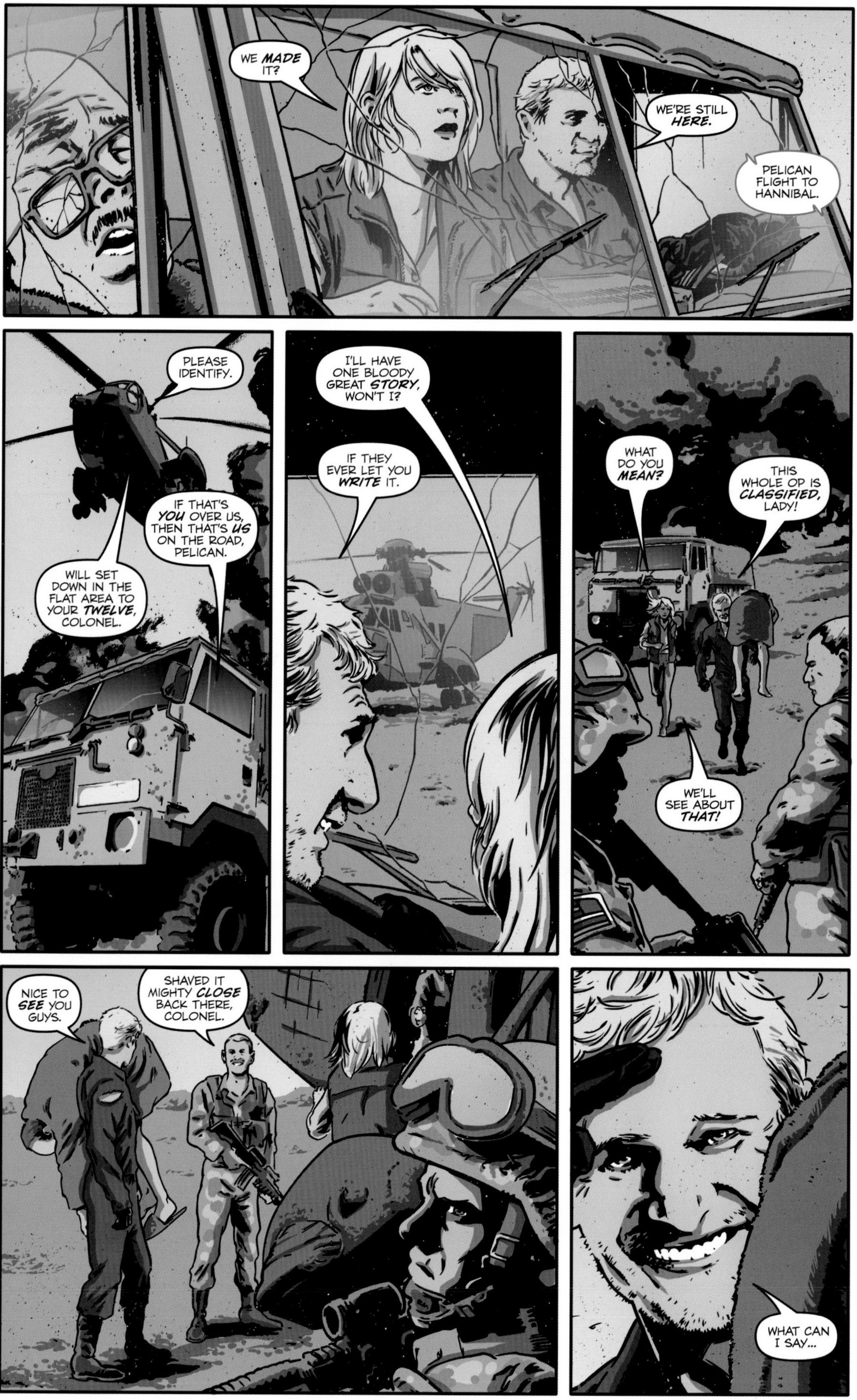
WE MADE IT?
WE'RE STILL HERE.
PELICAN FLIGHT TO HANNIBAL.
PLEASE IDENTIFY.
IF THAT'S YOU OVER US, THEN THAT'S US ON THE ROAD, PELICAN.
WILL SET DOWN IN THE FLAT AREA TO YOUR TWELVE, COLONEL.
I'LL HAVE ONE BLOODY GREAT STORY, WON'T I?
IF THEY EVER LET YOU WRITE IT.
WHAT DO YOU MEAN?
THIS WHOLE OP IS CLASSIFIED, LADY!
WE'LL SEE ABOUT THAT!
NICE TO SEE YOU GUYS.
SHAVED IT MIGHTY CLOSE BACK THERE, COLONEL.
WHAT CAN I SAY...

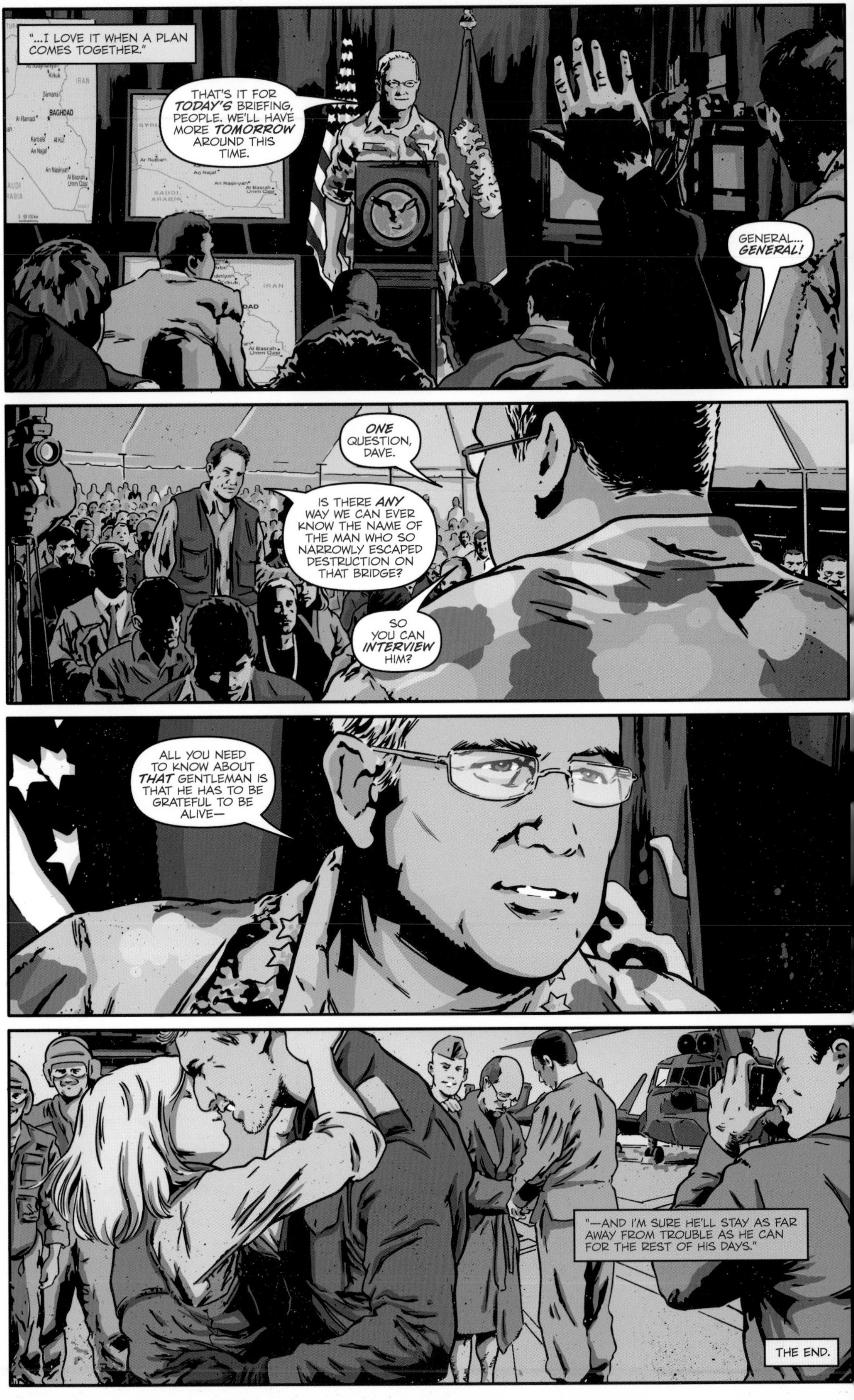
"...I LOVE IT WHEN A PLAN COMES TOGETHER."
THAT'S IT FOR TODAY'S BRIEFING, PEOPLE. WE'LL HAVE MORE TOMORROW AROUND THIS TIME.
GENERAL... GENERAL!
ONE QUESTION, DAVE.
IS THERE ANY WAY WE CAN EVER KNOW THE NAME OF THE MAN WHO SO NARROWLY ESCAPED DESTRUCTION ON THAT BRIDGE?
SO YOU CAN INTERVIEW HIM?
ALL YOU NEED TO KNOW ABOUT THAT GENTLEMAN IS THAT HE HAS TO BE GRATEFUL TO BE ALIVE—
"—AND I'M SURE HE'LL STAY AS FAR AWAY FROM TROUBLE AS HE CAN FOR THE REST OF HIS DAYS."
THE END.

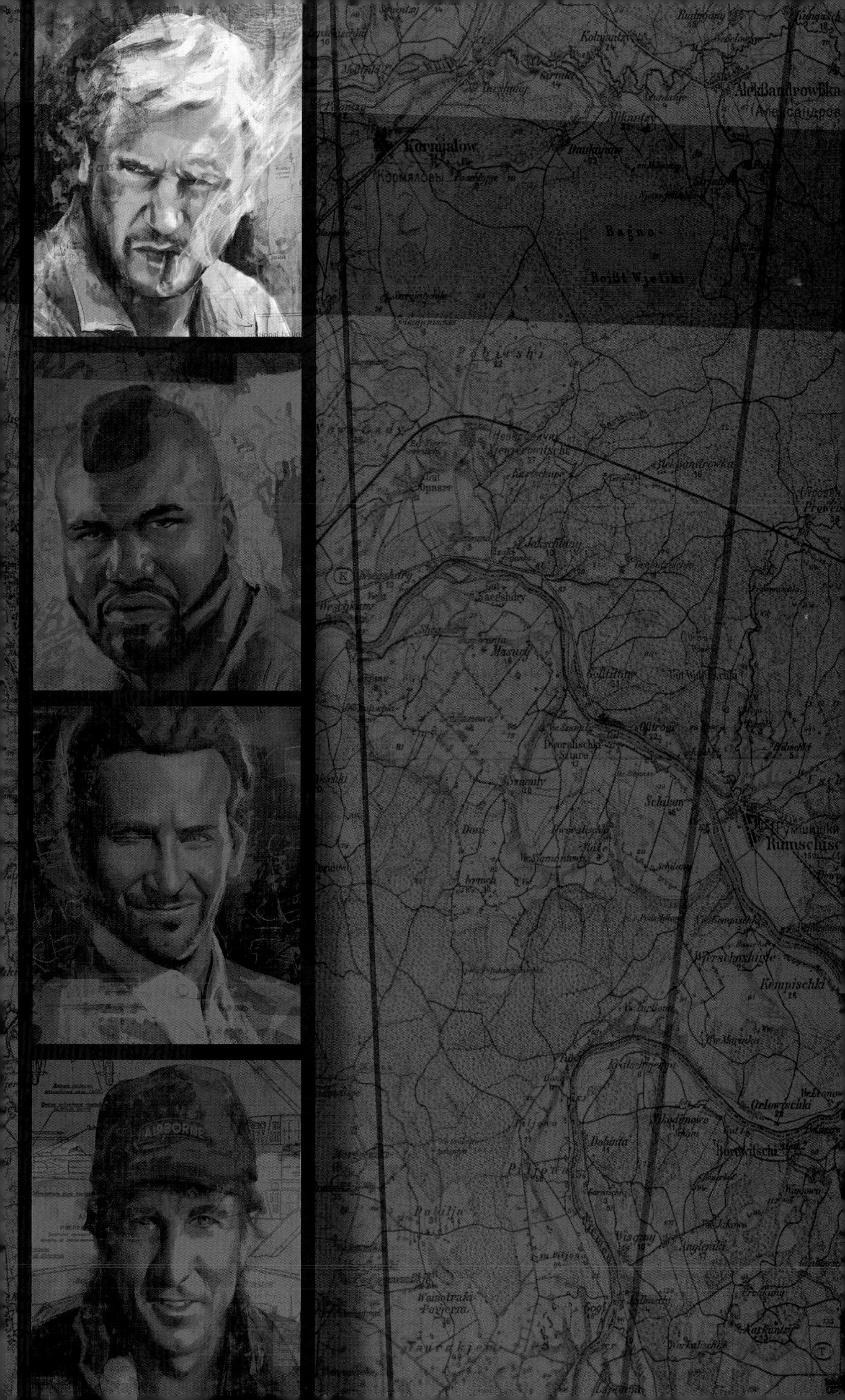

Kornjalow
Кормяловы
Bagno
Kempischki
Orlowischki
Schilany
Ostrogi
AIRBORNE

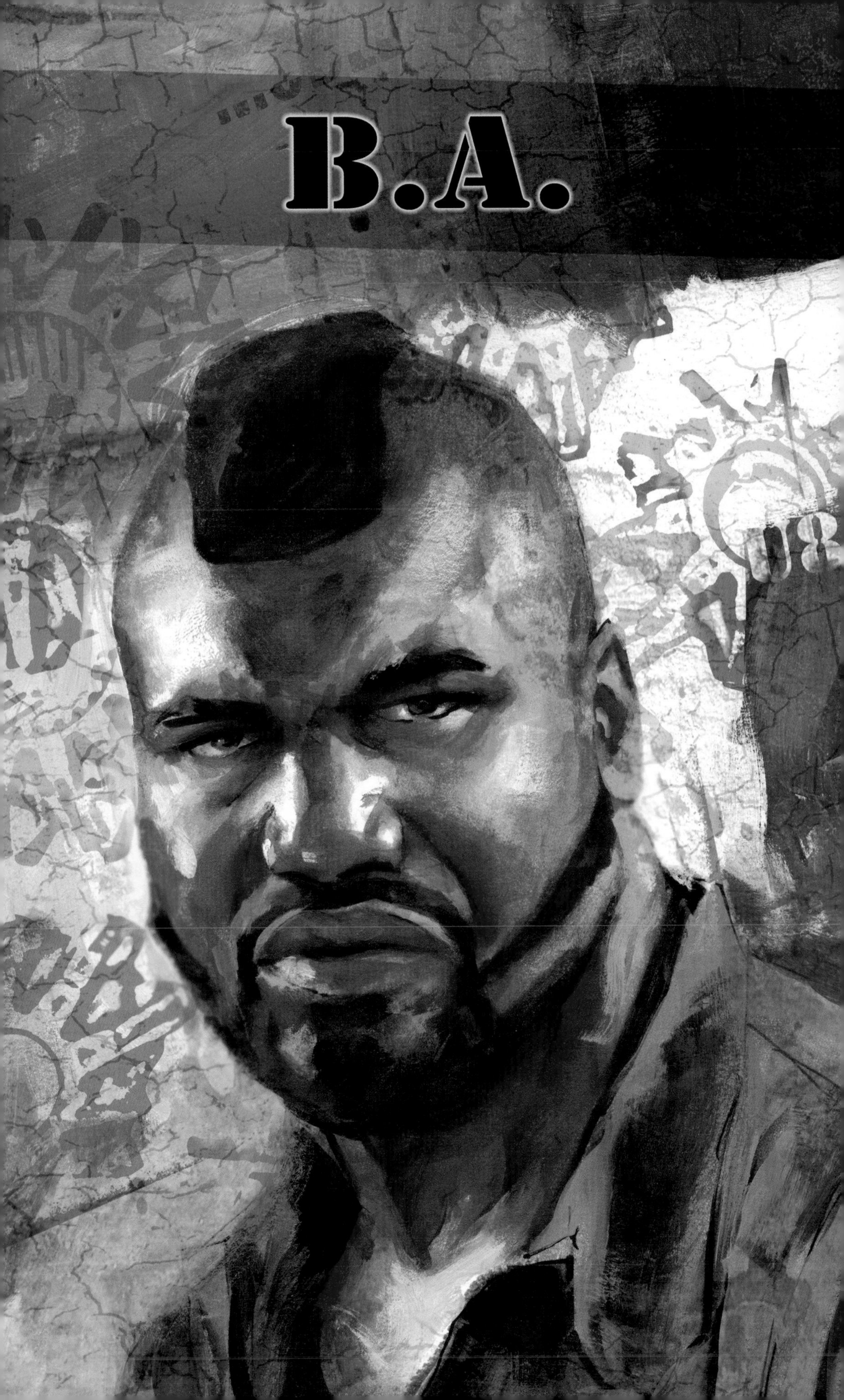
B.A.

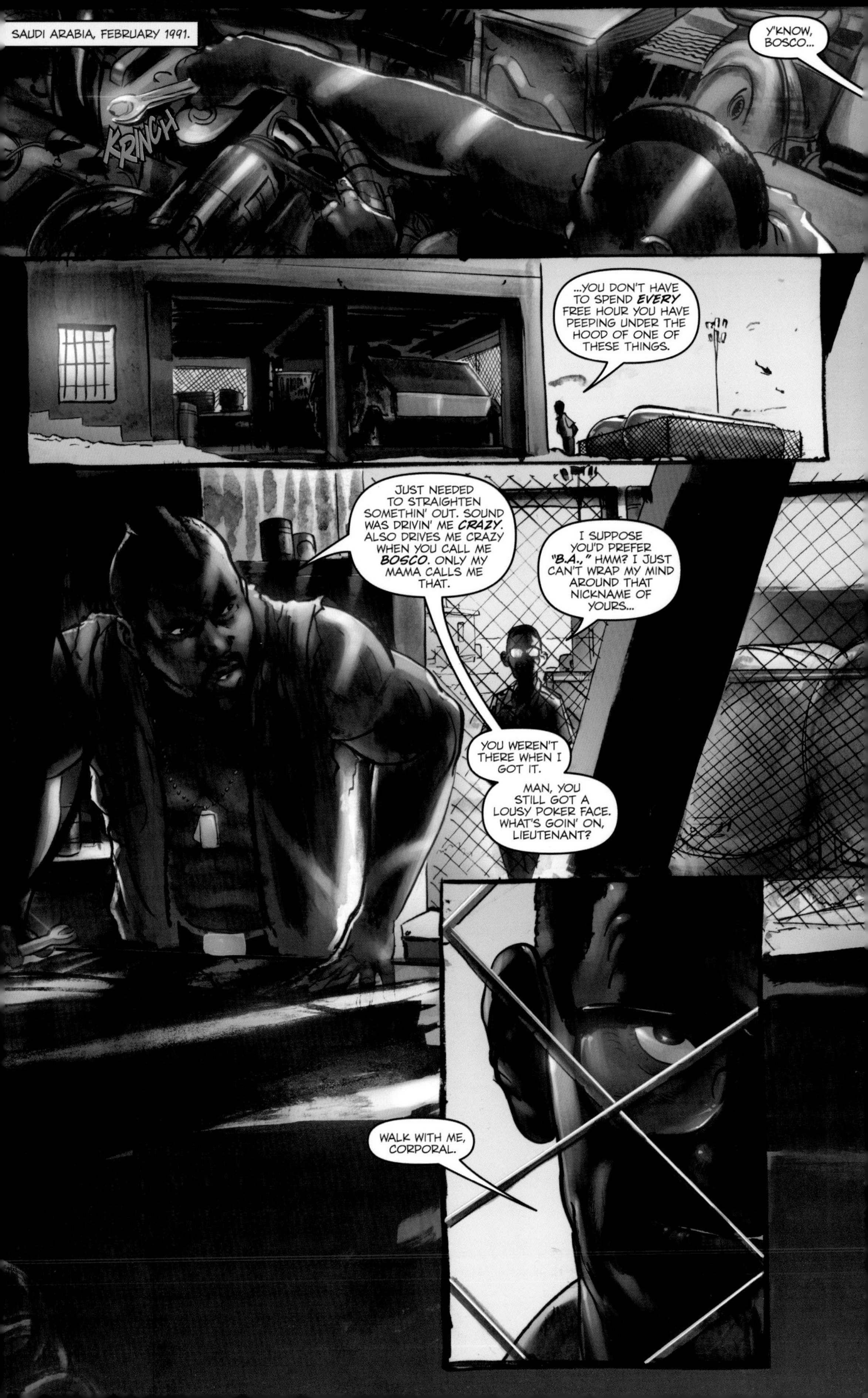

SAUDI ARABIA, FEBRUARY 1991.
Y'KNOW, BOSCO...
KRINCH
...YOU DON'T HAVE TO SPEND EVERY FREE HOUR YOU HAVE PEEPING UNDER THE HOOD OF ONE OF THESE THINGS.
JUST NEEDED TO STRAIGHTEN SOMETHIN' OUT. SOUND WAS DRIVIN' ME CRAZY. ALSO DRIVES ME CRAZY WHEN YOU CALL ME BOSCO. ONLY MY MAMA CALLS ME THAT.
I SUPPOSE YOU'D PREFER "B.A.," HMM? I JUST CAN'T WRAP MY MIND AROUND THAT NICKNAME OF YOURS...
YOU WEREN'T THERE WHEN I GOT IT.
MAN, YOU STILL GOT A LOUSY POKER FACE. WHAT'S GOIN' ON, LIEUTENANT?
WALK WITH ME, CORPORAL.

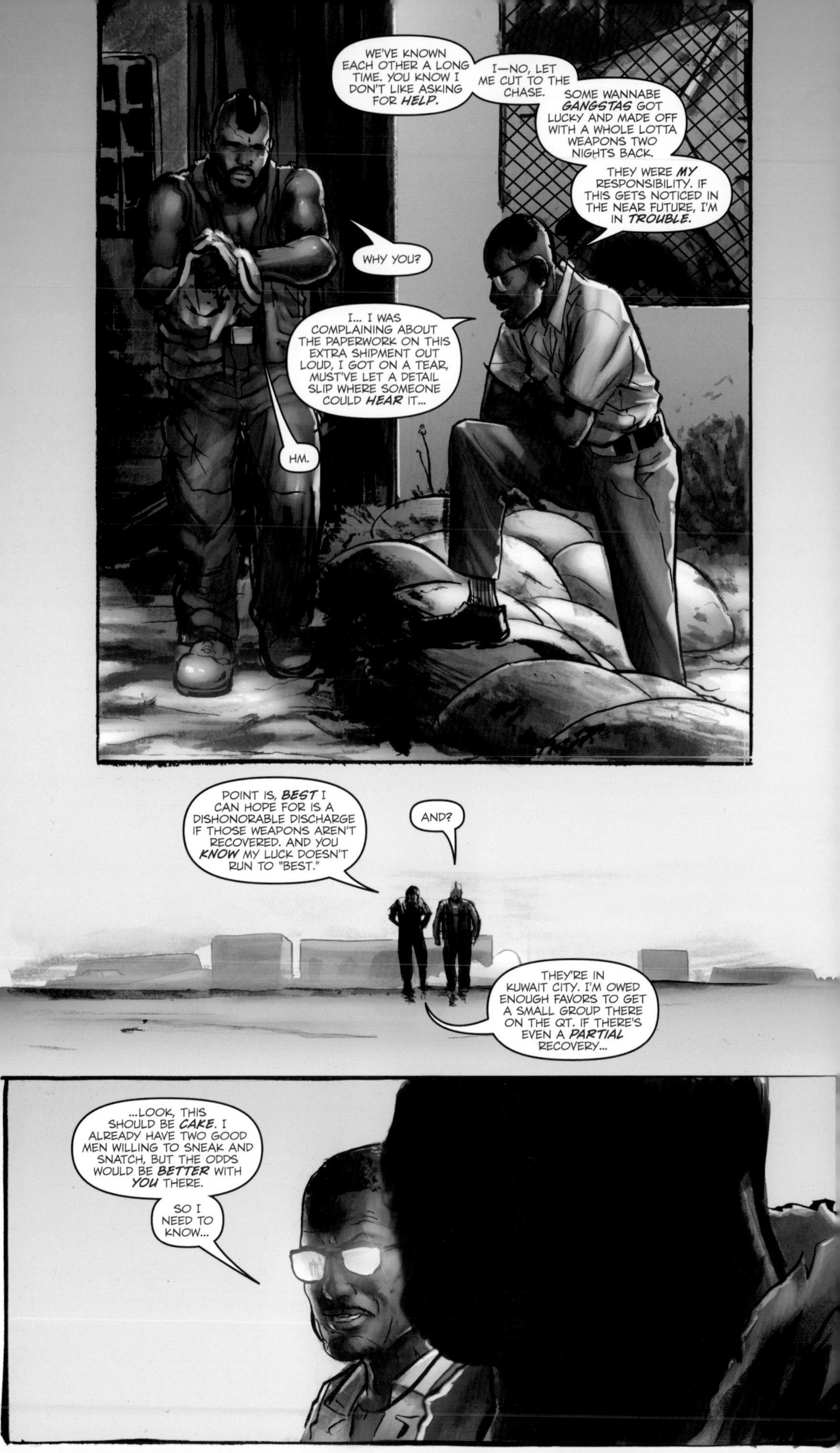
WE'VE KNOWN EACH OTHER A LONG TIME. YOU KNOW I DON'T LIKE ASKING FOR HELP.
I—NO, LET ME CUT TO THE CHASE.
SOME WANNABE GANGSTAS GOT LUCKY AND MADE OFF WITH A WHOLE LOTTA WEAPONS TWO NIGHTS BACK.
THEY WERE MY RESPONSIBILITY. IF THIS GETS NOTICED IN THE NEAR FUTURE, I'M IN TROUBLE.
WHY YOU?
I... I WAS COMPLAINING ABOUT THE PAPERWORK ON THIS EXTRA SHIPMENT OUT LOUD, I GOT ON A TEAR, MUST'VE LET A DETAIL SLIP WHERE SOMEONE COULD HEAR IT...
HM.
POINT IS, BEST I CAN HOPE FOR IS A DISHONORABLE DISCHARGE IF THOSE WEAPONS AREN'T RECOVERED. AND YOU KNOW MY LUCK DOESN'T RUN TO "BEST."
AND?
THEY'RE IN KUWAIT CITY. I'M OWED ENOUGH FAVORS TO GET A SMALL GROUP THERE ON THE QT. IF THERE'S EVEN A PARTIAL RECOVERY...
...LOOK, THIS SHOULD BE CAKE. I ALREADY HAVE TWO GOOD MEN WILLING TO SNEAK AND SNATCH, BUT THE ODDS WOULD BE BETTER WITH YOU THERE.
SO I NEED TO KNOW...

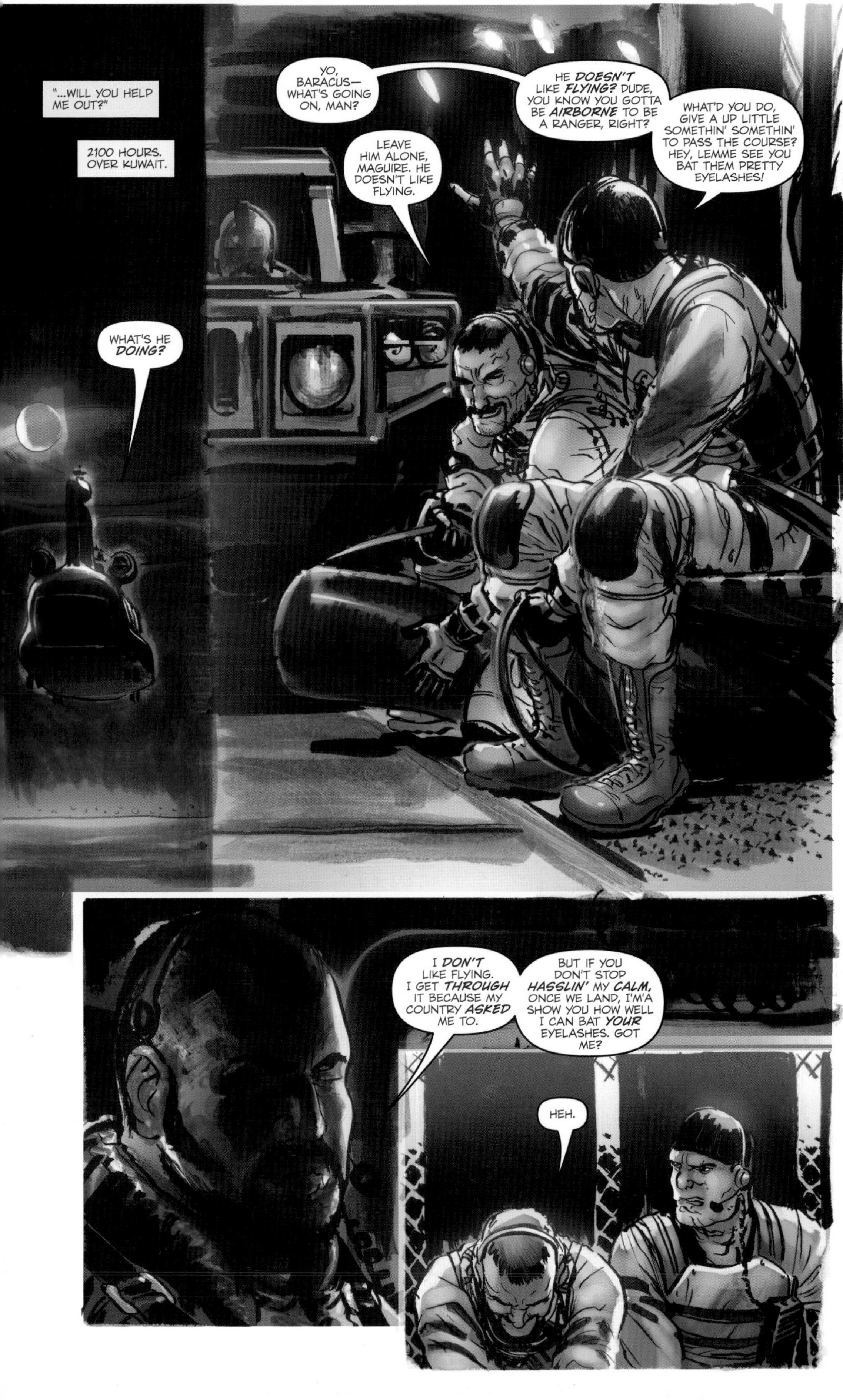

"...WILL YOU HELP ME OUT?"
2100 HOURS. OVER KUWAIT.
YO, BARACUS— WHAT'S GOING ON, MAN?
LEAVE HIM ALONE, MAGUIRE. HE DOESN'T LIKE FLYING.
HE DOESN'T LIKE FLYING? DUDE, YOU KNOW YOU GOTTA BE AIRBORNE TO BE A RANGER, RIGHT?
WHAT'D YOU DO, GIVE A UP LITTLE SOMETHIN' SOMETHIN' TO PASS THE COURSE? HEY, LEMME SEE YOU BAT THEM PRETTY EYELASHES!
WHAT'S HE DOING?
I DON'T LIKE FLYING. I GET THROUGH IT BECAUSE MY COUNTRY ASKED ME TO.
BUT IF YOU DON'T STOP HASSLIN' MY CALM, ONCE WE LAND, I'M'A SHOW YOU HOW WELL I CAN BAT YOUR EYELASHES. GOT ME?
HEH.

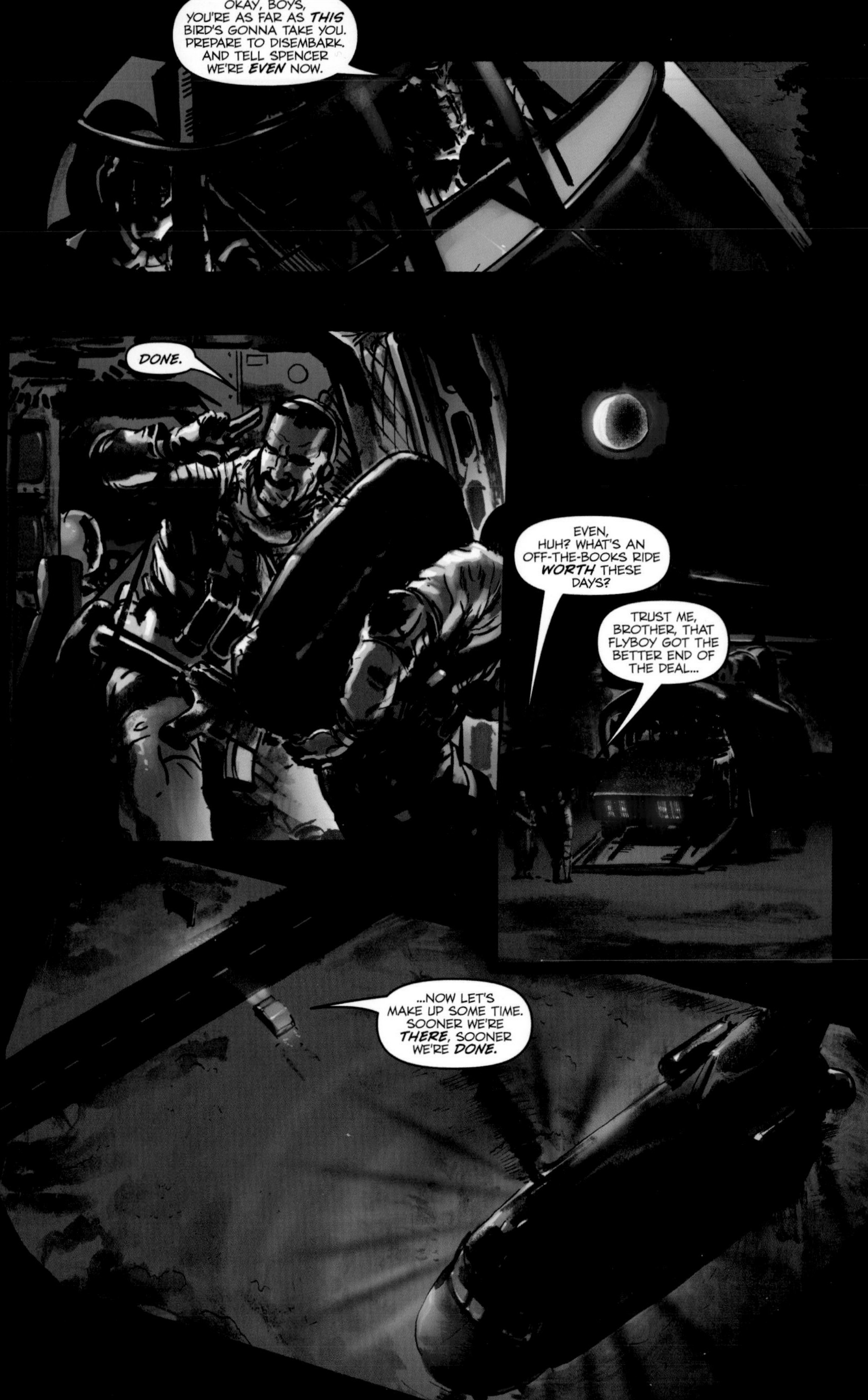
OKAY, BOYS, YOU'RE AS FAR AS THIS BIRD'S GONNA TAKE YOU. PREPARE TO DISEMBARK. AND TELL SPENCER WE'RE EVEN NOW.
DONE.
EVEN, HUH? WHAT'S AN OFF-THE-BOOKS RIDE WORTH THESE DAYS?
TRUST ME, BROTHER, THAT FLYBOY GOT THE BETTER END OF THE DEAL...
...NOW LET'S MAKE UP SOME TIME. SOONER WE'RE THERE, SOONER WE'RE DONE.

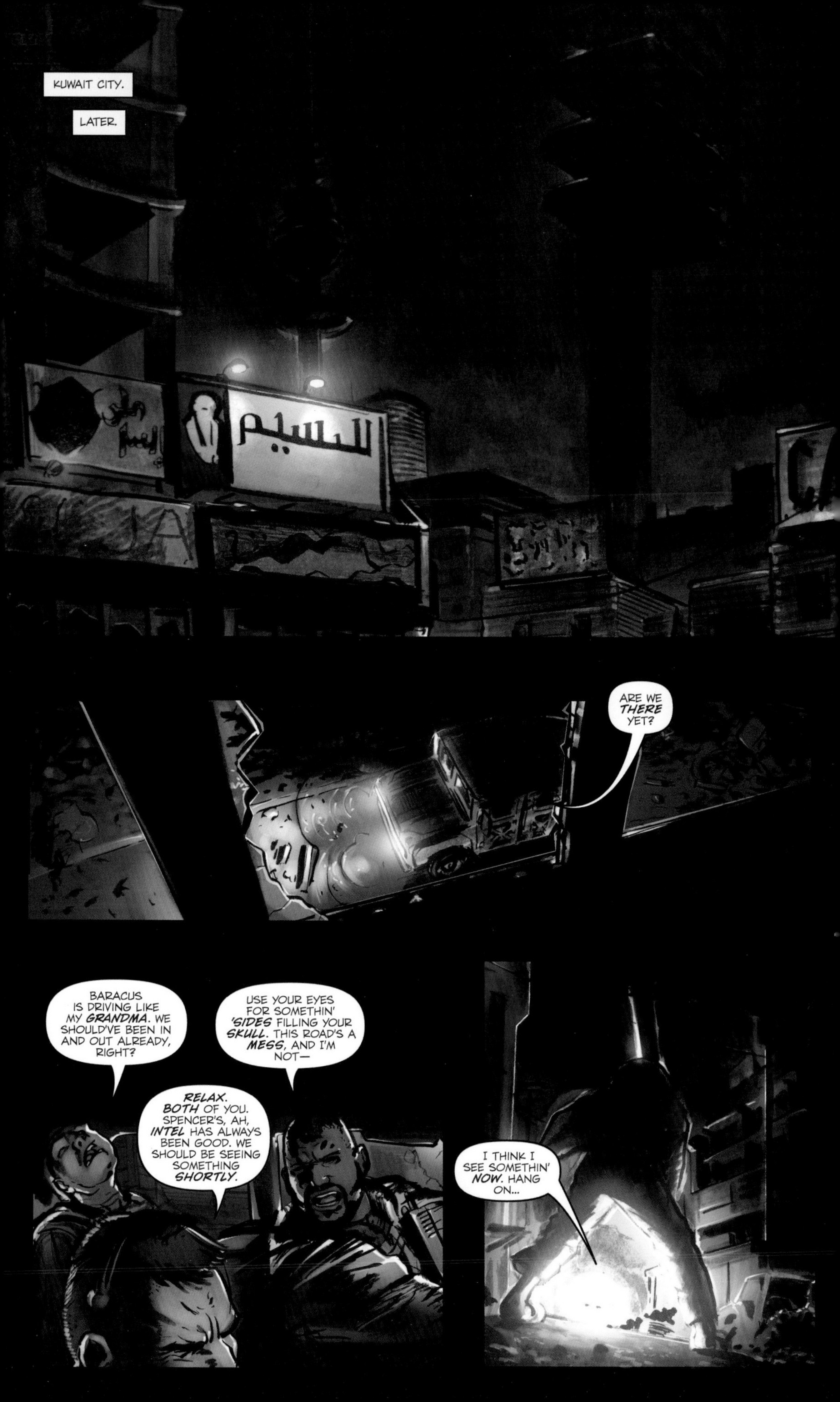
KUWAIT CITY.
LATER.
ARE WE THERE YET?
BARACUS IS DRIVING LIKE MY GRANDMA. WE SHOULD'VE BEEN IN AND OUT ALREADY, RIGHT?
USE YOUR EYES FOR SOMETHIN' 'SIDES FILLING YOUR SKULL. THIS ROAD'S A MESS, AND I'M NOT—
RELAX. BOTH OF YOU. SPENCER'S, AH, INTEL HAS ALWAYS BEEN GOOD. WE SHOULD BE SEEING SOMETHING SHORTLY.
I THINK I SEE SOMETHIN' NOW. HANG ON...

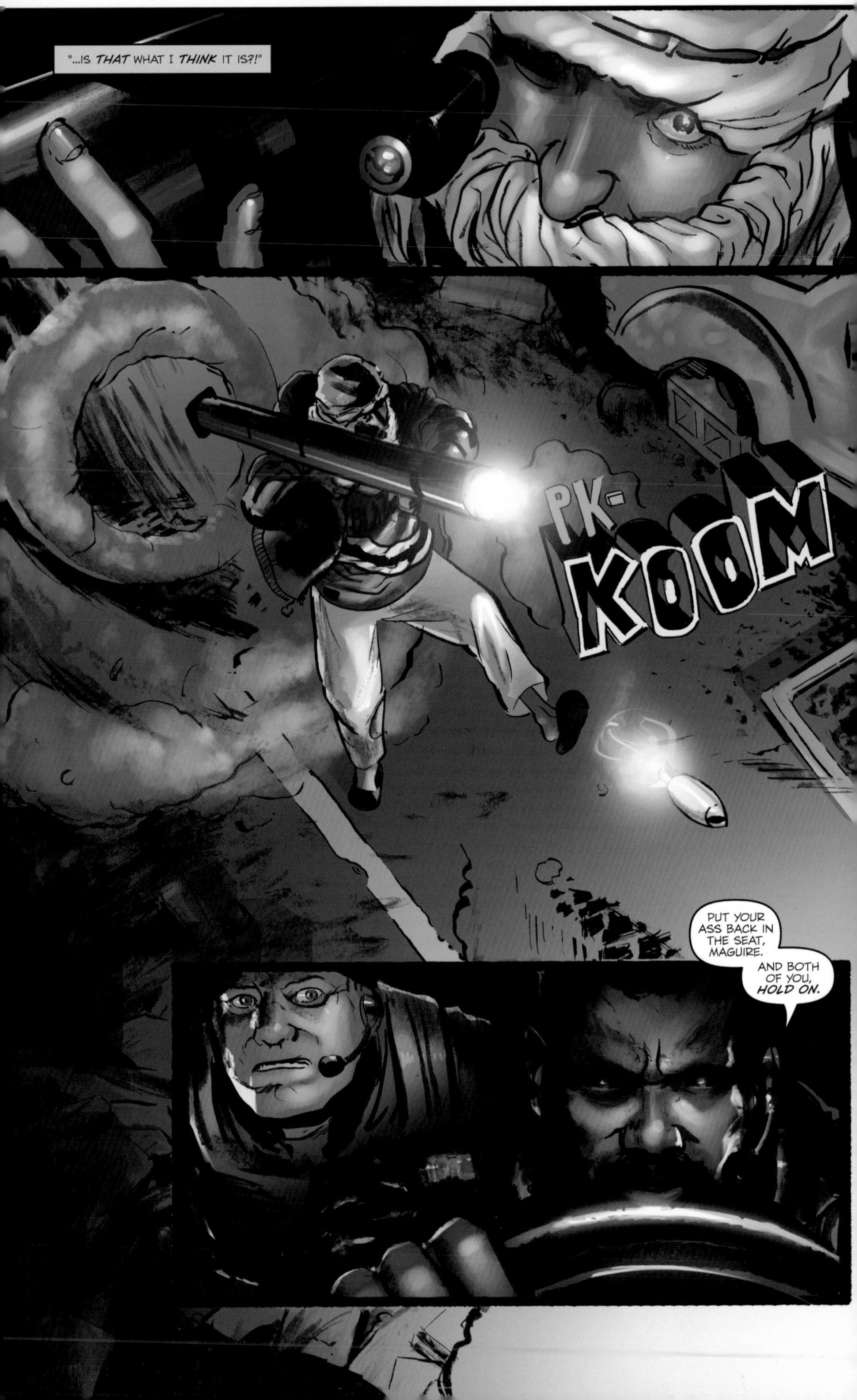
"...IS *THAT* WHAT I *THINK* IT IS?!"
PK-KOOM
PUT YOUR ASS BACK IN THE SEAT, MAGUIRE.
AND BOTH OF YOU, ***HOLD ON.***

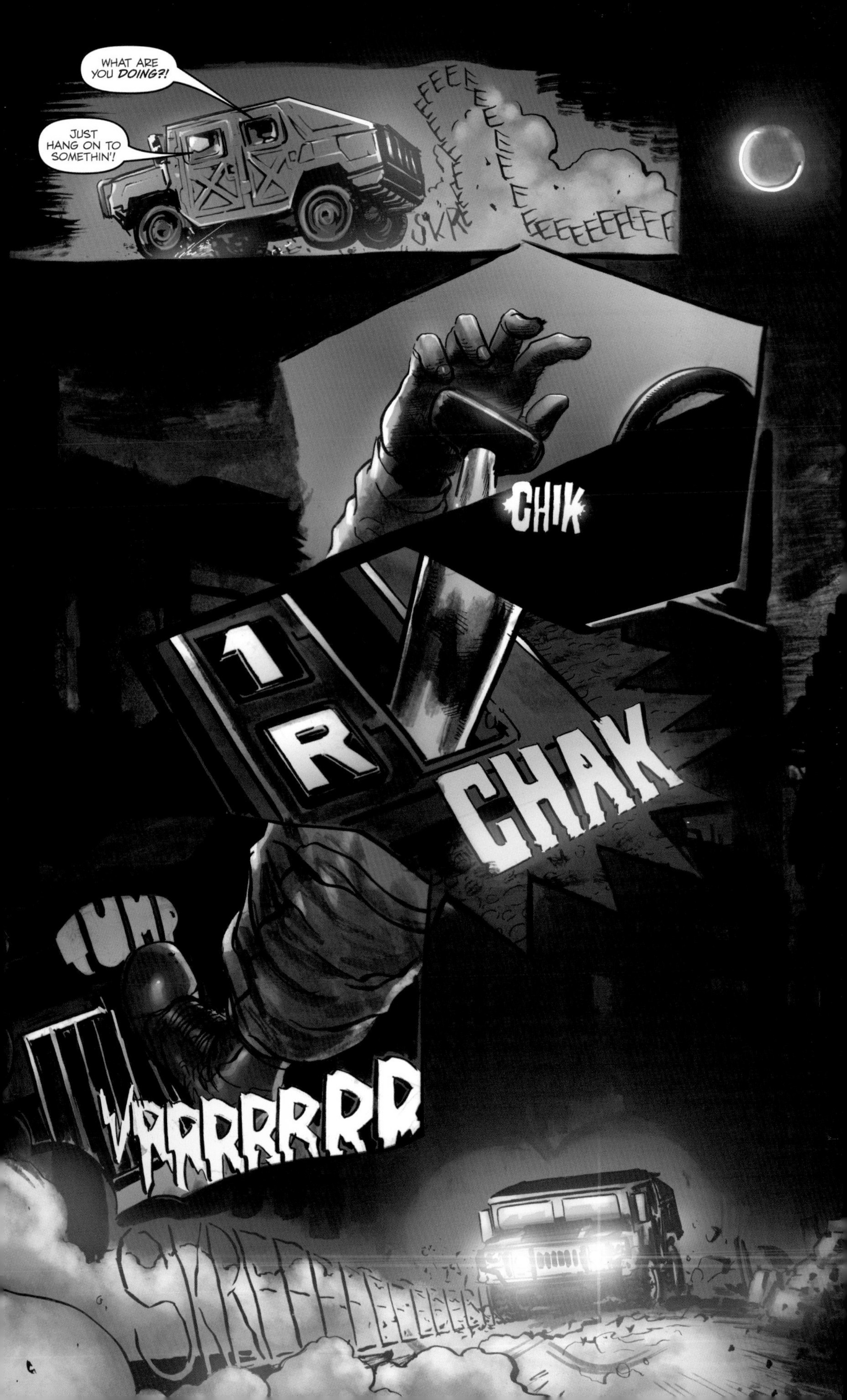
WHAT ARE YOU *DOING?!*
JUST HANG ON TO SOMETHIN'!
CHIK
CHAK

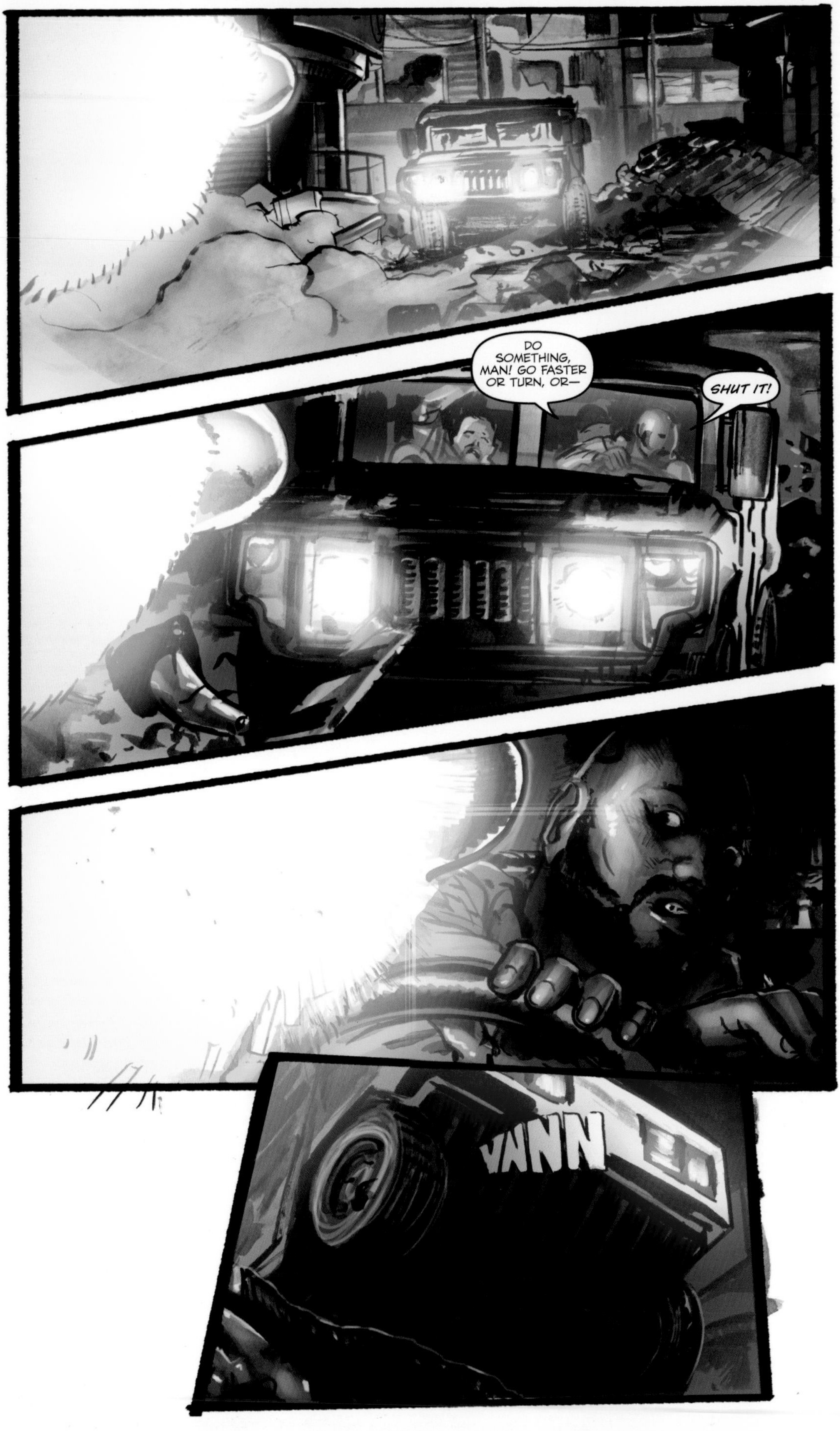

DO SOMETHING, MAN! GO FASTER OR TURN, OR—
SHUT IT!

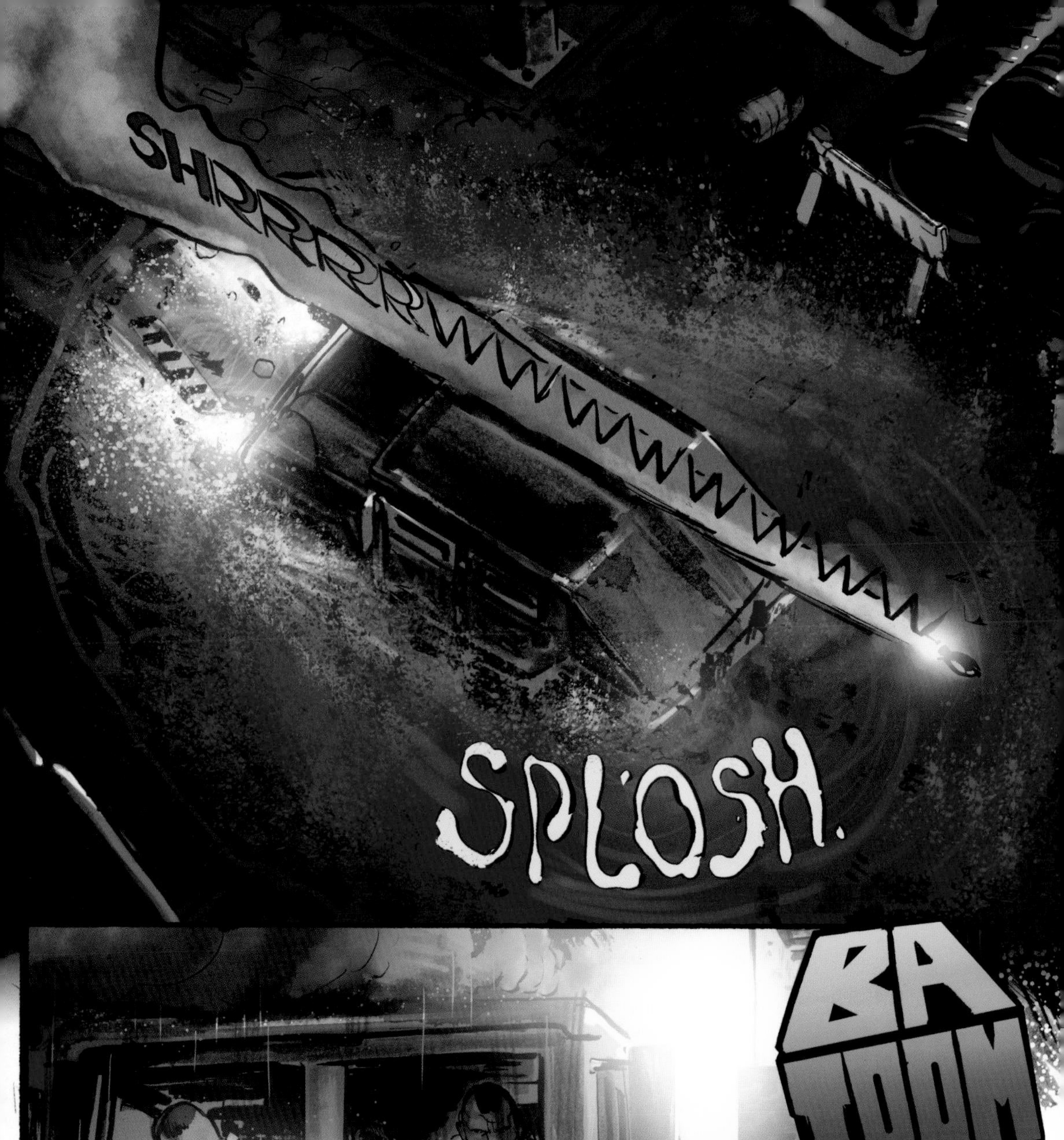
SHRRRRRWWWWWWWWW-WAW
SPLOSH.

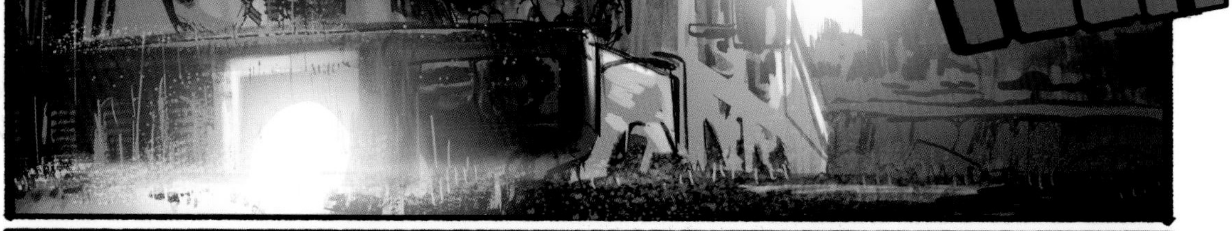
BA TOOM

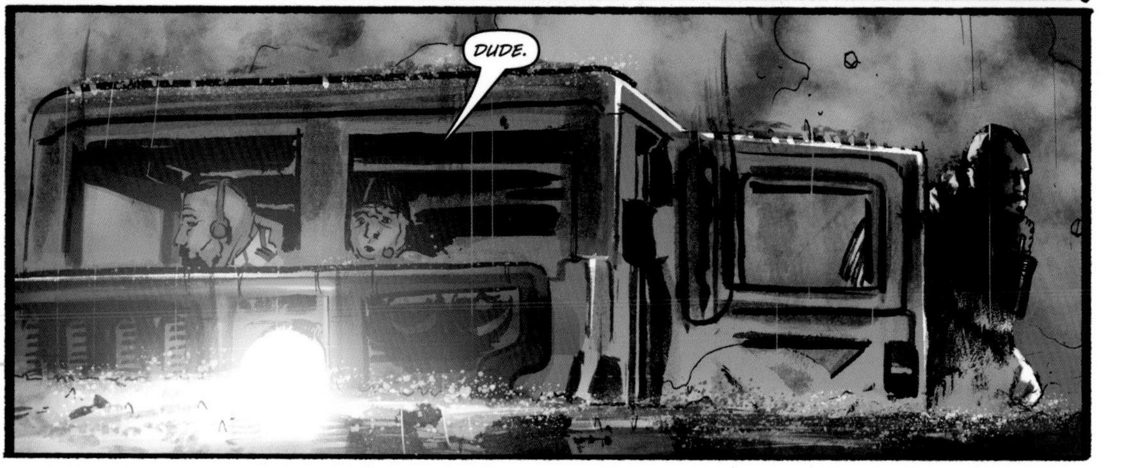
DUDE.

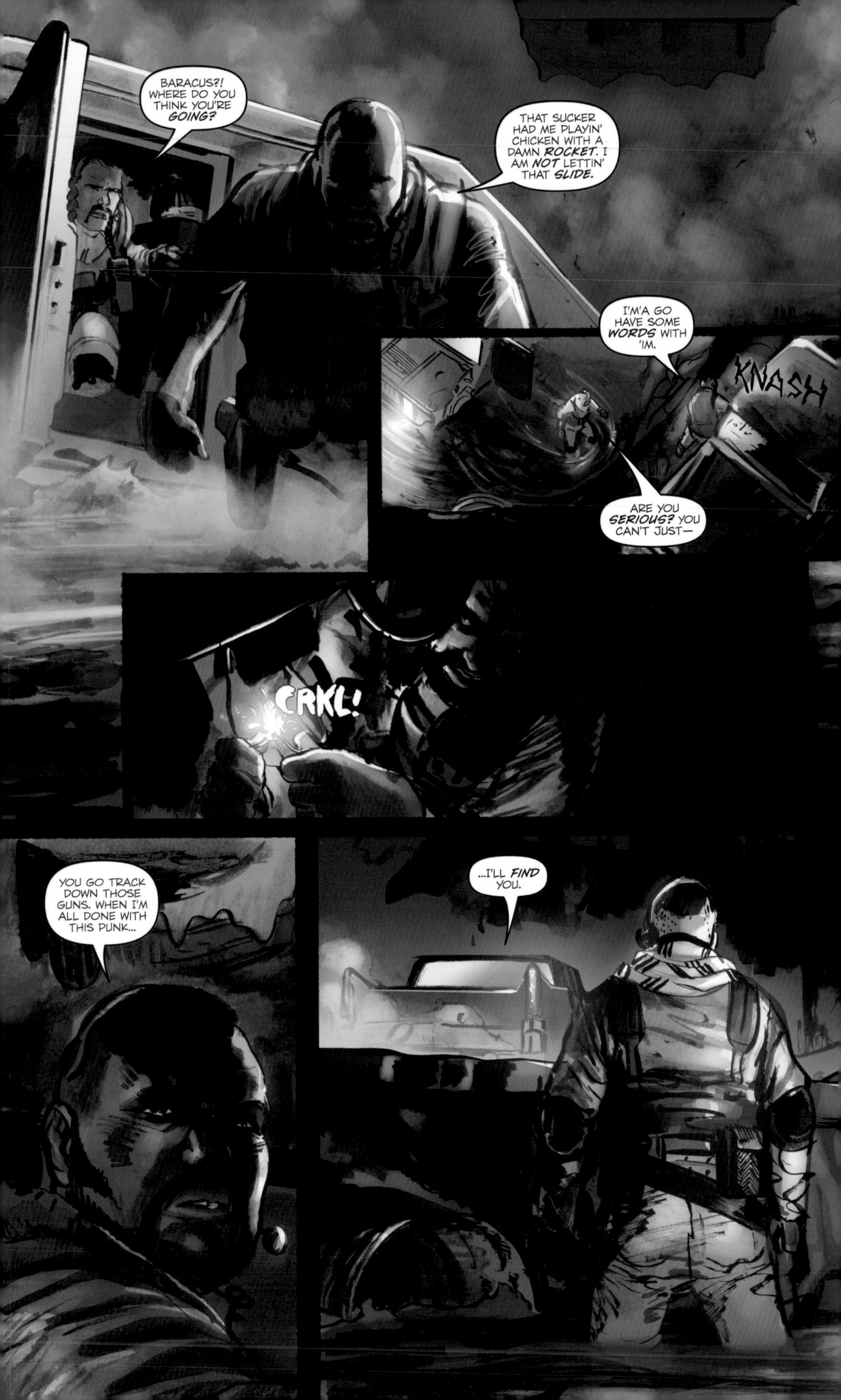
BARACUS?! WHERE DO YOU THINK YOU'RE GOING?
THAT SUCKER HAD ME PLAYIN' CHICKEN WITH A DAMN ROCKET. I AM NOT LETTIN' THAT SLIDE.
I'M'A GO HAVE SOME WORDS WITH 'IM.
KNASH
ARE YOU SERIOUS? YOU CAN'T JUST—
CRKL!
YOU GO TRACK DOWN THOSE GUNS. WHEN I'M ALL DONE WITH THIS PUNK...
...I'LL FIND YOU.

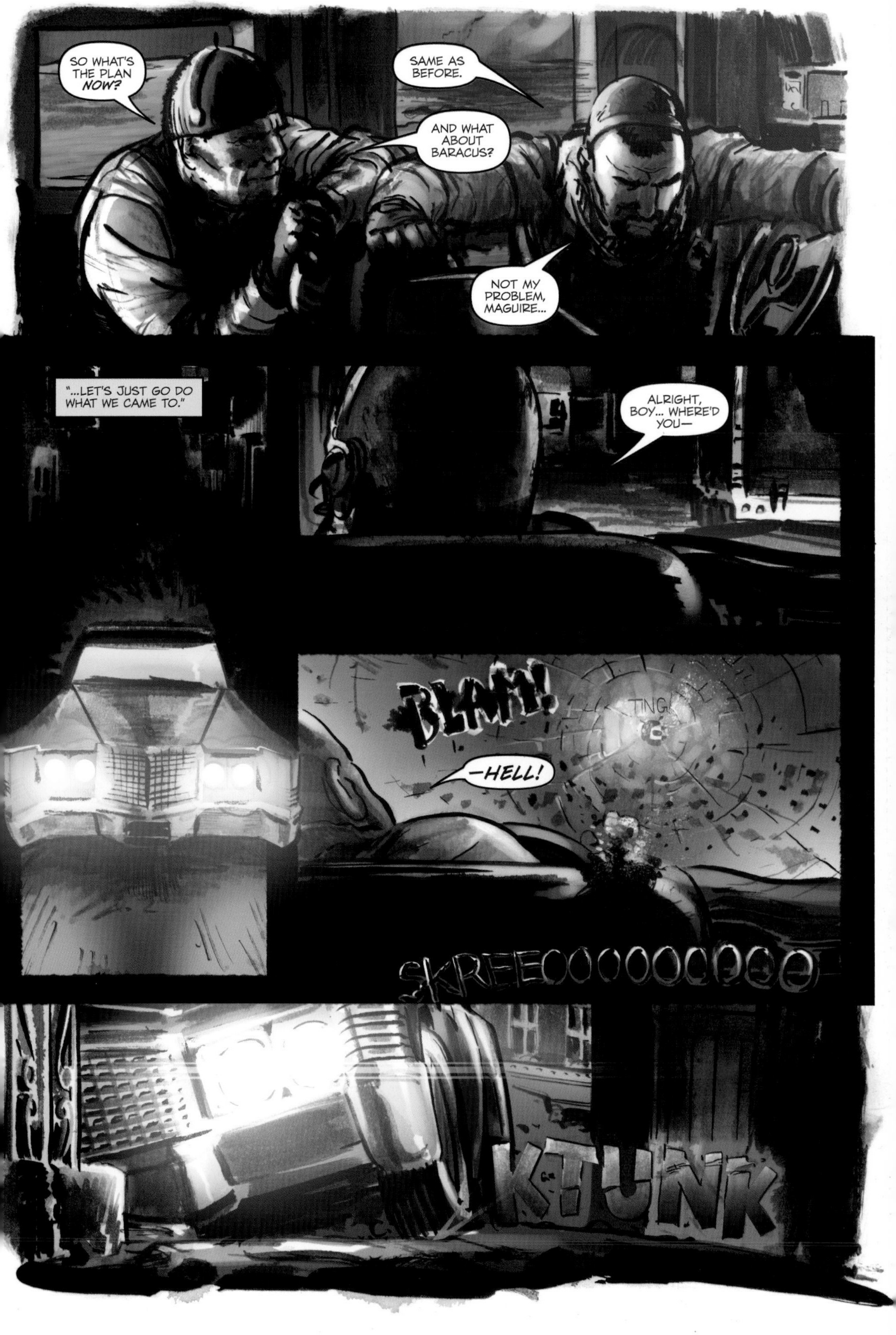
SO WHAT'S THE PLAN NOW?
SAME AS BEFORE.
AND WHAT ABOUT BARACUS?
NOT MY PROBLEM, MAGUIRE...
"...LET'S JUST GO DO WHAT WE CAME TO."
ALRIGHT, BOY... WHERE'D YOU—
BLAM!
TNG!
—HELL!
SKREEEOOOOOOOOOO
K-TUNK

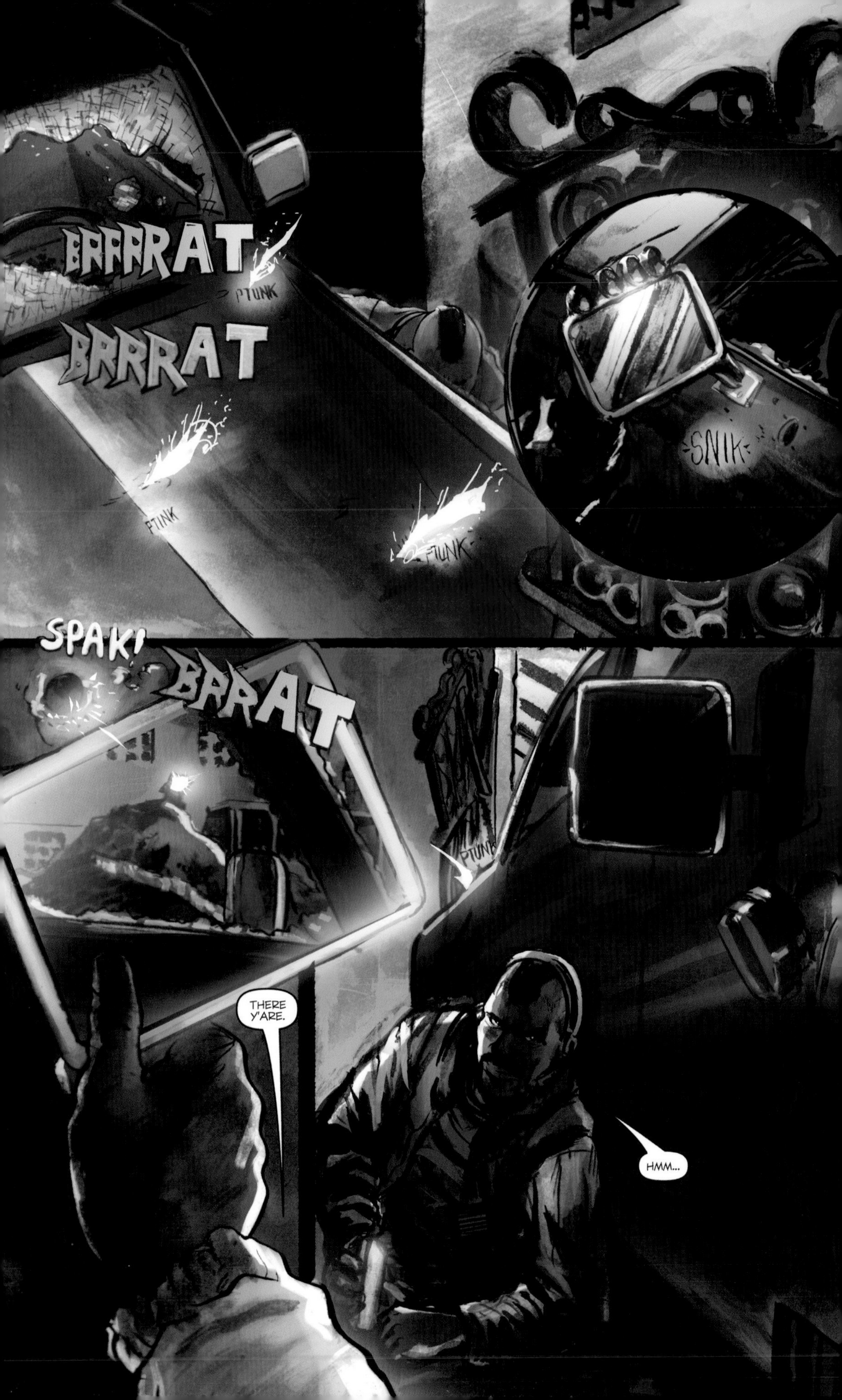
BRRRRAT
PTUNK
BRRRAT
PTUNK
PTUNK
SNIK
SPAK!
BRRAT
PTUNK
THERE Y'ARE.
HMM...

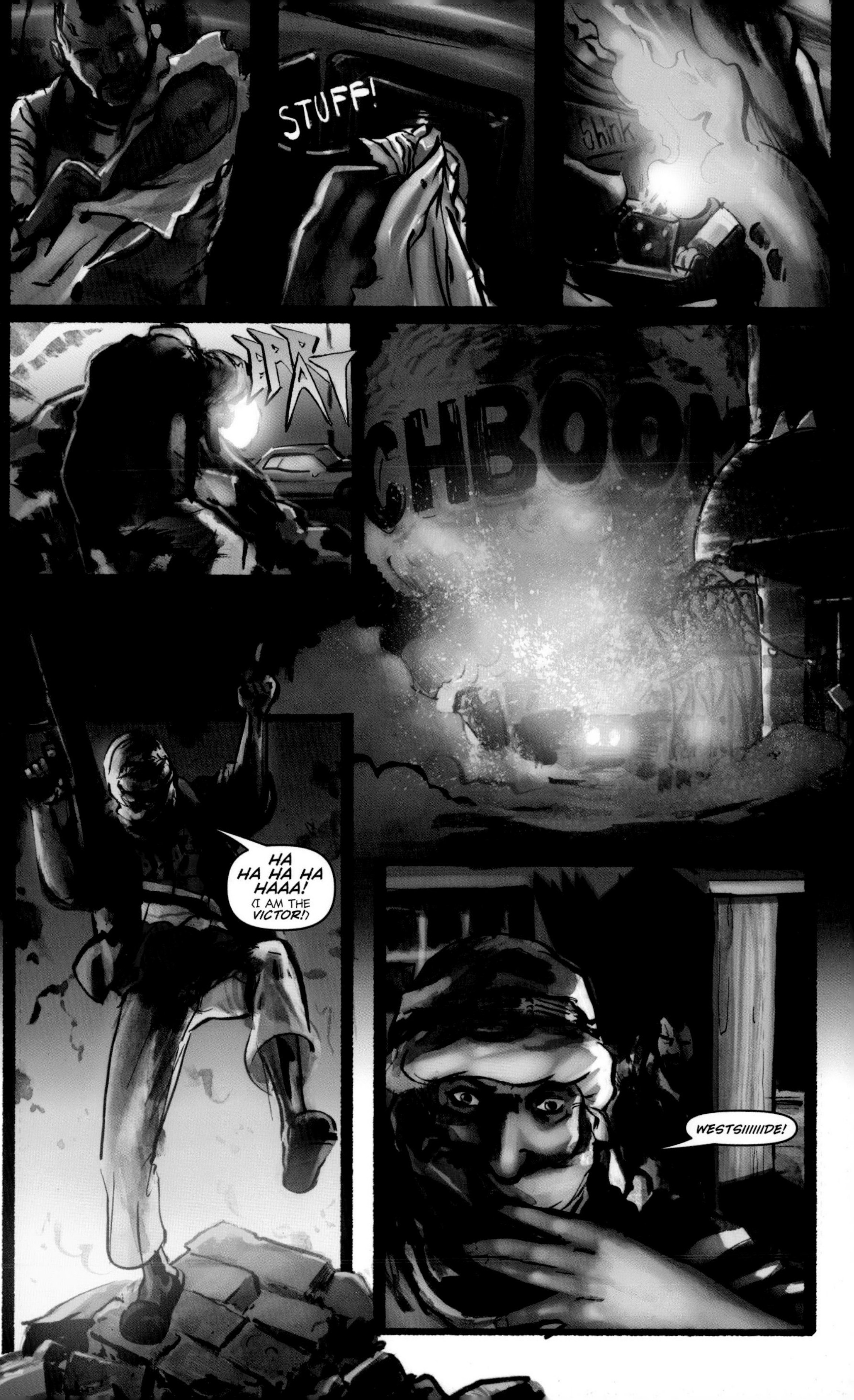
STUFF!
Shink
FPRAT
CHBOOM
HA HA HA HA HAAA! ‹I AM THE VICTOR!›
WESTSIIIIIIDE!

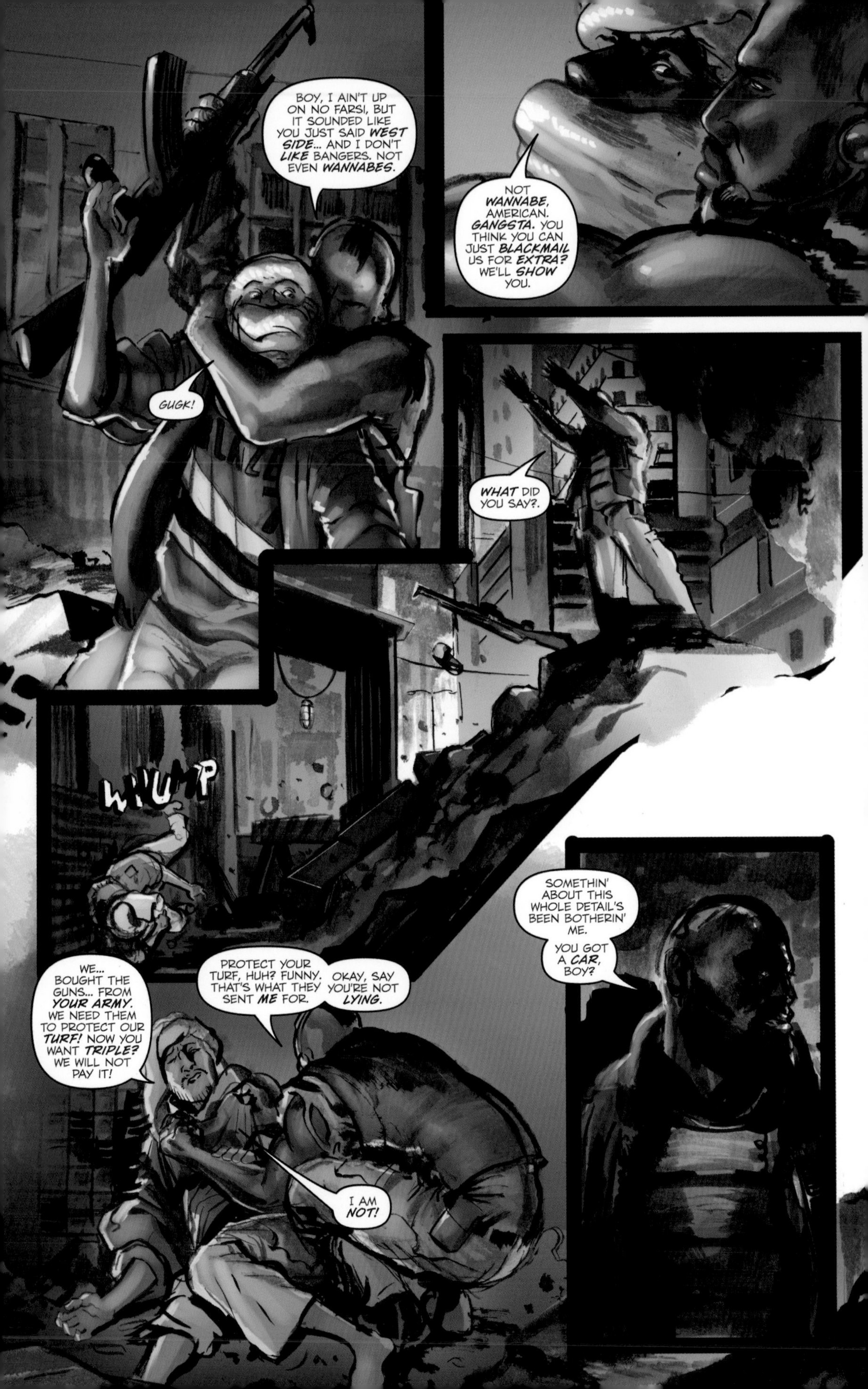
BOY, I AIN'T UP ON NO FARSI, BUT IT SOUNDED LIKE YOU JUST SAID WEST SIDE... AND I DON'T LIKE BANGERS. NOT EVEN WANNABES.
GUGK!
NOT WANNABE, AMERICAN. GANGSTA. YOU THINK YOU CAN JUST BLACKMAIL US FOR EXTRA? WE'LL SHOW YOU.
WHAT DID YOU SAY?.
WHUMP
WE... BOUGHT THE GUNS... FROM YOUR ARMY. WE NEED THEM TO PROTECT OUR TURF! NOW YOU WANT TRIPLE? WE WILL NOT PAY IT!
PROTECT YOUR TURF, HUH? FUNNY. THAT'S WHAT THEY SENT ME FOR.
OKAY, SAY YOU'RE NOT LYING.
I AM NOT!
SOMETHIN' ABOUT THIS WHOLE DETAIL'S BEEN BOTHERIN' ME.
YOU GOT A CAR, BOY?

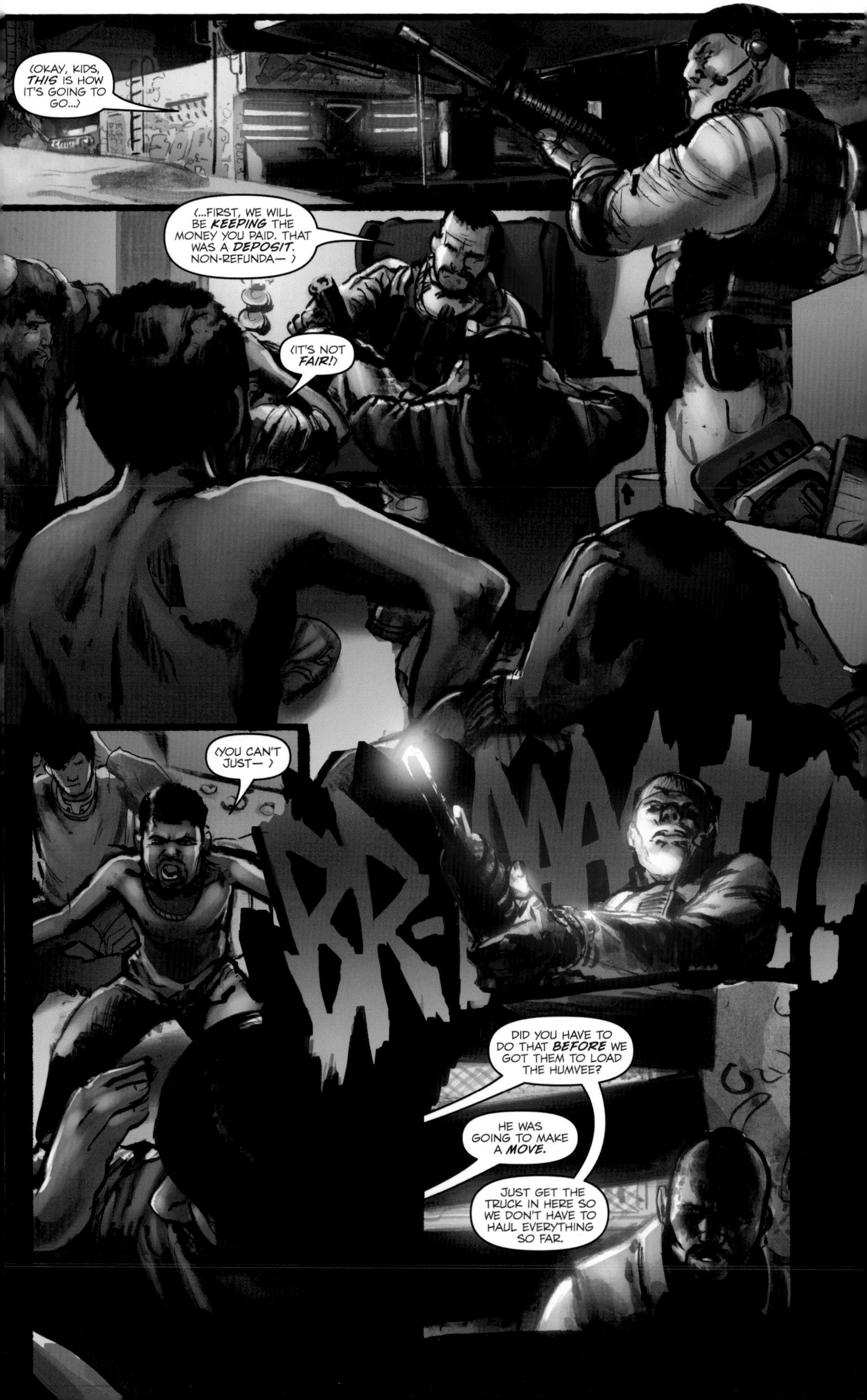

‹OKAY, KIDS, *THIS* IS HOW IT'S GOING TO GO...›
‹...FIRST, WE WILL BE *KEEPING* THE MONEY YOU PAID. THAT WAS A *DEPOSIT*. NON-REFUNDA— ›
‹IT'S NOT *FAIR!*›
‹YOU CAN'T JUST— ›
DID YOU HAVE TO DO THAT *BEFORE* WE GOT THEM TO LOAD THE HUMVEE?
HE WAS GOING TO MAKE A *MOVE.*
JUST GET THE TRUCK IN HERE SO WE DON'T HAVE TO HAUL EVERYTHING SO FAR.

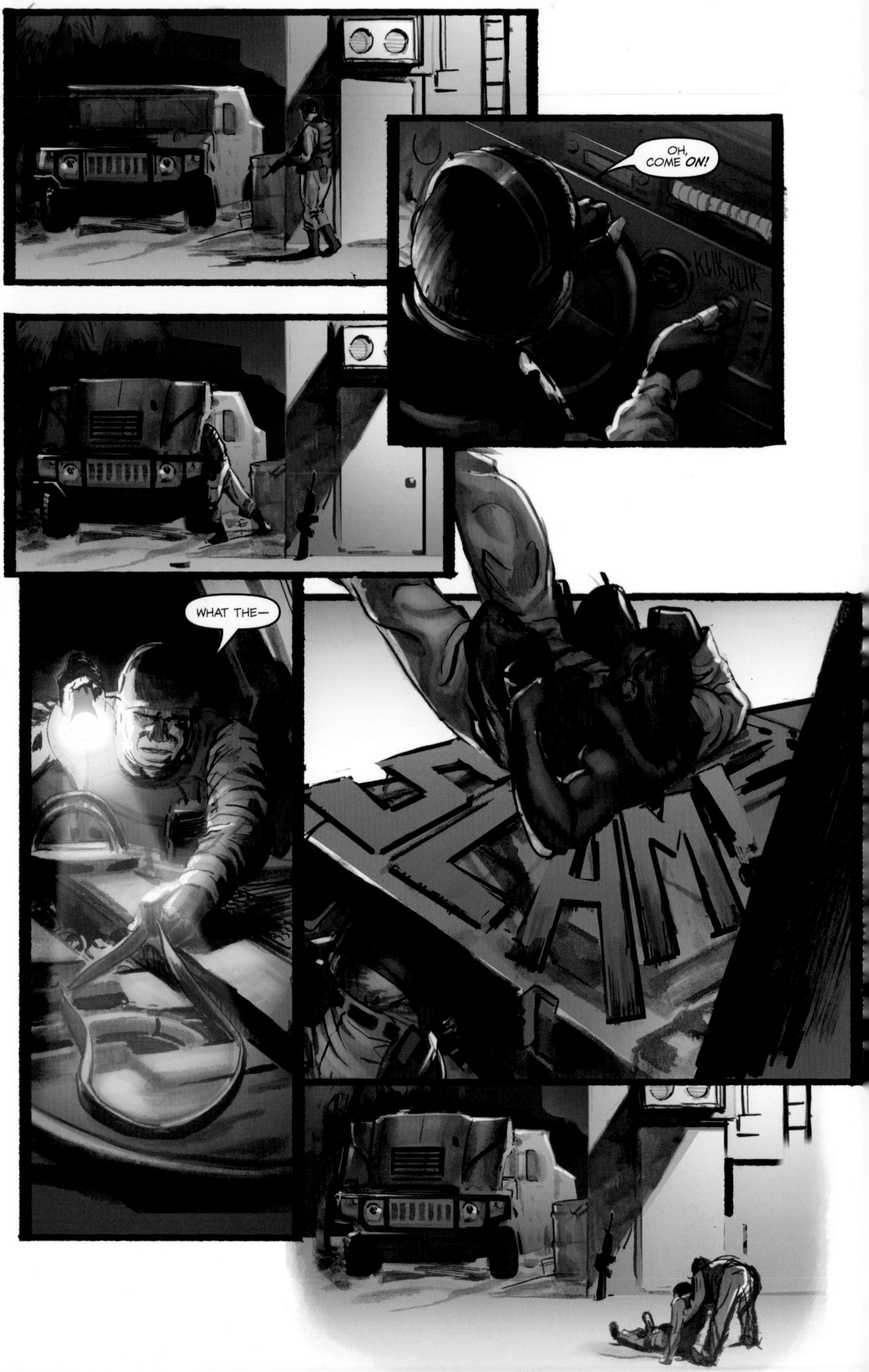
OH, COME ON!
KLIK KLIK
WHAT THE—

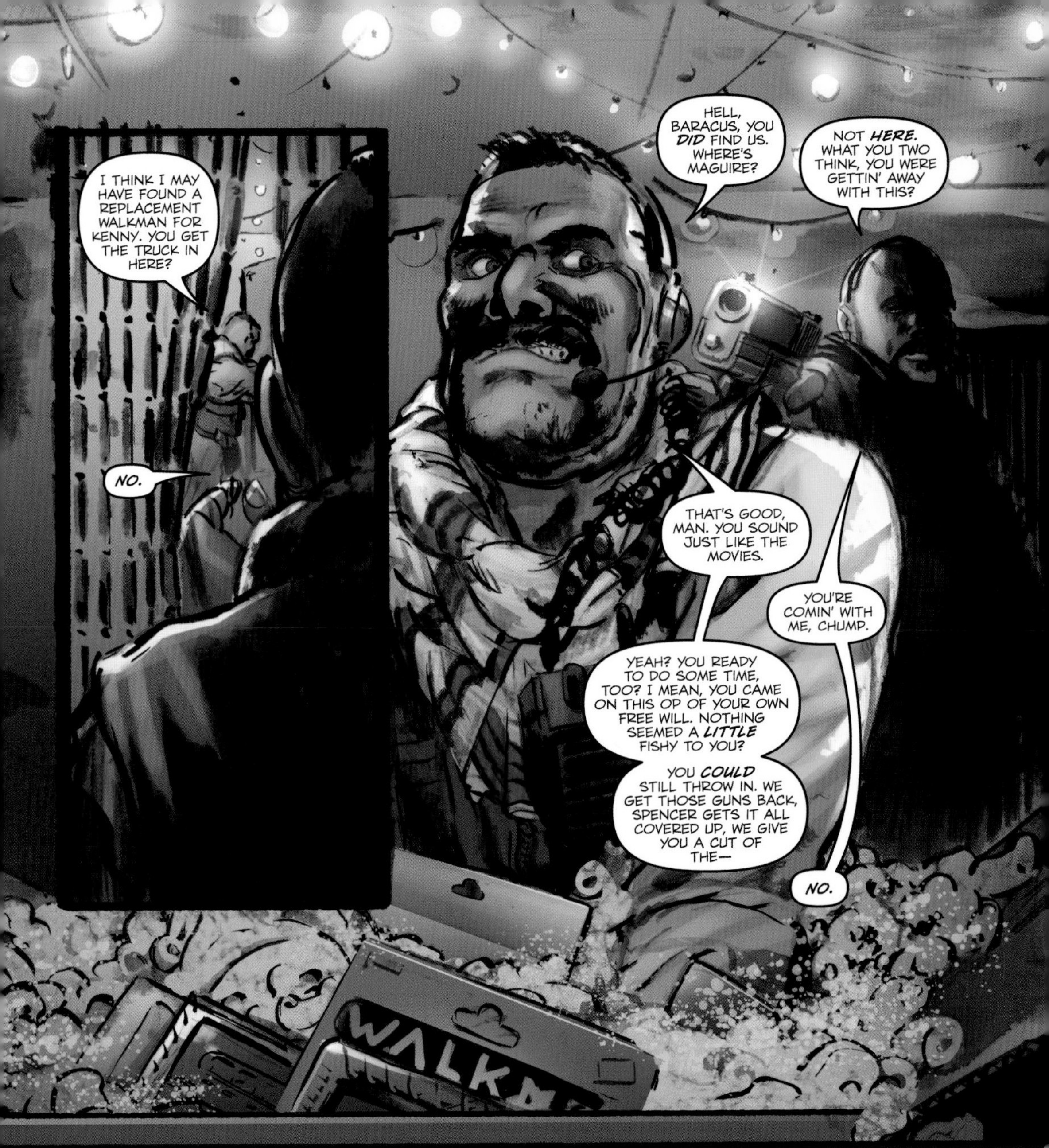
I THINK I MAY HAVE FOUND A REPLACEMENT WALKMAN FOR KENNY. YOU GET THE TRUCK IN HERE?
HELL, BARACUS, YOU *DID* FIND US. WHERE'S MAGUIRE?
NOT *HERE.* WHAT YOU TWO THINK, YOU WERE GETTIN' AWAY WITH THIS?
NO.
THAT'S GOOD, MAN. YOU SOUND JUST LIKE THE MOVIES.
YOU'RE COMIN' WITH ME, CHUMP.
YEAH? YOU READY TO DO SOME TIME, TOO? I MEAN, YOU CAME ON THIS OP OF YOUR OWN FREE WILL. NOTHING SEEMED A *LITTLE* FISHY TO YOU?
YOU *COULD* STILL THROW IN. WE GET THOSE GUNS BACK, SPENCER GETS IT ALL COVERED UP, WE GIVE YOU A CUT OF THE—
NO.
WALKM

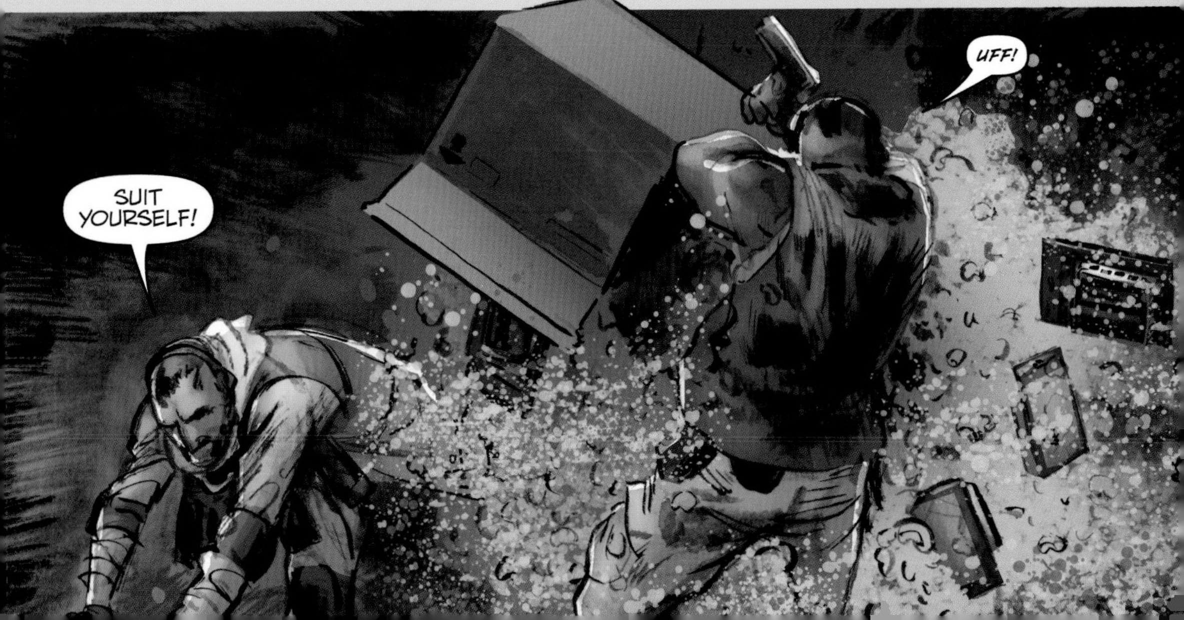
UFF!
SUIT YOURSELF!

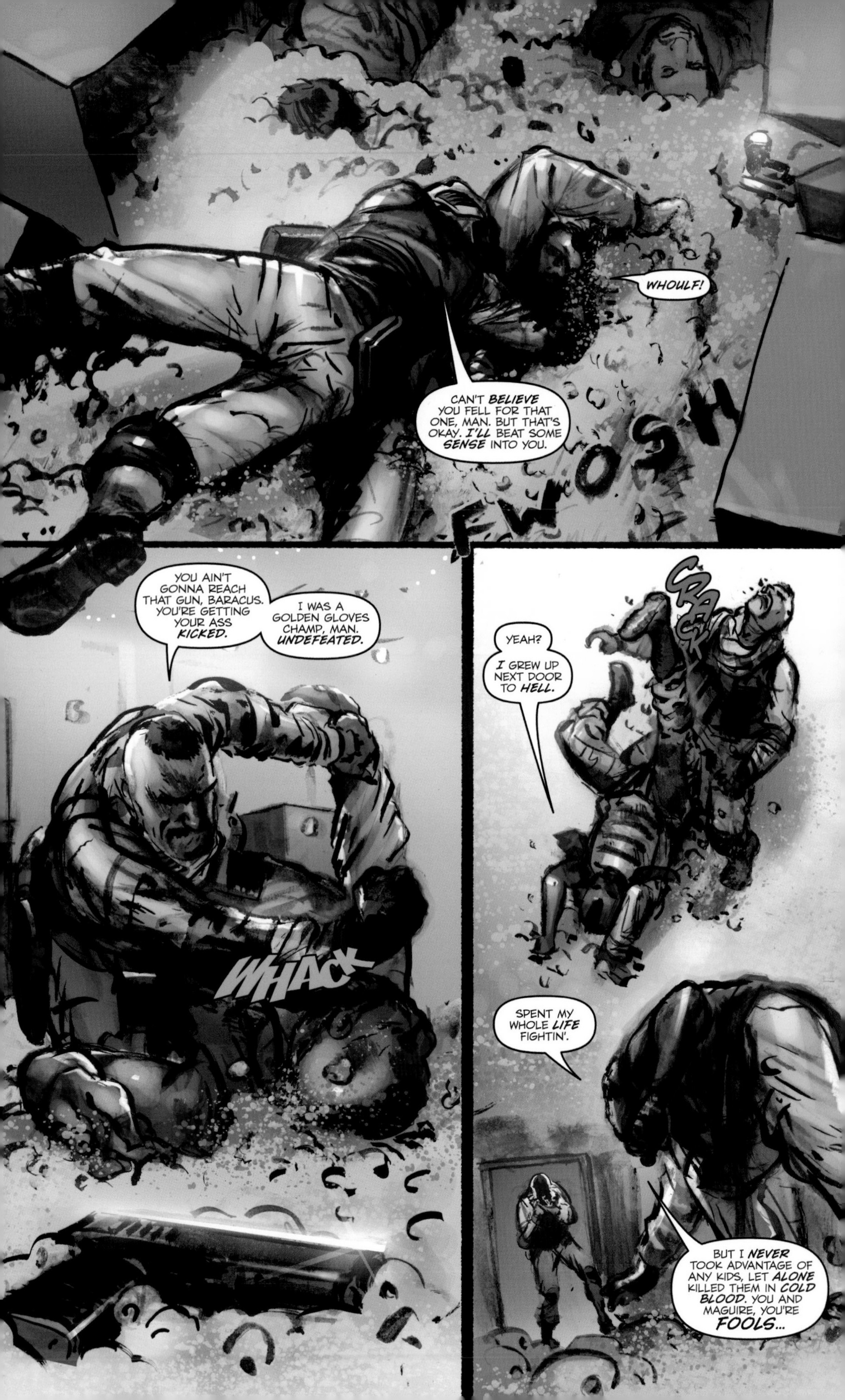
WHOULF!
CAN'T BELIEVE YOU FELL FOR THAT ONE, MAN. BUT THAT'S OKAY. I'LL BEAT SOME SENSE INTO YOU.
FWOOSH
YOU AIN'T GONNA REACH THAT GUN, BARACUS. YOU'RE GETTING YOUR ASS KICKED.
I WAS A GOLDEN GLOVES CHAMP, MAN. UNDEFEATED.
WHACK
CRACK
YEAH?
I GREW UP NEXT DOOR TO HELL.
SPENT MY WHOLE LIFE FIGHTIN'.
BUT I NEVER TOOK ADVANTAGE OF ANY KIDS, LET ALONE KILLED THEM IN COLD BLOOD. YOU AND MAGUIRE, YOU'RE FOOLS...

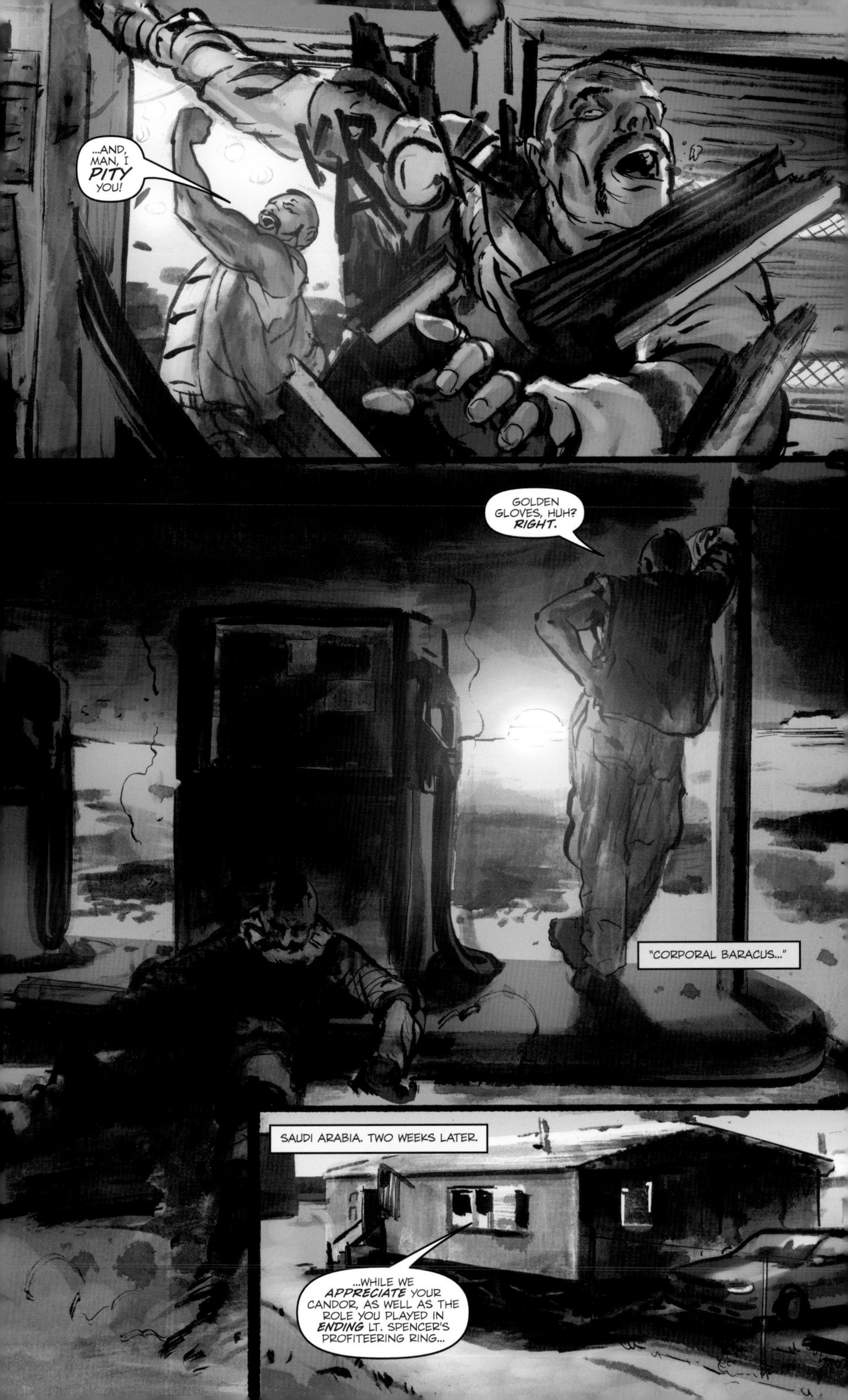
...AND, MAN, I PITY YOU!
GOLDEN GLOVES, HUH? RIGHT.
"CORPORAL BARACUS..."
SAUDI ARABIA. TWO WEEKS LATER.
...WHILE WE APPRECIATE YOUR CANDOR, AS WELL AS THE ROLE YOU PLAYED IN ENDING LT. SPENCER'S PROFITEERING RING...

...THE *FACT* OF THE MATTER IS, YOU *SHOULD* HAVE DISPLAYED *BETTER JUDGMENT* TO BEGIN WITH. THE UNITED STATES ARMY *EXPECTS* AS MUCH FROM ITS SOLDIERS.

IF YOU CAN'T EVEN MEET THAT EXPECTATION, CORPORAL, I'M AFRAID WE HAVE NO USE FOR YOU. THEREFORE IT IS THE JUDGMENT OF THIS COURT THAT YOU ARE TO BE *DISHONORABLY DISCHARGED* FROM SERVICE.

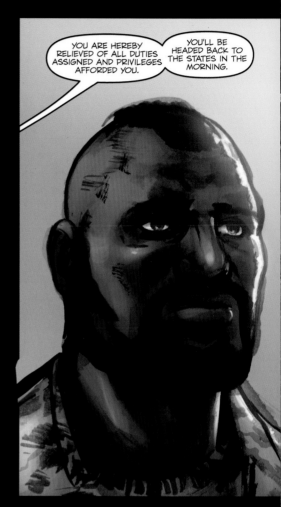

YOU ARE HEREBY RELIEVED OF ALL DUTIES ASSIGNED AND PRIVILEGES AFFORDED YOU.

YOU'LL BE HEADED BACK TO THE STATES IN THE MORNING.

LOS ANGELES.

TEN MONTHS LATER.

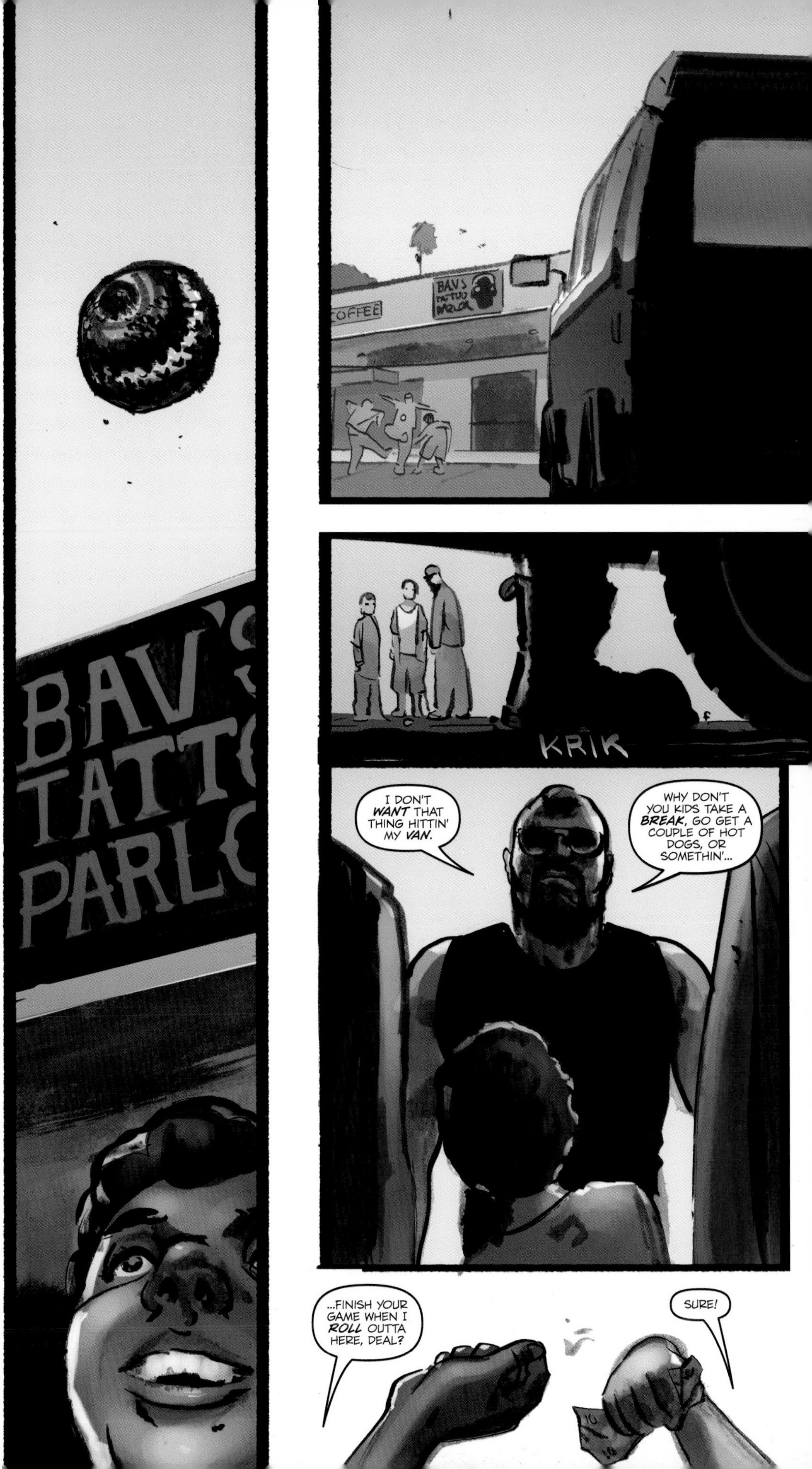
BAV'S TATTOO PARLOR
COFFEE
BAV'S TATTO PARLO
KRIK
I DON'T WANT THAT THING HITTIN' MY VAN.
WHY DON'T YOU KIDS TAKE A BREAK, GO GET A COUPLE OF HOT DOGS, OR SOMETHIN'...
...FINISH YOUR GAME WHEN I ROLL OUTTA HERE, DEAL?
SURE!

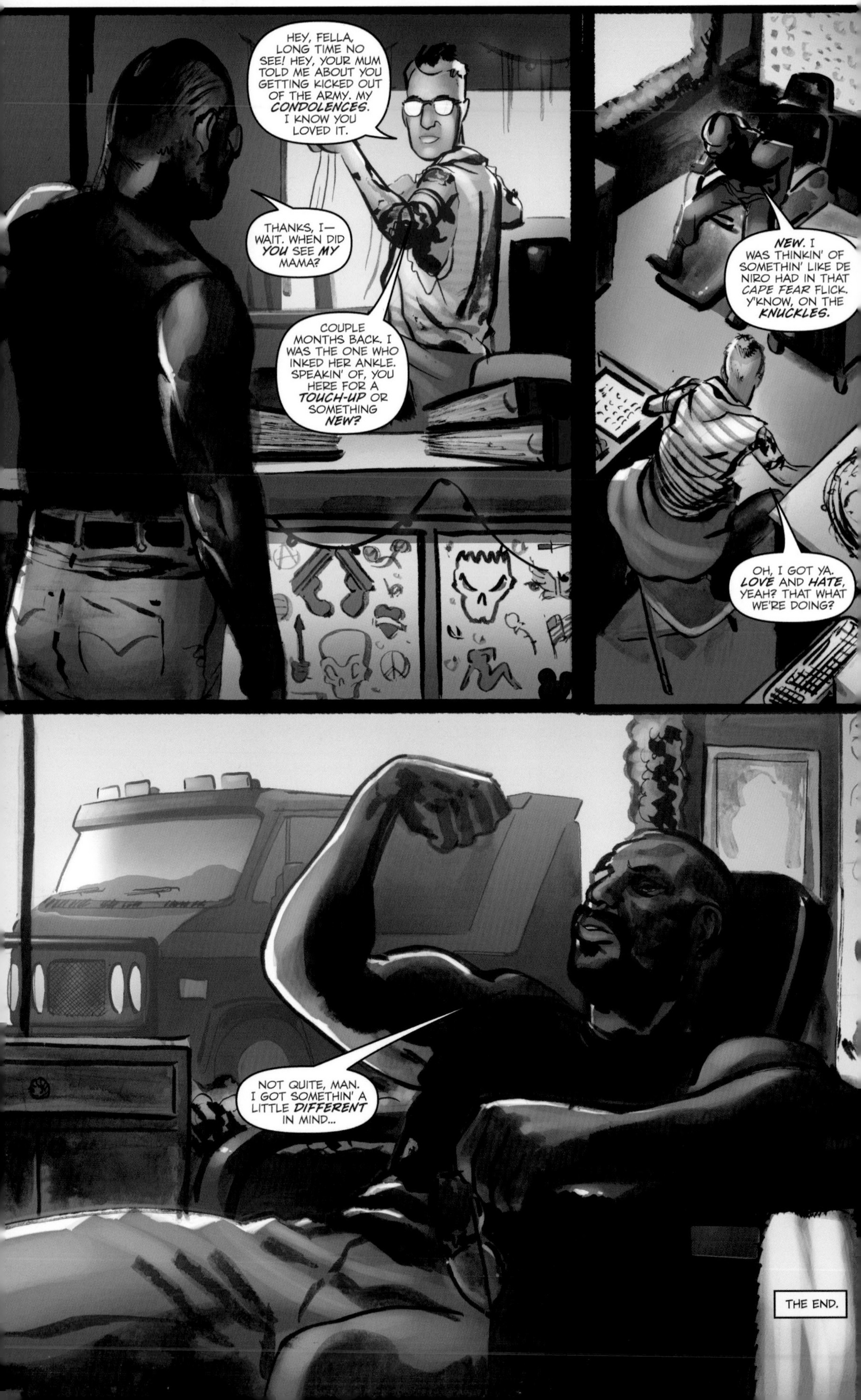

HEY, FELLA, LONG TIME NO SEE! HEY, YOUR MUM TOLD ME ABOUT YOU GETTING KICKED OUT OF THE ARMY. MY CONDOLENCES. I KNOW YOU LOVED IT.
THANKS, I— WAIT. WHEN DID YOU SEE MY MAMA?
COUPLE MONTHS BACK. I WAS THE ONE WHO INKED HER ANKLE. SPEAKIN' OF, YOU HERE FOR A TOUCH-UP OR SOMETHING NEW?
NEW. I WAS THINKIN' OF SOMETHIN' LIKE DE NIRO HAD IN THAT CAPE FEAR FLICK. Y'KNOW, ON THE KNUCKLES.
OH, I GOT YA. LOVE AND HATE, YEAH? THAT WHAT WE'RE DOING?
NOT QUITE, MAN. I GOT SOMETHIN' A LITTLE DIFFERENT IN MIND...
THE END.

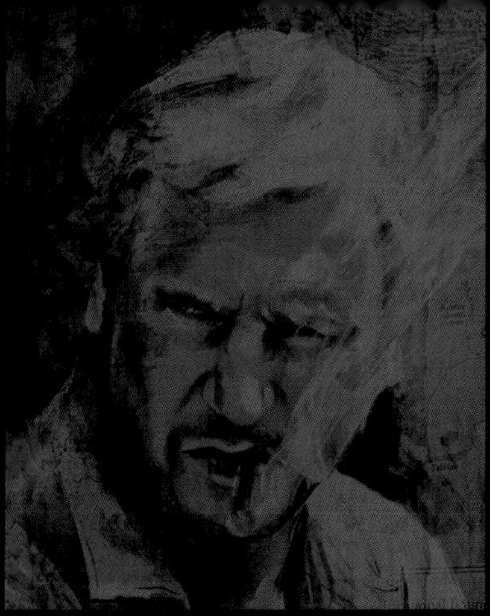

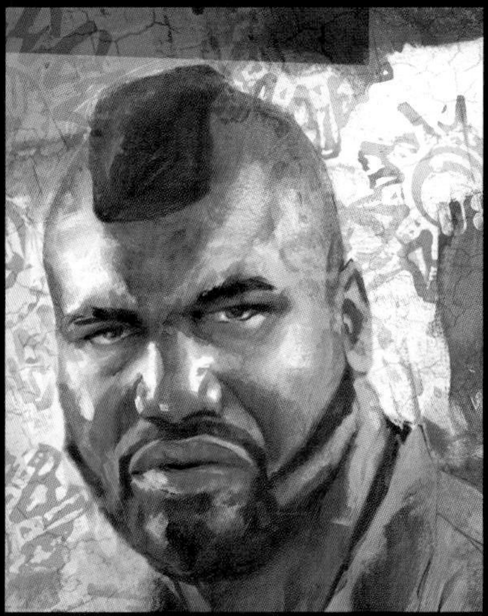

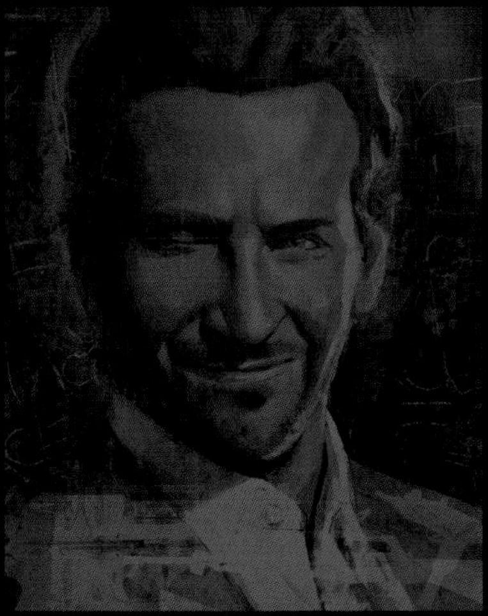

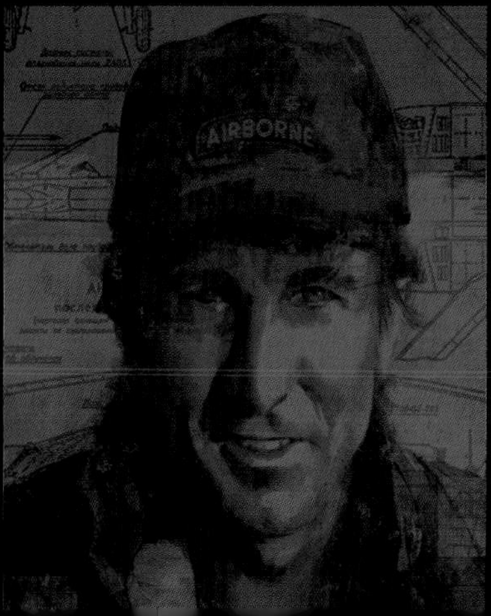
AIRBORNE

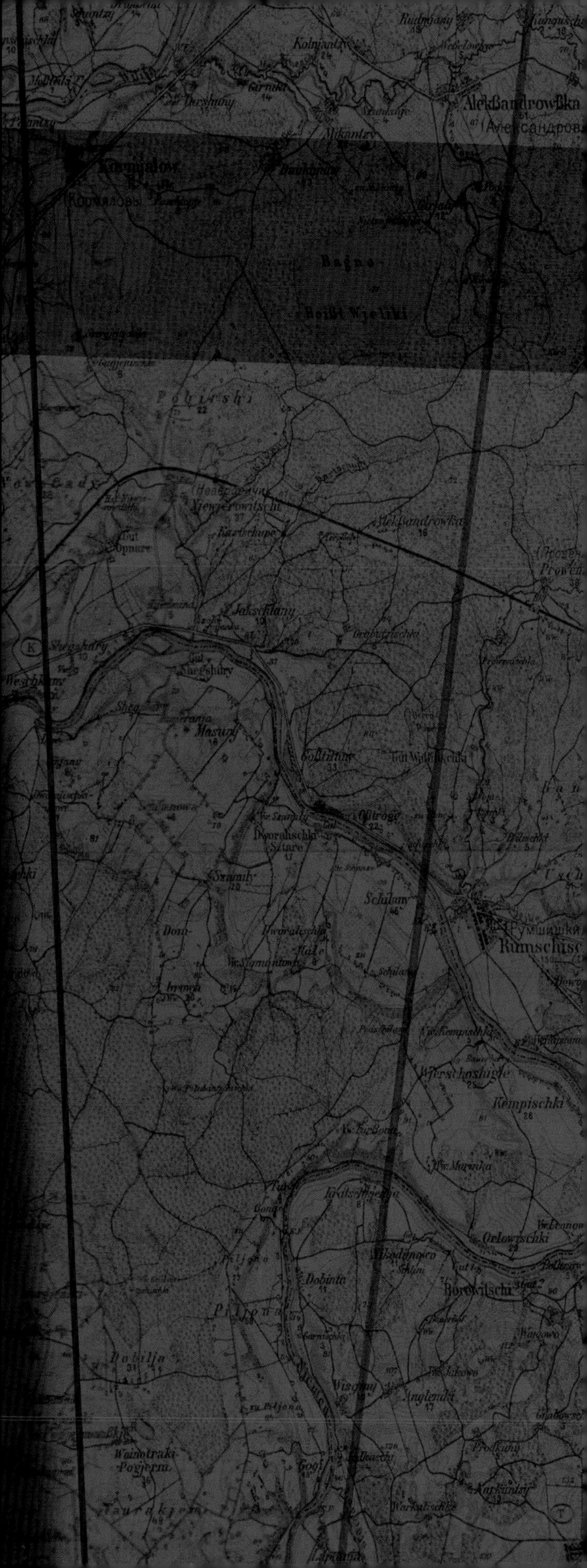
Bagno
Jakschlany
Masury
Szumily
Schilany
Orlowschki
Kempischki
Borowitschi
Dobinta
Anglenki

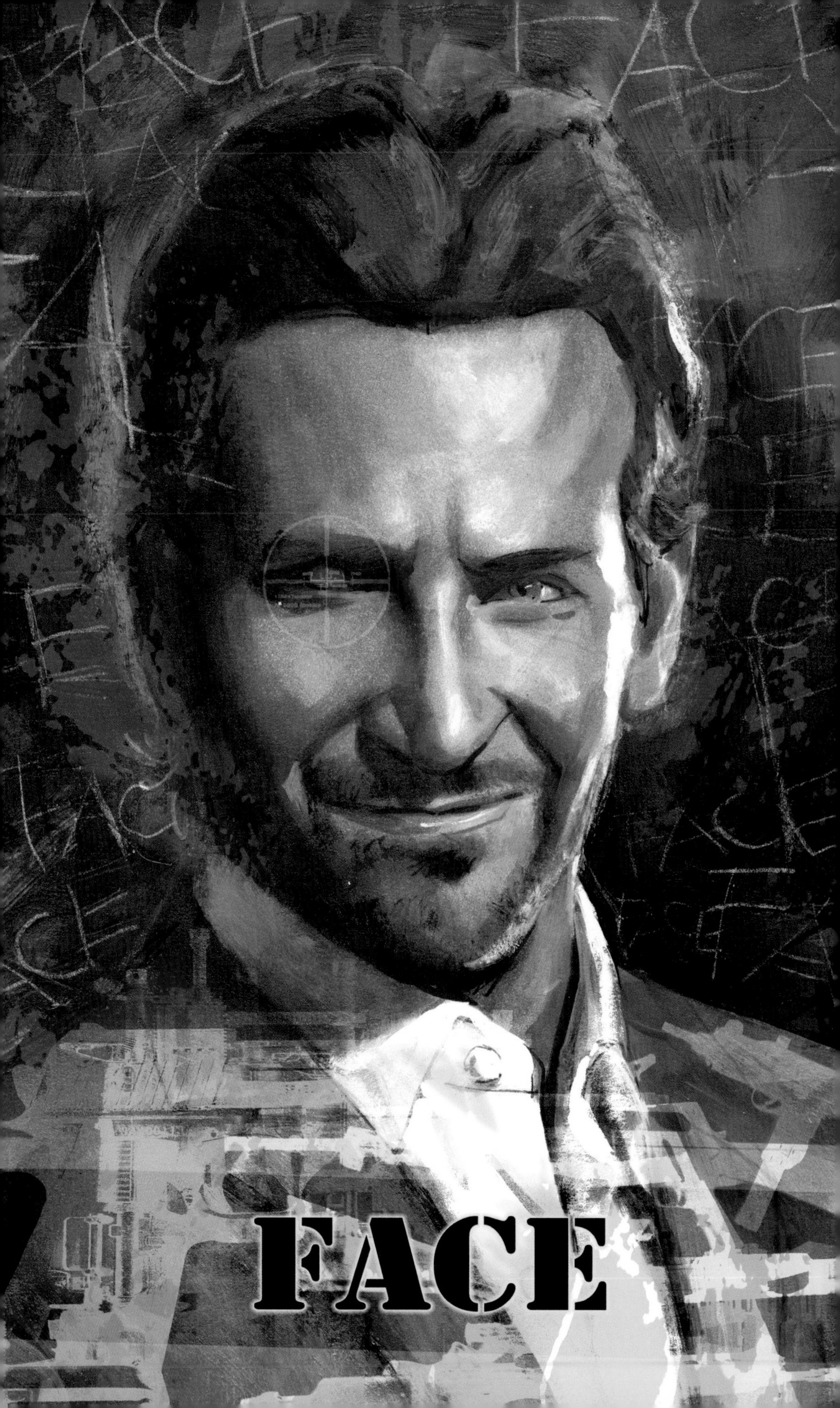
FACE

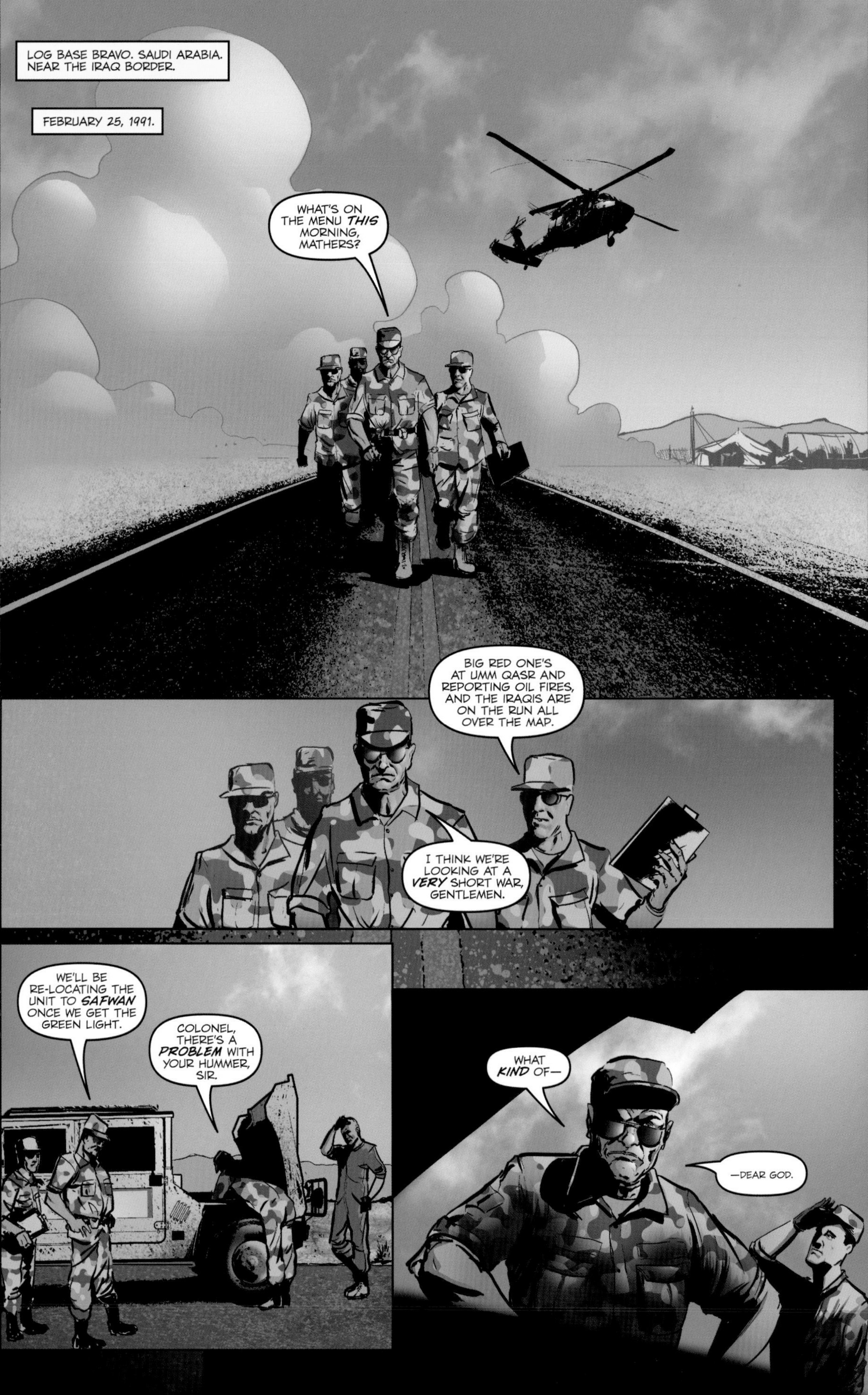
LOG BASE BRAVO. SAUDI ARABIA. NEAR THE IRAQ BORDER.
FEBRUARY 25, 1991.
WHAT'S ON THE MENU THIS MORNING, MATHERS?
BIG RED ONE'S AT UMM QASR AND REPORTING OIL FIRES, AND THE IRAQIS ARE ON THE RUN ALL OVER THE MAP.
I THINK WE'RE LOOKING AT A VERY SHORT WAR, GENTLEMEN.
WE'LL BE RE-LOCATING THE UNIT TO SAFWAN ONCE WE GET THE GREEN LIGHT.
COLONEL, THERE'S A PROBLEM WITH YOUR HUMMER, SIR.
WHAT KIND OF—
—DEAR GOD.

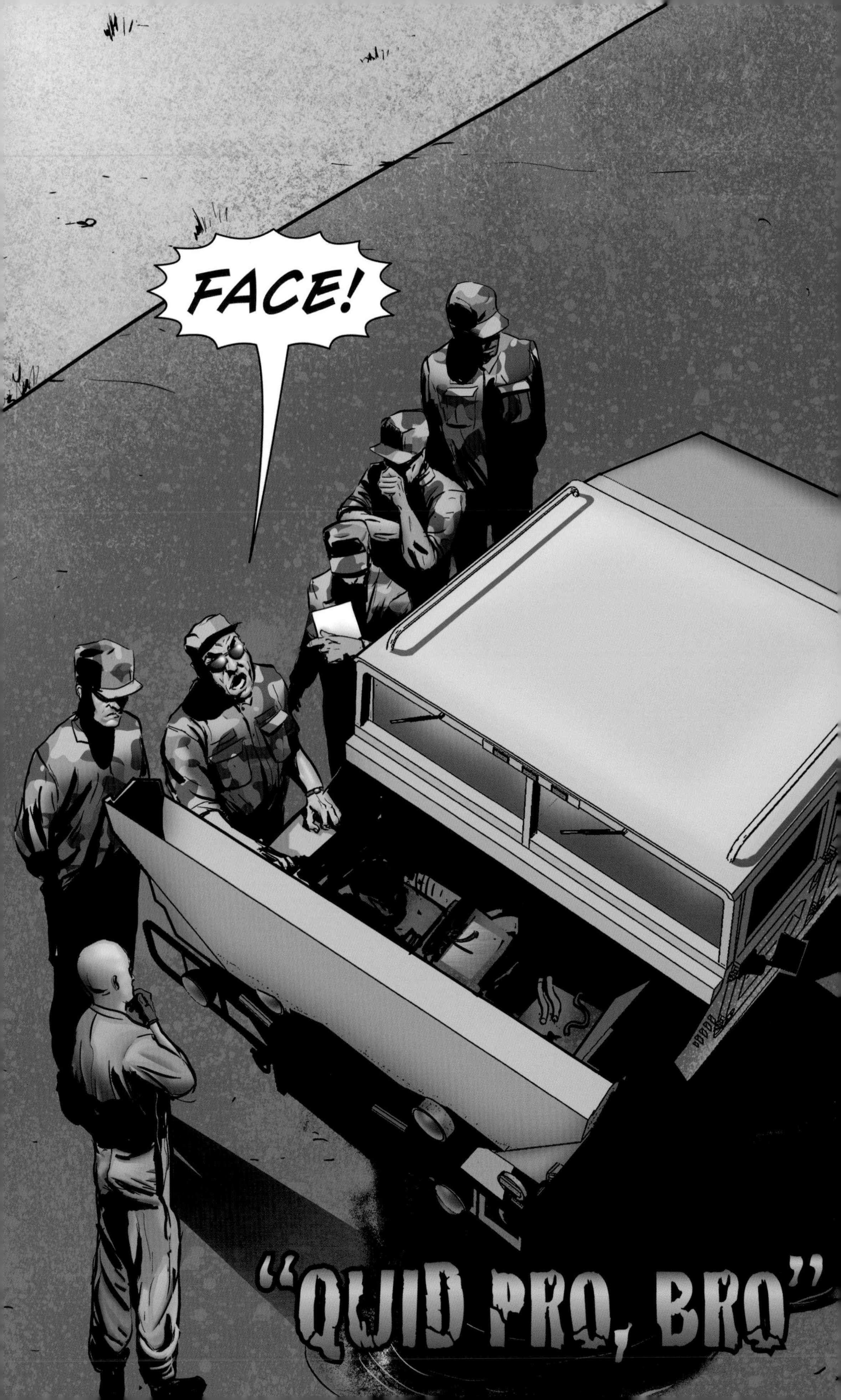
FACE!
"QUID PRO, BRO"

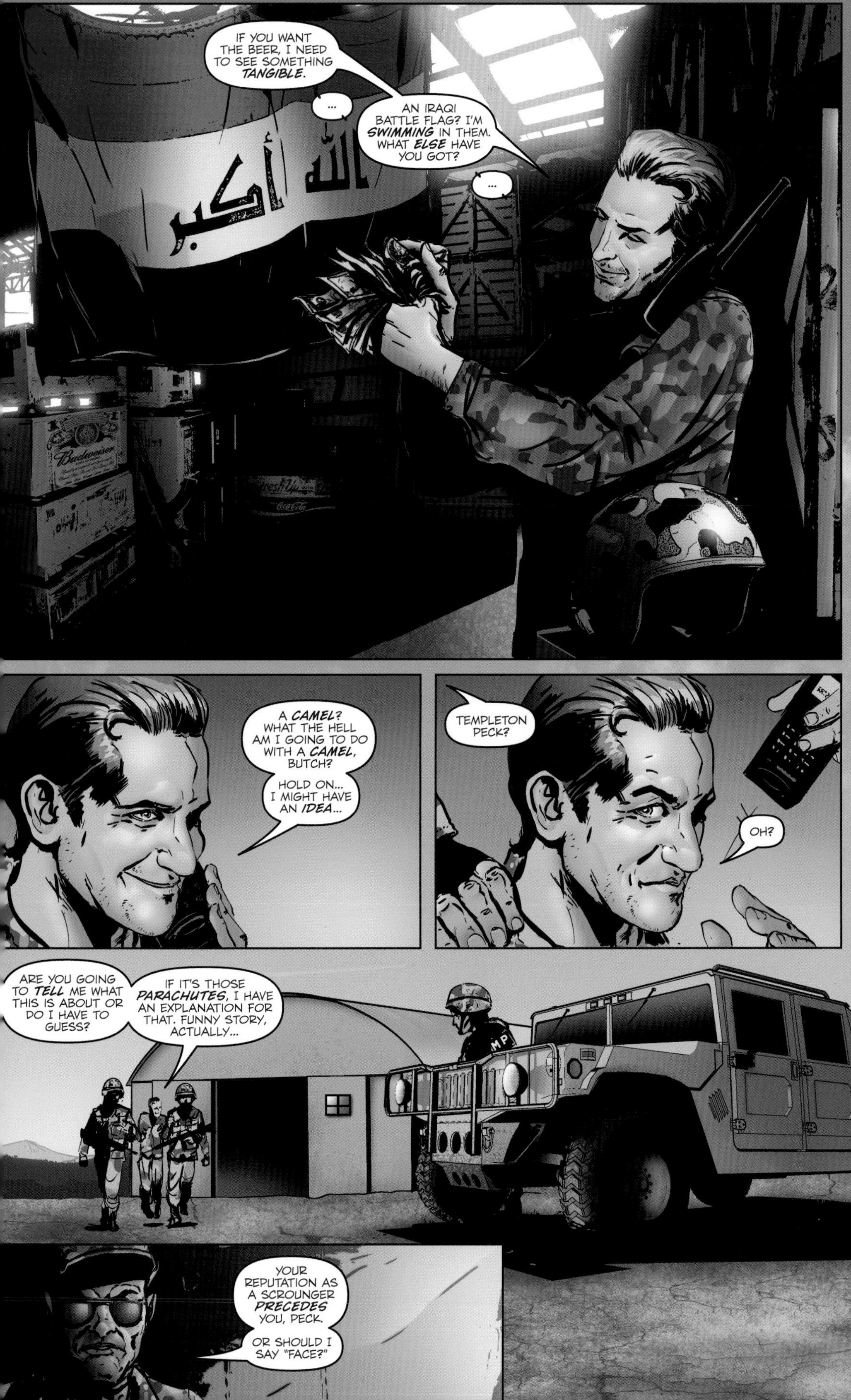

IF YOU WANT THE BEER, I NEED TO SEE SOMETHING *TANGIBLE*.
...
AN IRAQI BATTLE FLAG? I'M *SWIMMING* IN THEM. WHAT *ELSE* HAVE YOU GOT?
...
الله أكبر
Budweiser
Coca-Cola
A *CAMEL*? WHAT THE HELL AM I GOING TO DO WITH A *CAMEL*, BUTCH?
HOLD ON... I MIGHT HAVE AN *IDEA*...
TEMPLETON PECK?
OH?
ARE YOU GOING TO *TELL* ME WHAT THIS IS ABOUT OR DO I HAVE TO GUESS?
IF IT'S THOSE *PARACHUTES*, I HAVE AN EXPLANATION FOR THAT. FUNNY STORY, ACTUALLY...
MP
YOUR REPUTATION AS A SCROUNGER *PRECEDES* YOU, PECK.
OR SHOULD I SAY "FACE?"

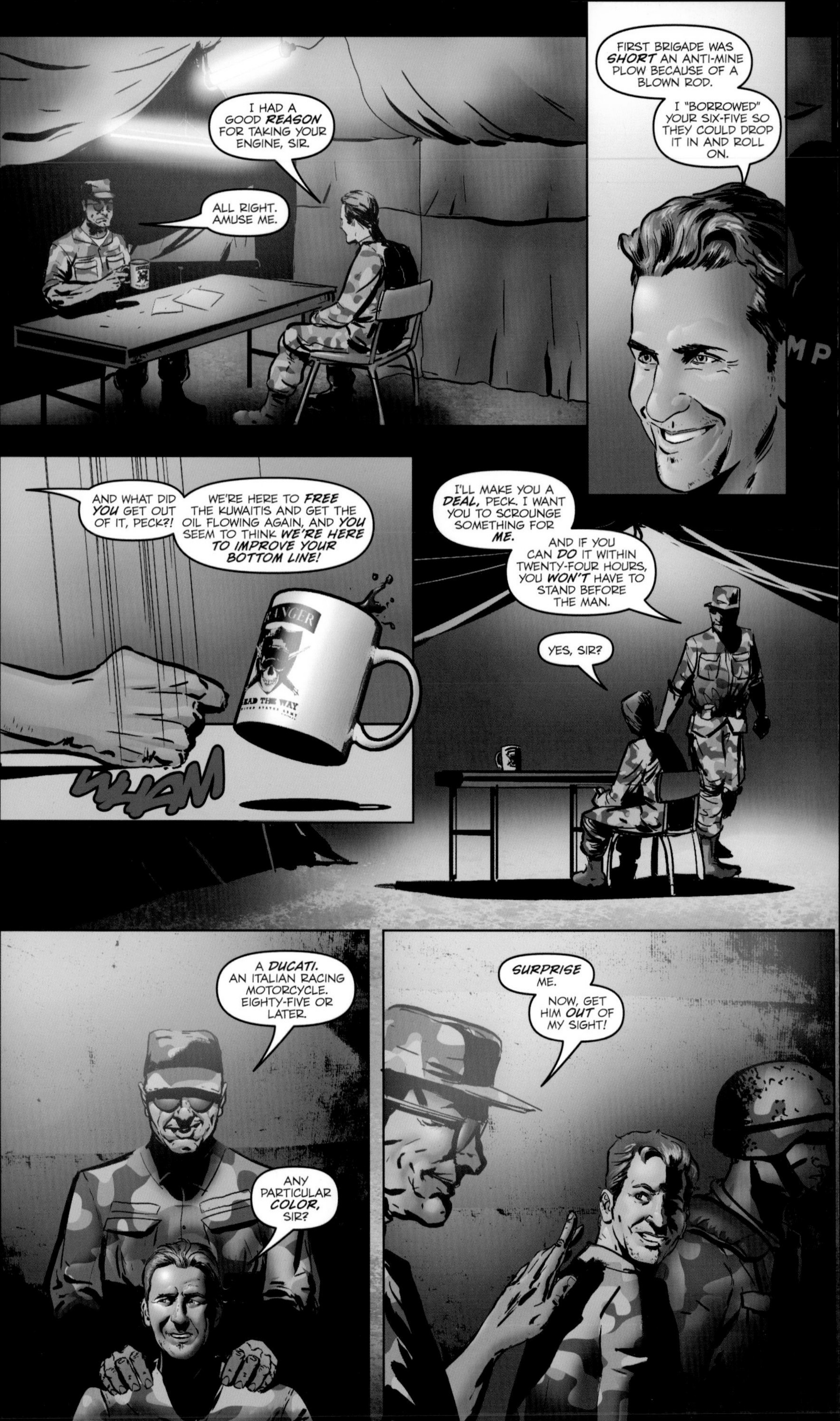
I HAD A GOOD REASON FOR TAKING YOUR ENGINE, SIR.
ALL RIGHT. AMUSE ME.
FIRST BRIGADE WAS SHORT AN ANTI-MINE PLOW BECAUSE OF A BLOWN ROD.
I "BORROWED" YOUR SIX-FIVE SO THEY COULD DROP IT IN AND ROLL ON.
MP
AND WHAT DID YOU GET OUT OF IT, PECK?!
WE'RE HERE TO FREE THE KUWAITIS AND GET THE OIL FLOWING AGAIN, AND YOU SEEM TO THINK WE'RE HERE TO IMPROVE YOUR BOTTOM LINE!
RANGER
LEAD THE WAY
WHAM
I'LL MAKE YOU A DEAL, PECK. I WANT YOU TO SCROUNGE SOMETHING FOR ME.
AND IF YOU CAN DO IT WITHIN TWENTY-FOUR HOURS, YOU WON'T HAVE TO STAND BEFORE THE MAN.
YES, SIR?
A DUCATI. AN ITALIAN RACING MOTORCYCLE. EIGHTY-FIVE OR LATER.
ANY PARTICULAR COLOR, SIR?
SURPRISE ME.
NOW, GET HIM OUT OF MY SIGHT!

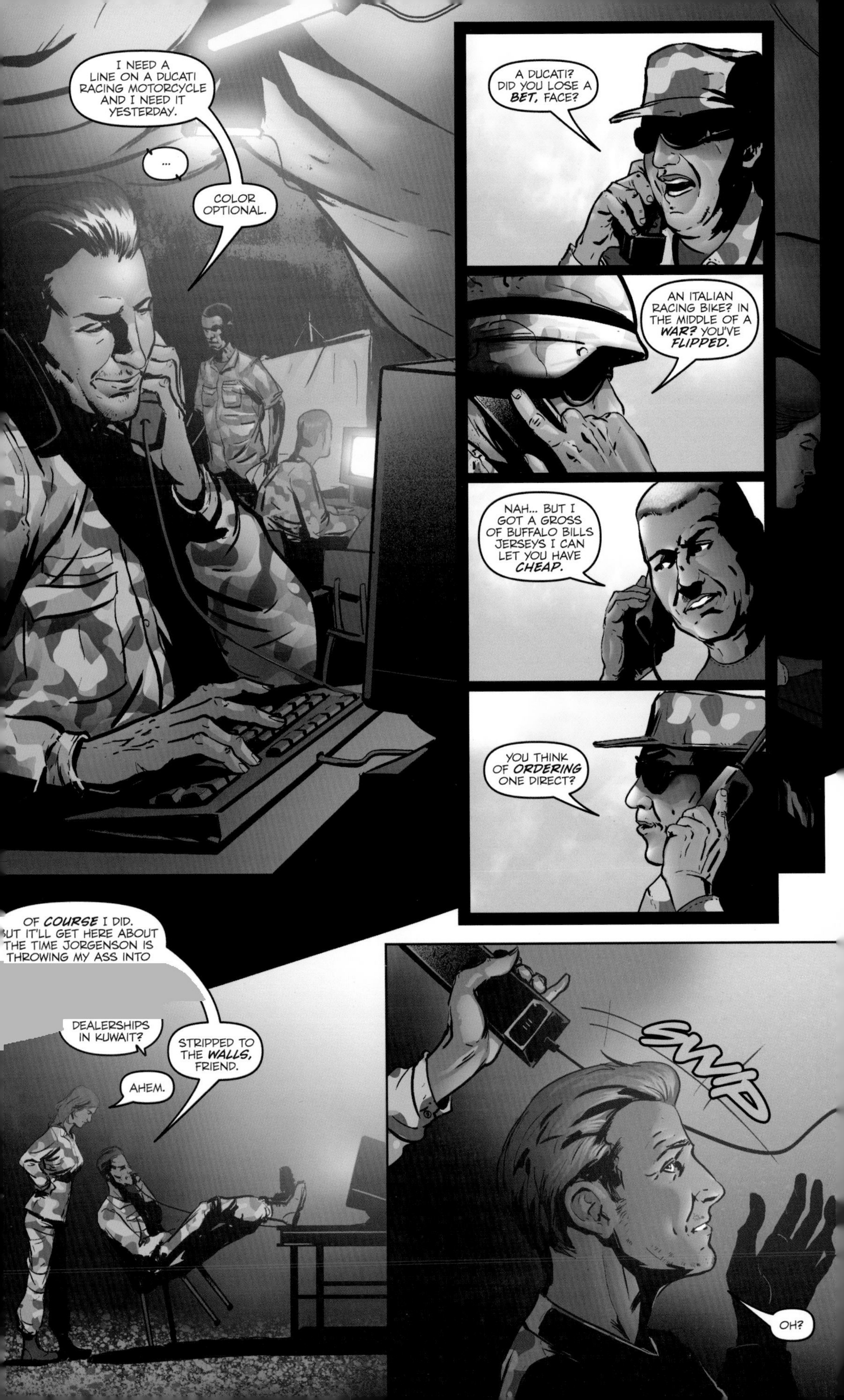

I NEED A LINE ON A DUCATI RACING MOTORCYCLE AND I NEED IT YESTERDAY.
...
COLOR OPTIONAL.
A DUCATI? DID YOU LOSE A BET, FACE?
AN ITALIAN RACING BIKE? IN THE MIDDLE OF A WAR? YOU'VE FLIPPED.
NAH... BUT I GOT A GROSS OF BUFFALO BILLS JERSEYS I CAN LET YOU HAVE CHEAP.
YOU THINK OF ORDERING ONE DIRECT?
OF COURSE I DID. UT IT'LL GET HERE ABOUT THE TIME JORGENSON IS THROWING MY ASS INTO
DEALERSHIPS IN KUWAIT?
STRIPPED TO THE WALLS, FRIEND.
AHEM.
SWIP
OH?

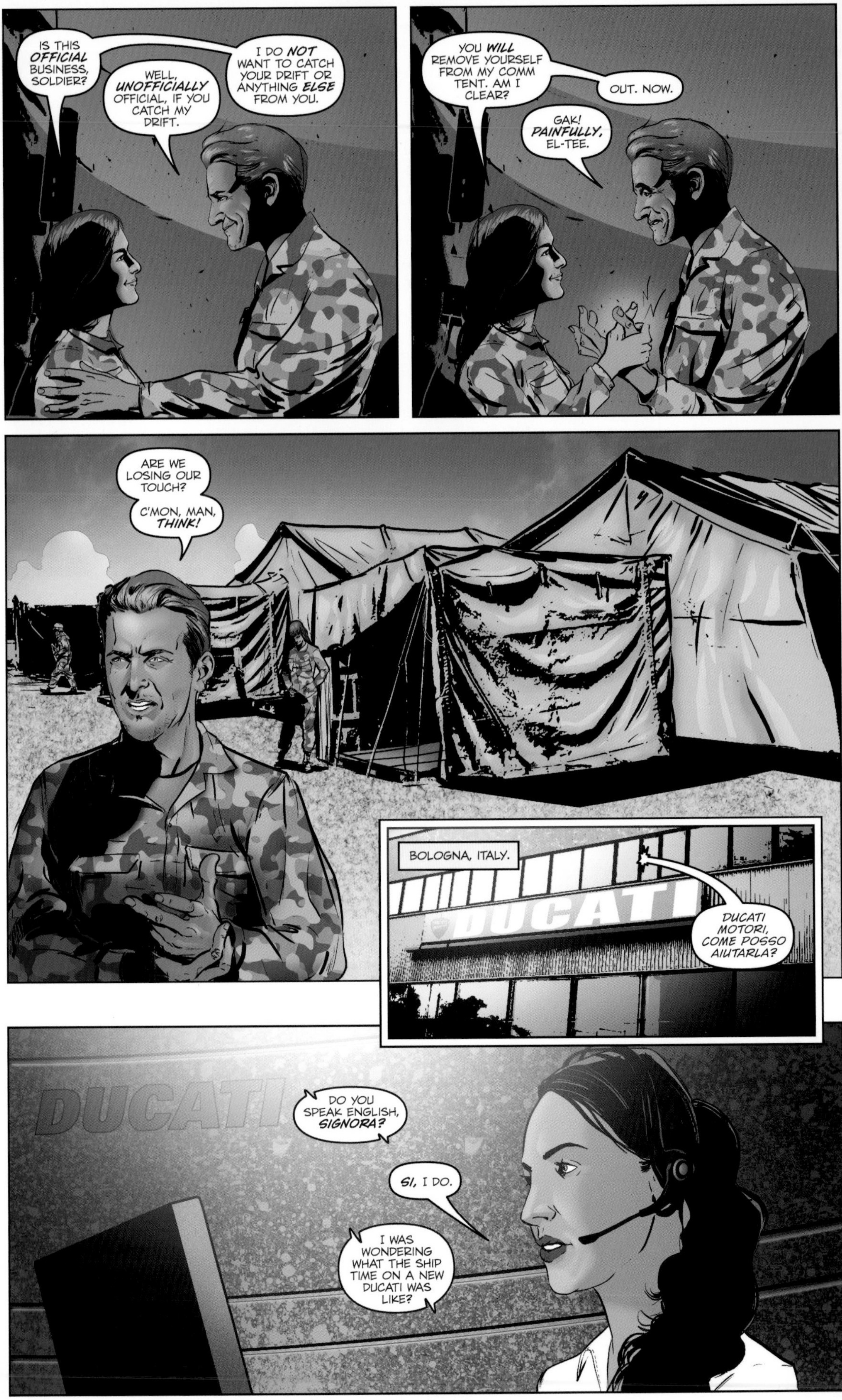
IS THIS OFFICIAL BUSINESS, SOLDIER?
WELL, UNOFFICIALLY OFFICIAL, IF YOU CATCH MY DRIFT.
I DO NOT WANT TO CATCH YOUR DRIFT OR ANYTHING ELSE FROM YOU.
YOU WILL REMOVE YOURSELF FROM MY COMM TENT. AM I CLEAR?
OUT. NOW.
GAK! PAINFULLY, EL-TEE.
ARE WE LOSING OUR TOUCH?
C'MON, MAN, THINK!
BOLOGNA, ITALY.
DUCATI
DUCATI MOTORI, COME POSSO AIUTARLA?
DUCATI
DO YOU SPEAK ENGLISH, SIGNORA?
SI, I DO.
I WAS WONDERING WHAT THE SHIP TIME ON A NEW DUCATI WAS LIKE?

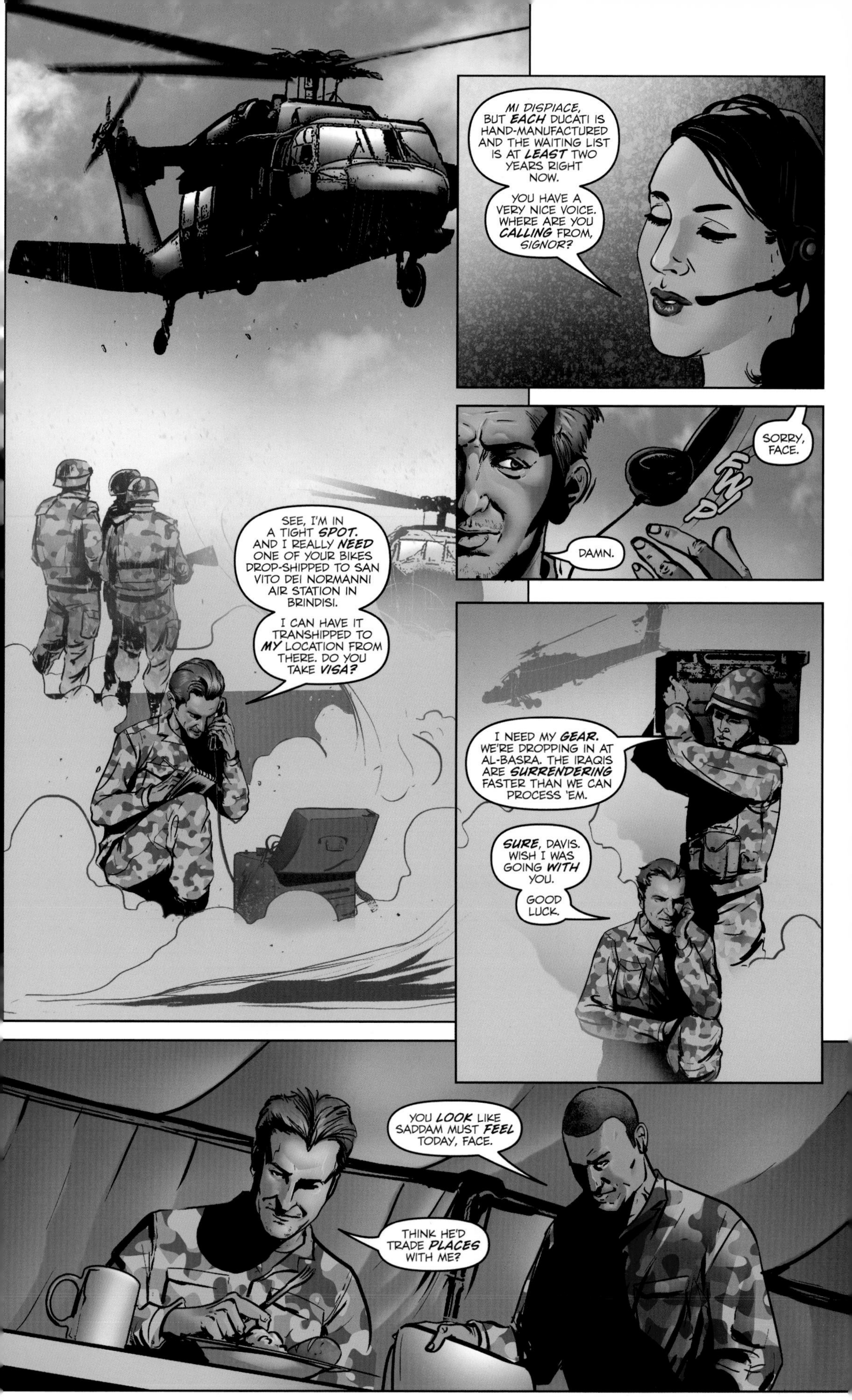
MI DISPIACE, BUT EACH DUCATI IS HAND-MANUFACTURED AND THE WAITING LIST IS AT LEAST TWO YEARS RIGHT NOW.
YOU HAVE A VERY NICE VOICE. WHERE ARE YOU CALLING FROM, SIGNOR?
SEE, I'M IN A TIGHT SPOT. AND I REALLY NEED ONE OF YOUR BIKES DROP-SHIPPED TO SAN VITO DEI NORMANNI AIR STATION IN BRINDISI.
I CAN HAVE IT TRANSHIPPED TO MY LOCATION FROM THERE. DO YOU TAKE VISA?
SORRY, FACE.
FWP
DAMN.
I NEED MY GEAR. WE'RE DROPPING IN AT AL-BASRA. THE IRAQIS ARE SURRENDERING FASTER THAN WE CAN PROCESS 'EM.
SURE, DAVIS. WISH I WAS GOING WITH YOU.
GOOD LUCK.
YOU LOOK LIKE SADDAM MUST FEEL TODAY, FACE.
THINK HE'D TRADE PLACES WITH ME?

COLONEL VOGEL WANTS ME TO HAND HIM UP A DUCATI BY TOMORROW *MORNING* OR I'LL BE SERVING MY TOUR FROM A *JAIL* CELL.

A *DUCATI?* IF THERE WAS *ONE*, IT'S ON ITS WAY TO *BAGHDAD* BY NOW.

SADDAM'S GOONS CLEANED OUT KUWAIT LIKE AN *ENEMA*. YOU ARE *OUT* OF LUCK, BRO.

MAYBE *NOT*, ERNIE.

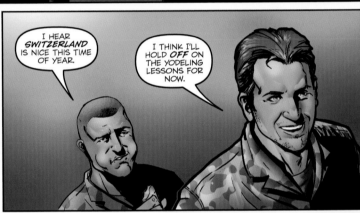

I HEAR *SWITZERLAND* IS NICE THIS TIME OF YEAR.

I THINK I'LL HOLD *OFF* ON THE YODELING LESSONS FOR NOW.

...ET AUCUN ARTICLE N'EST SÛR DES VOLEURS QUI PARCOURENT LES RUES...

Les Iraquiens pillent la ville de Koweit.

I NEVER TOOK *YOU* FOR A THRILL JUNKIE, FACE.

THIS IS A *SPECIAL* CASE, MORGAN.

HERE'S THE *DHAJEEF* SECTION. YOU SURE YOUR CONTACT IS HERE?

THEIR NETWORK IN PARIS SAID THEIR LAST *REPORT* WAS FROM THIS STREET.

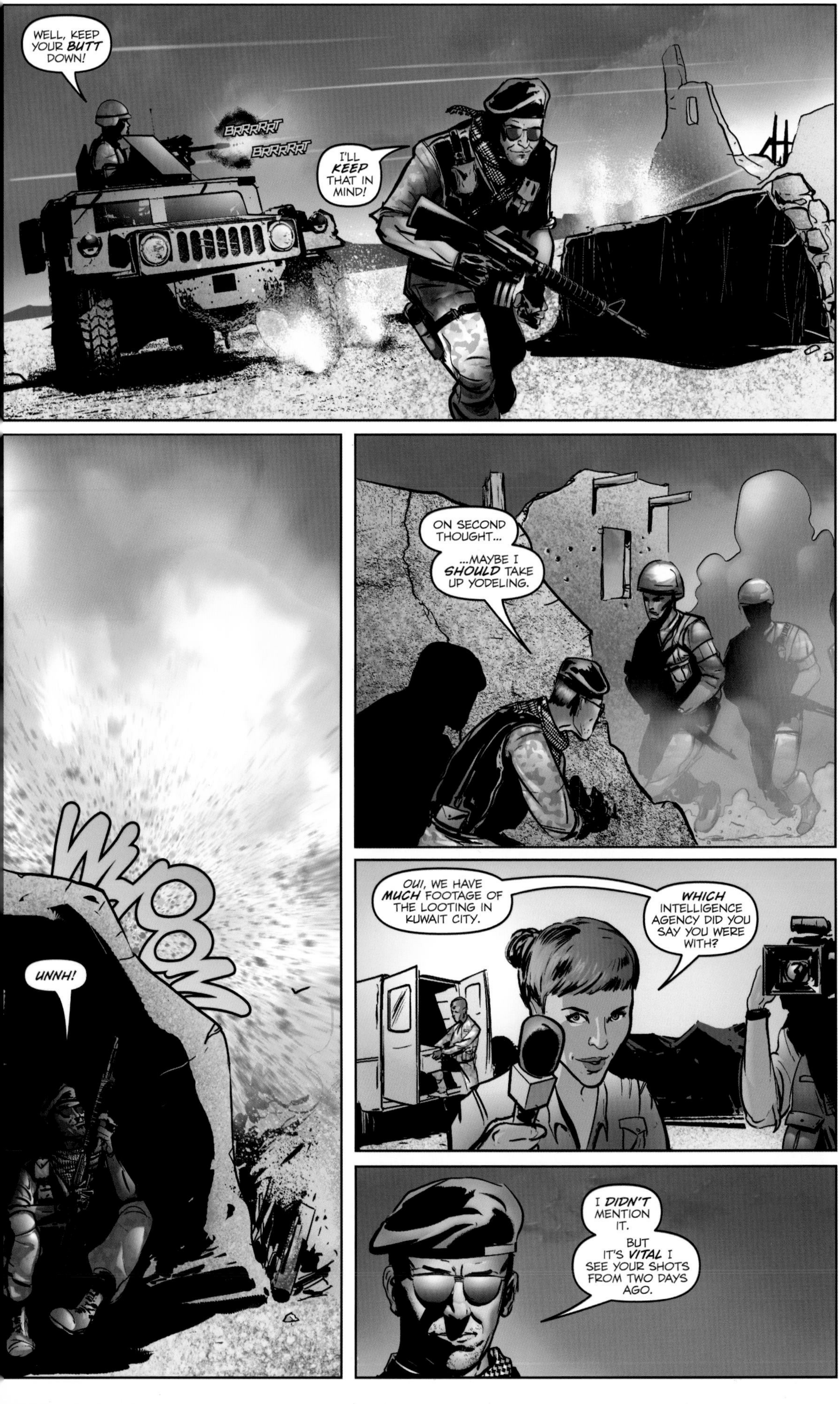

WELL, KEEP YOUR BUTT DOWN!
BRRRRRT
BRRRRRT
I'LL KEEP THAT IN MIND!
WHOOM
UNNH!
ON SECOND THOUGHT...
...MAYBE I SHOULD TAKE UP YODELING.
OUI, WE HAVE MUCH FOOTAGE OF THE LOOTING IN KUWAIT CITY.
WHICH INTELLIGENCE AGENCY DID YOU SAY YOU WERE WITH?
I DIDN'T MENTION IT.
BUT IT'S VITAL I SEE YOUR SHOTS FROM TWO DAYS AGO.

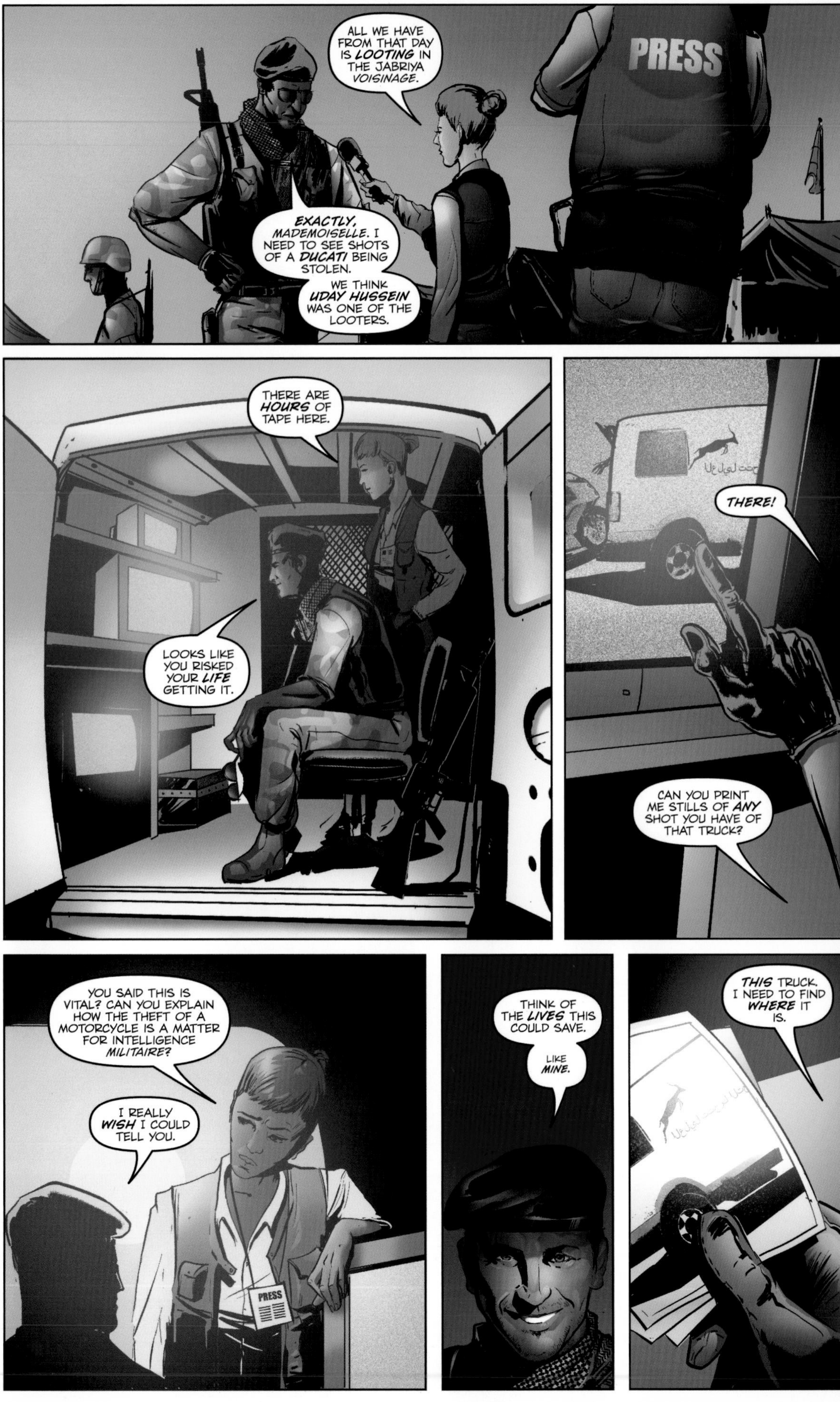
ALL WE HAVE FROM THAT DAY IS LOOTING IN THE JABRIYA VOISINAGE.
EXACTLY, MADEMOISELLE. I NEED TO SEE SHOTS OF A DUCATI BEING STOLEN.
WE THINK UDAY HUSSEIN WAS ONE OF THE LOOTERS.
PRESS
THERE ARE HOURS OF TAPE HERE.
LOOKS LIKE YOU RISKED YOUR LIFE GETTING IT.
THERE!
CAN YOU PRINT ME STILLS OF ANY SHOT YOU HAVE OF THAT TRUCK?
YOU SAID THIS IS VITAL? CAN YOU EXPLAIN HOW THE THEFT OF A MOTORCYCLE IS A MATTER FOR INTELLIGENCE MILITAIRE?
I REALLY WISH I COULD TELL YOU.
PRESS
THINK OF THE LIVES THIS COULD SAVE.
LIKE MINE.
THIS TRUCK. I NEED TO FIND WHERE IT IS.

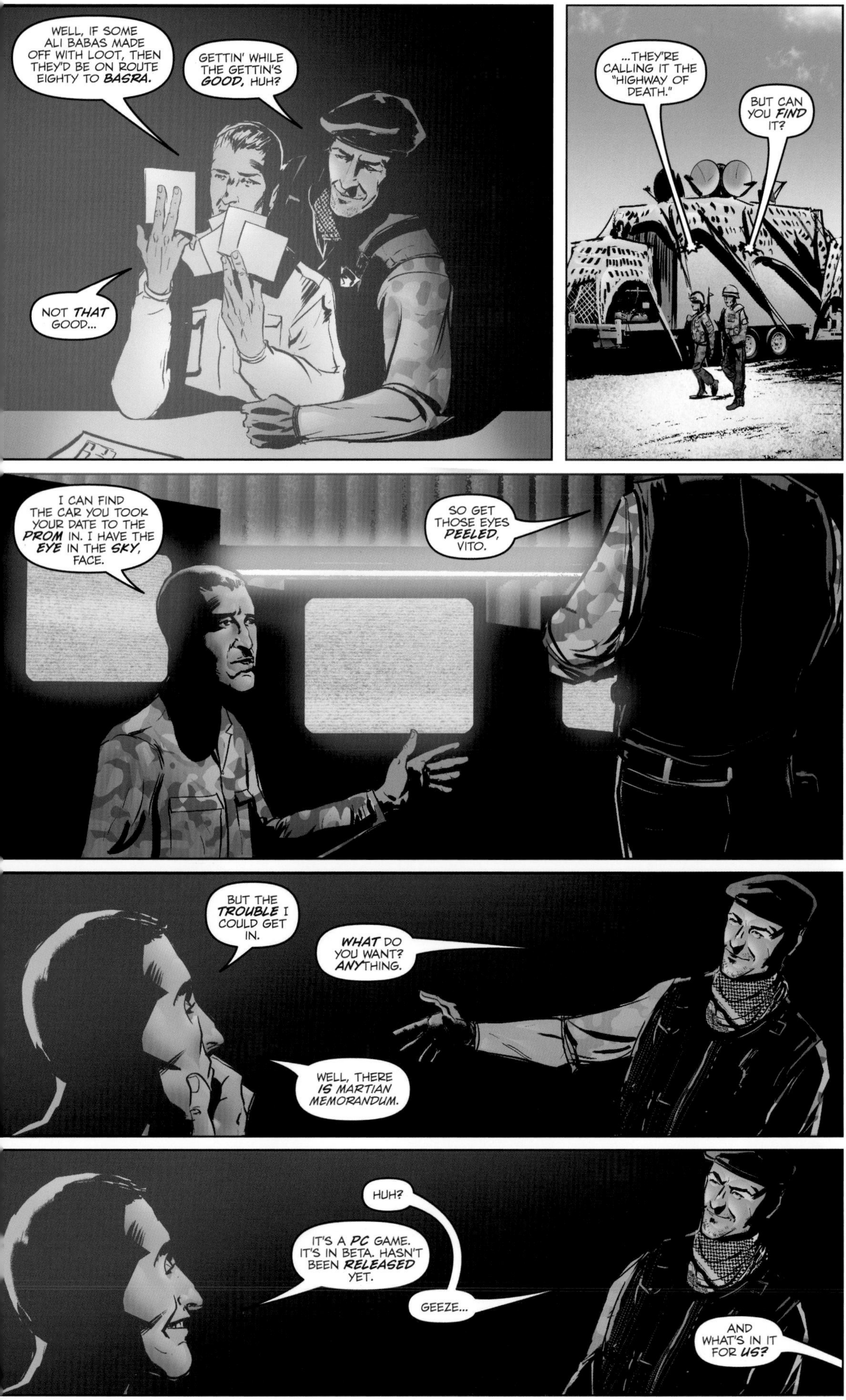

WELL, IF SOME ALI BABAS MADE OFF WITH LOOT, THEN THEY'D BE ON ROUTE EIGHTY TO BASRA.
GETTIN' WHILE THE GETTIN'S GOOD, HUH?
NOT THAT GOOD...
...THEY'RE CALLING IT THE "HIGHWAY OF DEATH."
BUT CAN YOU FIND IT?
I CAN FIND THE CAR YOU TOOK YOUR DATE TO THE PROM IN. I HAVE THE EYE IN THE SKY, FACE.
SO GET THOSE EYES PEELED, VITO.
BUT THE TROUBLE I COULD GET IN.
WHAT DO YOU WANT? ANYTHING.
WELL, THERE IS MARTIAN MEMORANDUM.
HUH?
IT'S A PC GAME. IT'S IN BETA. HASN'T BEEN RELEASED YET.
GEEZE...
AND WHAT'S IN IT FOR US?

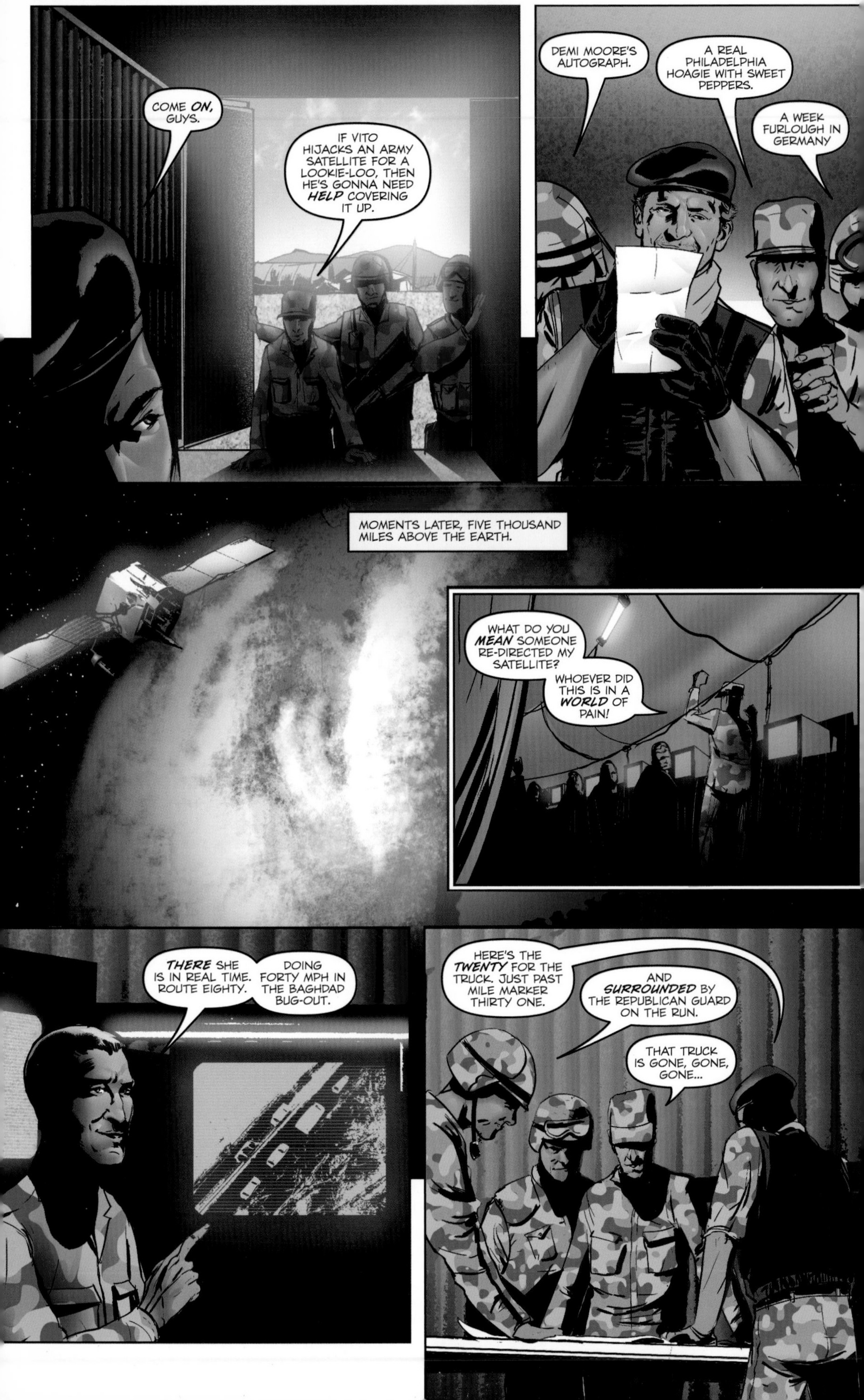
COME ON, GUYS.
IF VITO HIJACKS AN ARMY SATELLITE FOR A LOOKIE-LOO, THEN HE'S GONNA NEED HELP COVERING IT UP.
DEMI MOORE'S AUTOGRAPH.
A REAL PHILADELPHIA HOAGIE WITH SWEET PEPPERS.
A WEEK FURLOUGH IN GERMANY
MOMENTS LATER, FIVE THOUSAND MILES ABOVE THE EARTH.
WHAT DO YOU MEAN SOMEONE RE-DIRECTED MY SATELLITE?
WHOEVER DID THIS IS IN A WORLD OF PAIN!
THERE SHE IS IN REAL TIME. ROUTE EIGHTY.
DOING FORTY MPH IN THE BAGHDAD BUG-OUT.
HERE'S THE TWENTY FOR THE TRUCK. JUST PAST MILE MARKER THIRTY ONE.
AND SURROUNDED BY THE REPUBLICAN GUARD ON THE RUN.
THAT TRUCK IS GONE, GONE, GONE...

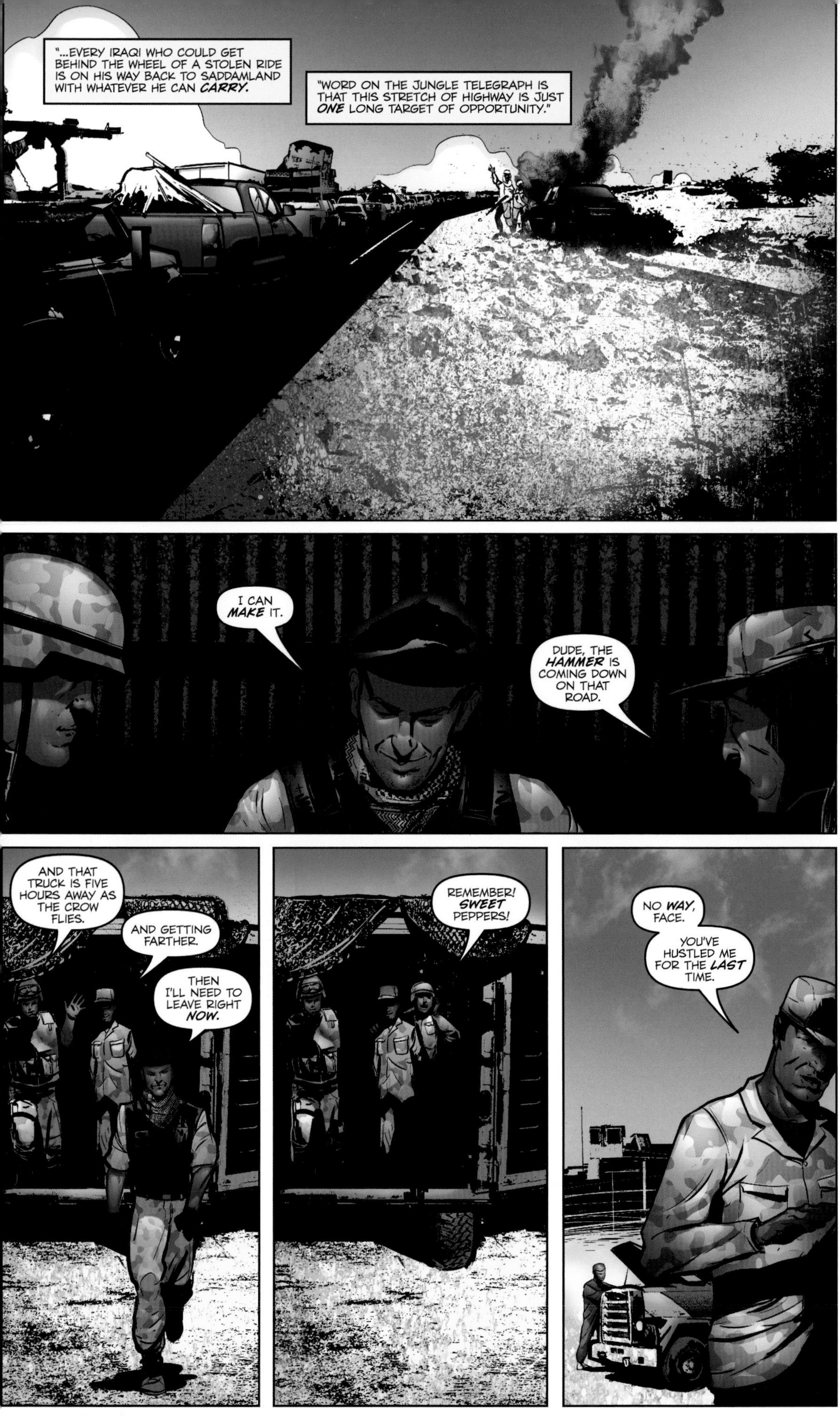
"...EVERY IRAQI WHO COULD GET BEHIND THE WHEEL OF A STOLEN RIDE IS ON HIS WAY BACK TO SADDAMLAND WITH WHATEVER HE CAN CARRY.
"WORD ON THE JUNGLE TELEGRAPH IS THAT THIS STRETCH OF HIGHWAY IS JUST ONE LONG TARGET OF OPPORTUNITY."
I CAN MAKE IT.
DUDE, THE HAMMER IS COMING DOWN ON THAT ROAD.
AND THAT TRUCK IS FIVE HOURS AWAY AS THE CROW FLIES.
AND GETTING FARTHER.
THEN I'LL NEED TO LEAVE RIGHT NOW.
REMEMBER! SWEET PEPPERS!
NO WAY, FACE.
YOU'VE HUSTLED ME FOR THE LAST TIME.

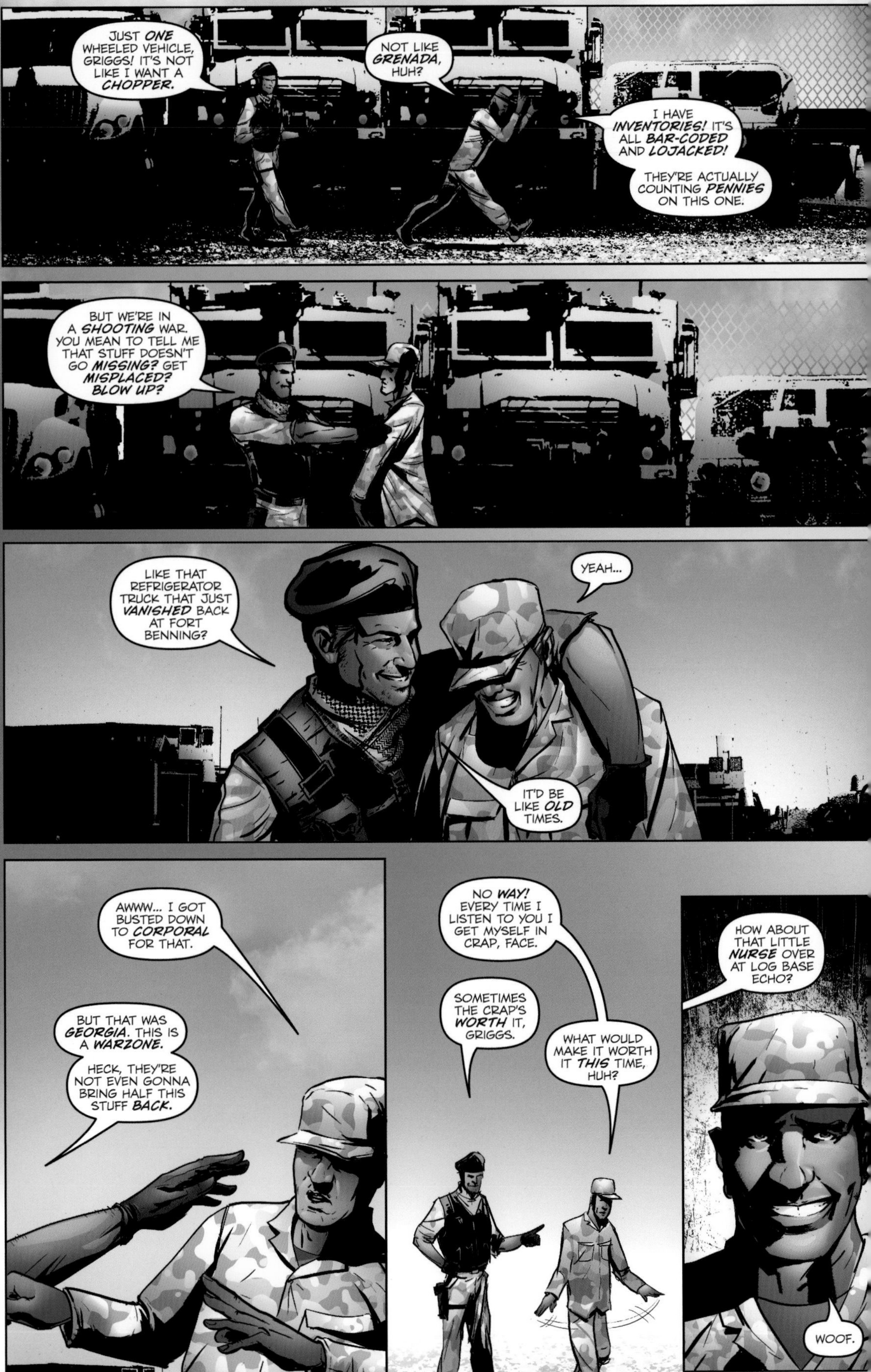
JUST ONE WHEELED VEHICLE, GRIGGS! IT'S NOT LIKE I WANT A CHOPPER.
NOT LIKE GRENADA, HUH?
I HAVE INVENTORIES! IT'S ALL BAR-CODED AND LOJACKED!
THEY'RE ACTUALLY COUNTING PENNIES ON THIS ONE.
BUT WE'RE IN A SHOOTING WAR. YOU MEAN TO TELL ME THAT STUFF DOESN'T GO MISSING? GET MISPLACED? BLOW UP?
LIKE THAT REFRIGERATOR TRUCK THAT JUST VANISHED BACK AT FORT BENNING?
YEAH...
IT'D BE LIKE OLD TIMES.
AWWW... I GOT BUSTED DOWN TO CORPORAL FOR THAT.
BUT THAT WAS GEORGIA. THIS IS A WARZONE.
HECK, THEY'RE NOT EVEN GONNA BRING HALF THIS STUFF BACK.
NO WAY! EVERY TIME I LISTEN TO YOU I GET MYSELF IN CRAP, FACE.
SOMETIMES THE CRAP'S WORTH IT, GRIGGS.
WHAT WOULD MAKE IT WORTH IT THIS TIME, HUH?
HOW ABOUT THAT LITTLE NURSE OVER AT LOG BASE ECHO?
WOOF.

NORTH OF RHAWDATA.

WHAT THE HELL AM I *DOING?*

EVEN IF I *FIND* THE TRUCK I HAVE NO REAL PLAN.

THEY MIGHT *NOTICE* A GUY RIDING A RACING MOTORCYCLE THE WRONG WAY.

POINT OF NO RETURN.

THE ROAD TO BASRA.

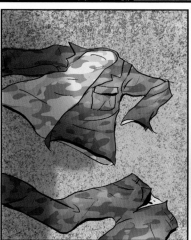

YOU CAN *DO* THIS.

IT'S JUST LIKE ANY *OTHER* CON, RIGHT?

MAKE *MYSELF* BELIEVE IT AND THEY'LL FALL IN LINE.

NO REASON FOR THEM TO TAKE A SECOND LOOK.

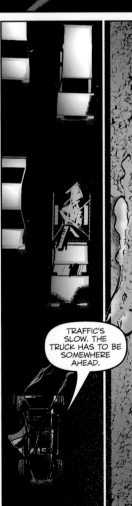

TRAFFIC'S SLOW. THE TRUCK HAS TO BE SOMEWHERE AHEAD.

119 K

FIND THE TRUCK. WORRY ABOUT THE REST *WHEN* I FIND IT.

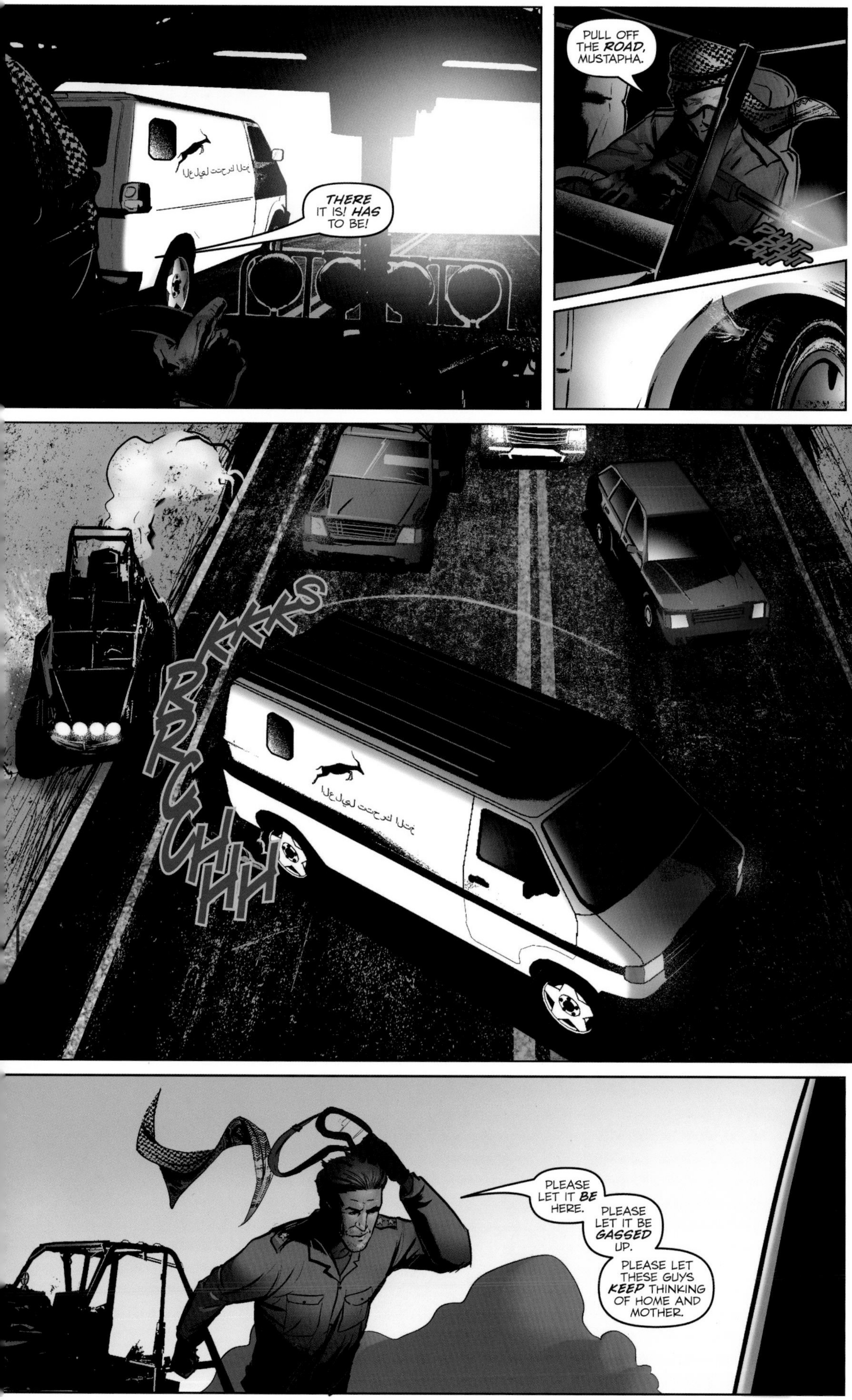
THERE IT IS! HAS TO BE!
PULL OFF THE ROAD, MUSTAPHA.
PHHT PHHT
KKKS BRRUHHH
PLEASE LET IT BE HERE.
PLEASE LET IT BE GASSED UP.
PLEASE LET THESE GUYS KEEP THINKING OF HOME AND MOTHER.

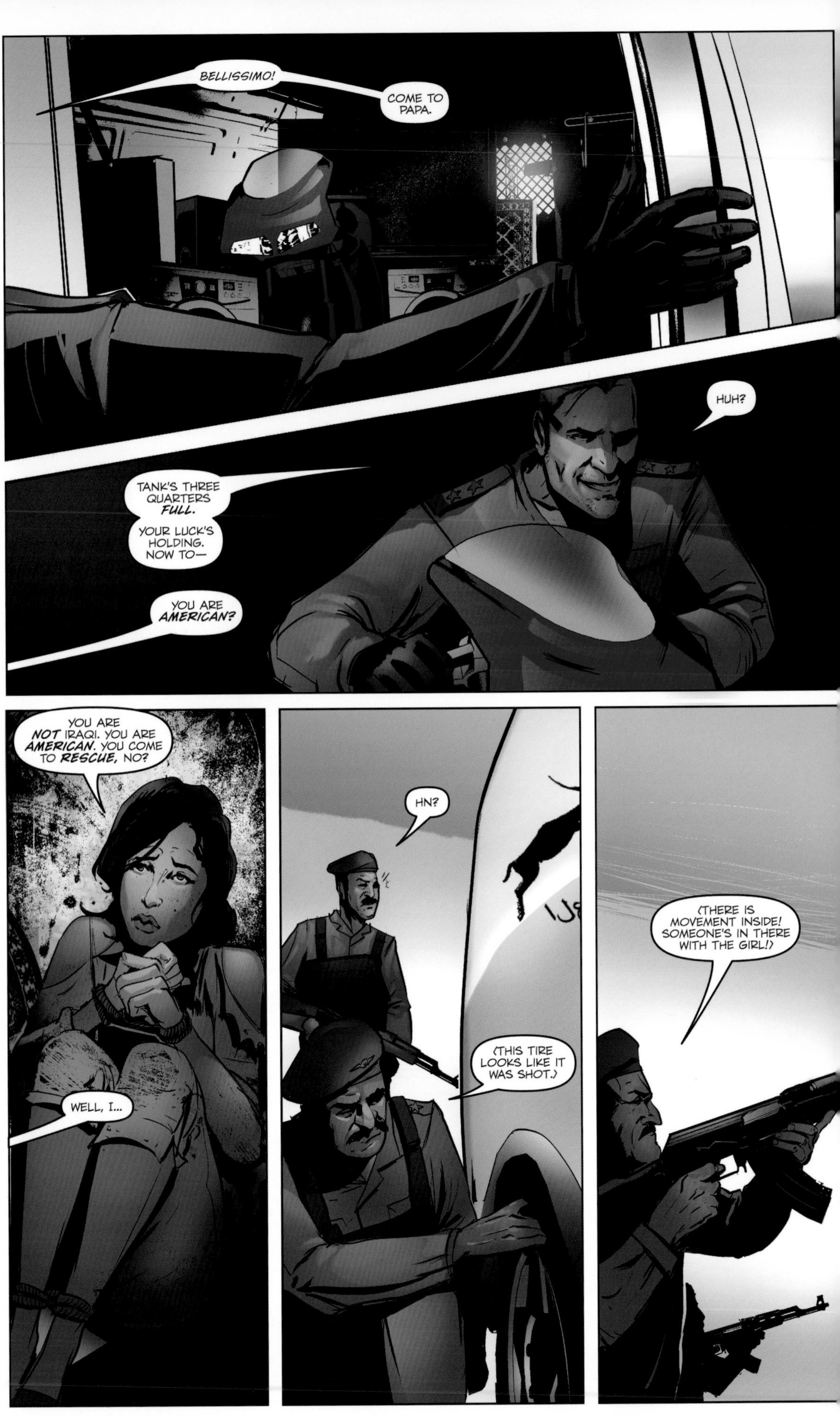
BELLISSIMO!
COME TO PAPA.
HUH?
TANK'S THREE QUARTERS *FULL.*
YOUR LUCK'S HOLDING. NOW TO—
YOU ARE *AMERICAN?*
YOU ARE *NOT* IRAQI. YOU ARE *AMERICAN*. YOU COME TO *RESCUE,* NO?
WELL, I...
HN?
(THIS TIRE LOOKS LIKE IT WAS SHOT.)
(THERE IS MOVEMENT INSIDE! SOMEONE'S IN THERE WITH THE GIRL!)

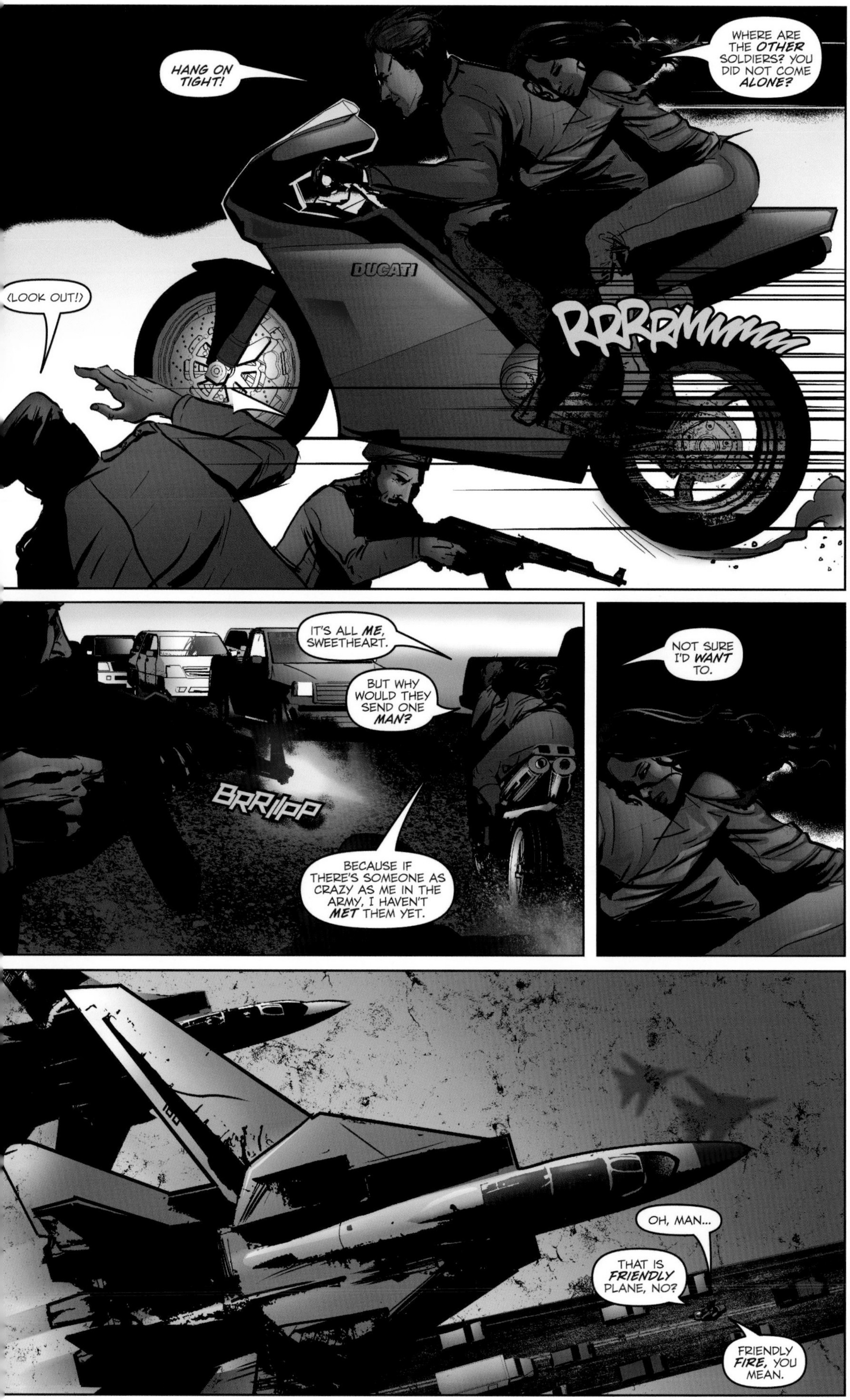
HANG ON TIGHT!
WHERE ARE THE OTHER SOLDIERS? YOU DID NOT COME ALONE?
DUCATI
(LOOK OUT!)
RRRRMMMMMM
IT'S ALL ME, SWEETHEART.
BUT WHY WOULD THEY SEND ONE MAN?
BRRIIPP
BECAUSE IF THERE'S SOMEONE AS CRAZY AS ME IN THE ARMY, I HAVEN'T MET THEM YET.
NOT SURE I'D WANT TO.
OH, MAN...
THAT IS FRIENDLY PLANE, NO?
FRIENDLY FIRE, YOU MEAN.

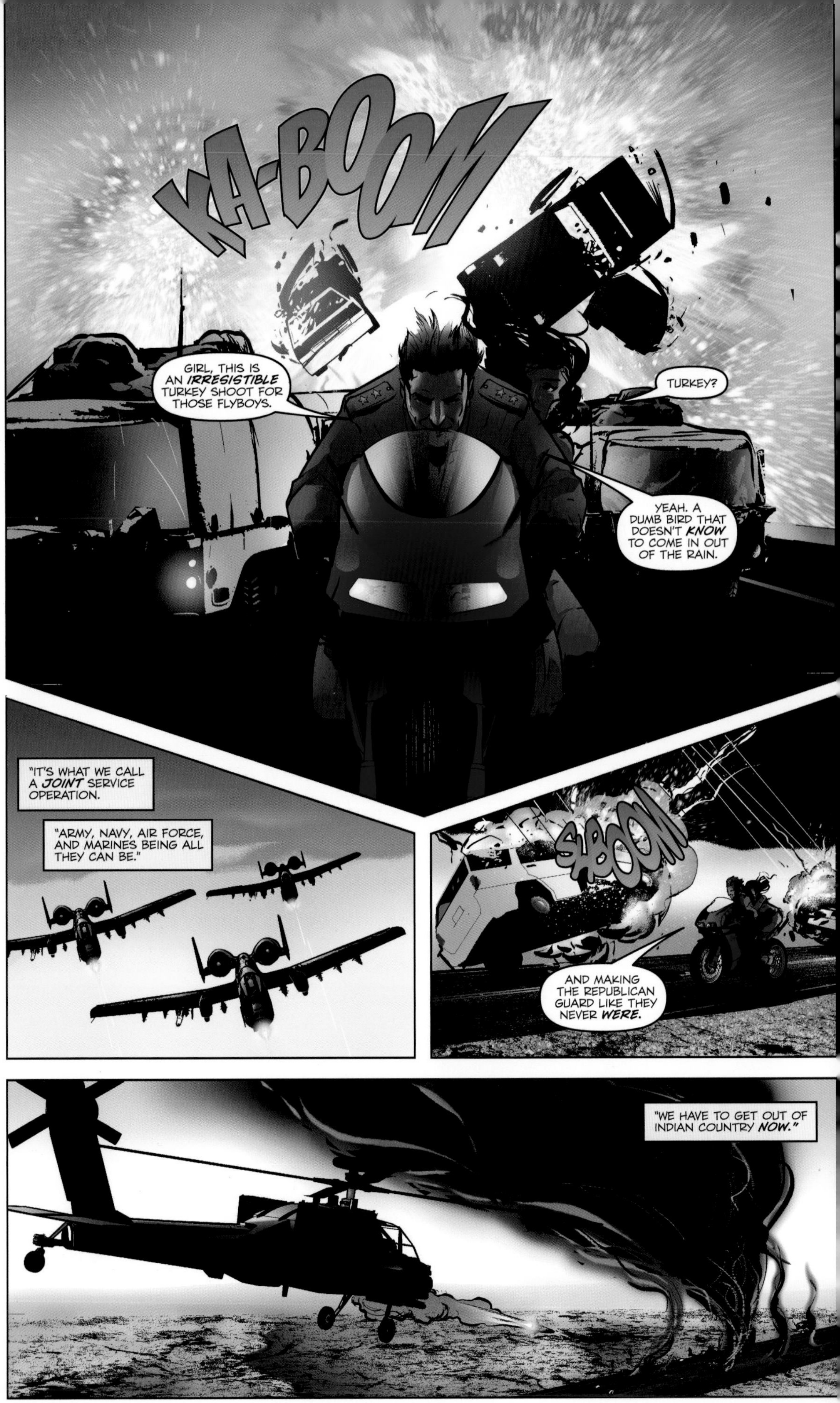
KA-BOOM
GIRL, THIS IS AN IRRESISTIBLE TURKEY SHOOT FOR THOSE FLYBOYS.
TURKEY?
YEAH. A DUMB BIRD THAT DOESN'T KNOW TO COME IN OUT OF THE RAIN.
"IT'S WHAT WE CALL A JOINT SERVICE OPERATION.
"ARMY, NAVY, AIR FORCE, AND MARINES BEING ALL THEY CAN BE."
SHBOOM
AND MAKING THE REPUBLICAN GUARD LIKE THEY NEVER WERE.
"WE HAVE TO GET OUT OF INDIAN COUNTRY NOW."

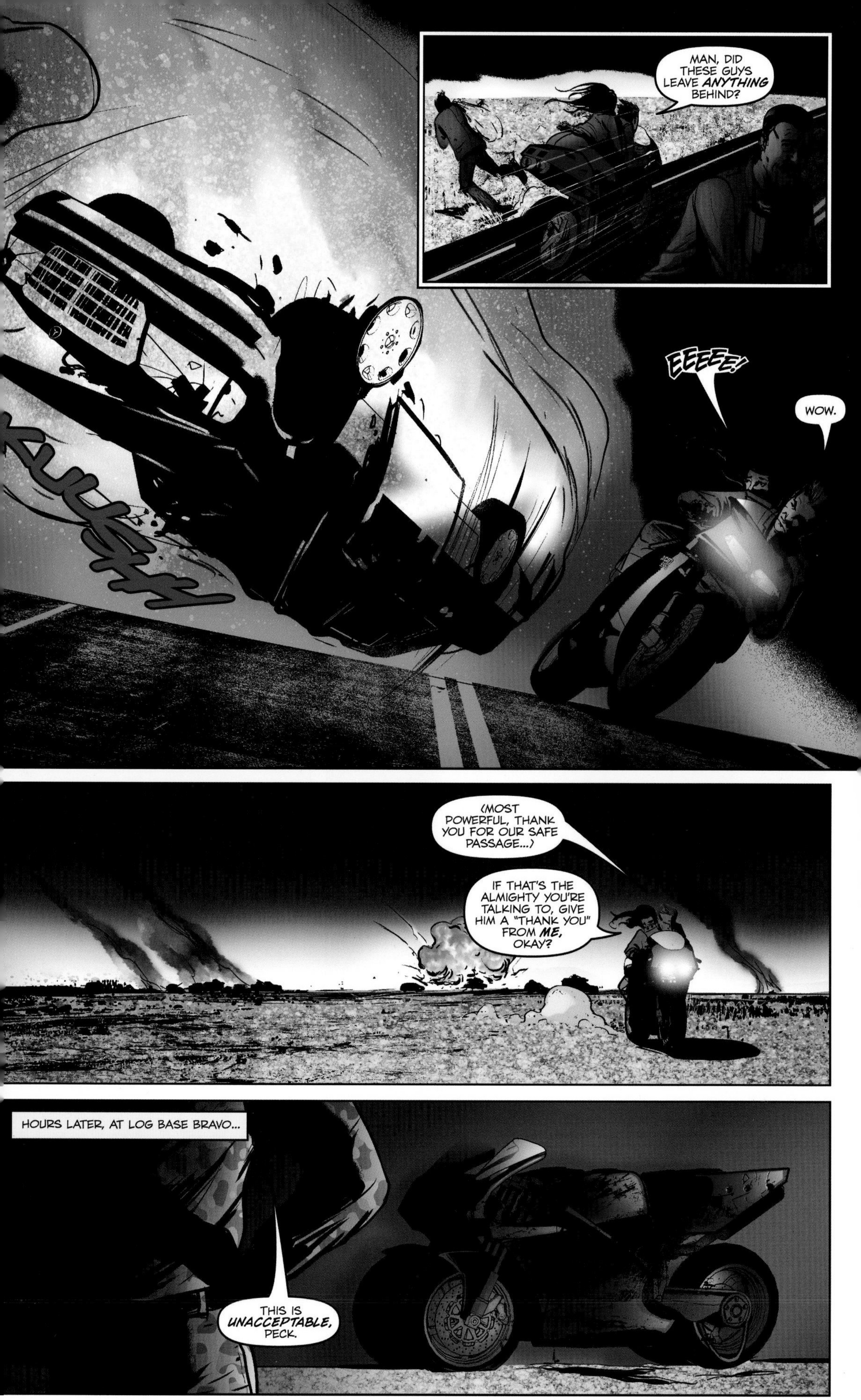

MAN, DID THESE GUYS LEAVE ANYTHING BEHIND?
KKUSHH
EEEEE!
WOW.
(MOST POWERFUL, THANK YOU FOR OUR SAFE PASSAGE...)
IF THAT'S THE ALMIGHTY YOU'RE TALKING TO, GIVE HIM A "THANK YOU" FROM ME, OKAY?
HOURS LATER, AT LOG BASE BRAVO...
THIS IS UNACCEPTABLE, PECK.

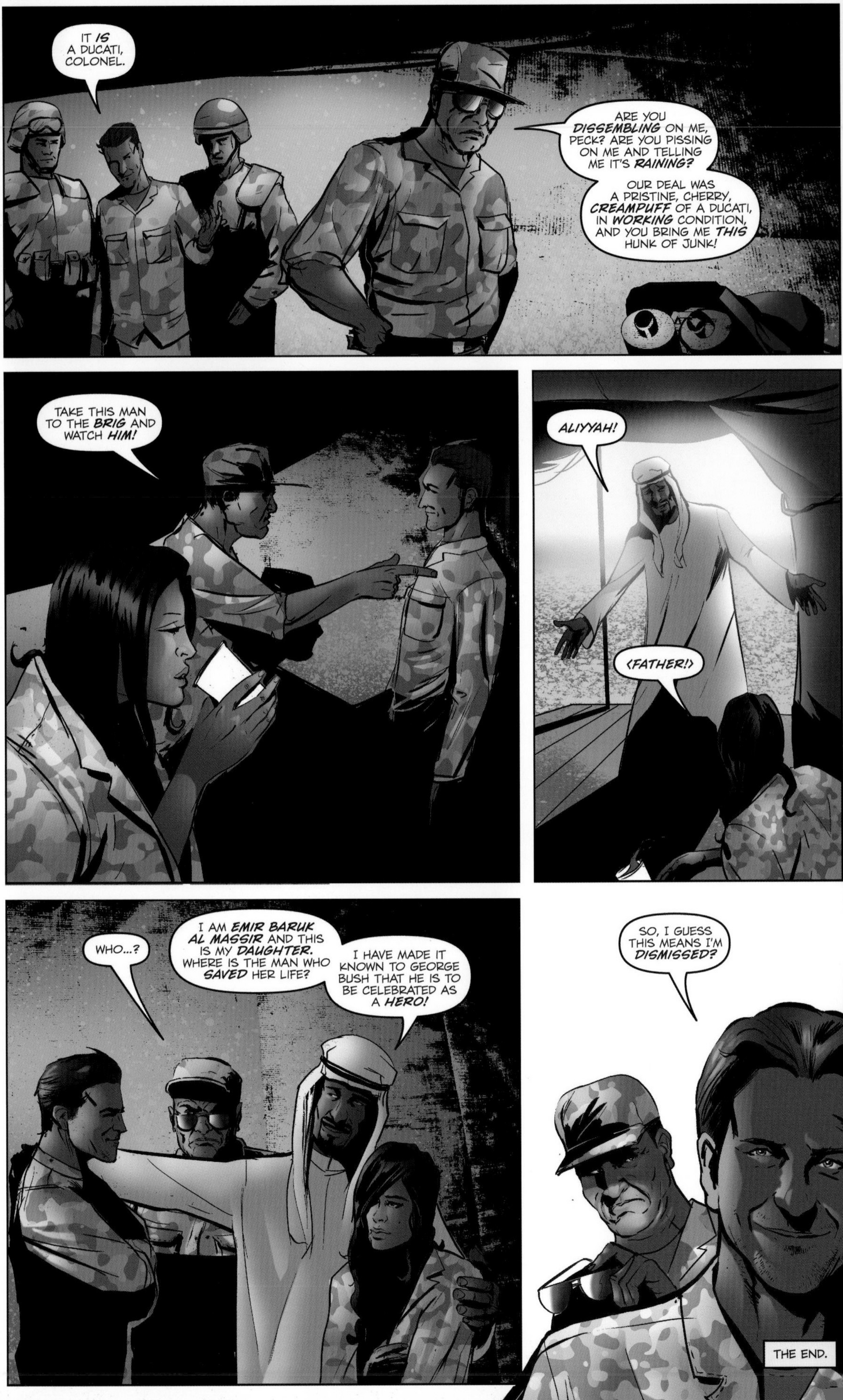
IT IS A DUCATI, COLONEL.
ARE YOU DISSEMBLING ON ME, PECK? ARE YOU PISSING ON ME AND TELLING ME IT'S RAINING?
OUR DEAL WAS A PRISTINE, CHERRY, CREAMPUFF OF A DUCATI, IN WORKING CONDITION, AND YOU BRING ME THIS HUNK OF JUNK!
TAKE THIS MAN TO THE BRIG AND WATCH HIM!
ALIYYAH!
<FATHER!>
WHO...?
I AM EMIR BARUK AL MASSIR AND THIS IS MY DAUGHTER. WHERE IS THE MAN WHO SAVED HER LIFE?
I HAVE MADE IT KNOWN TO GEORGE BUSH THAT HE IS TO BE CELEBRATED AS A HERO!
SO, I GUESS THIS MEANS I'M DISMISSED?
THE END.

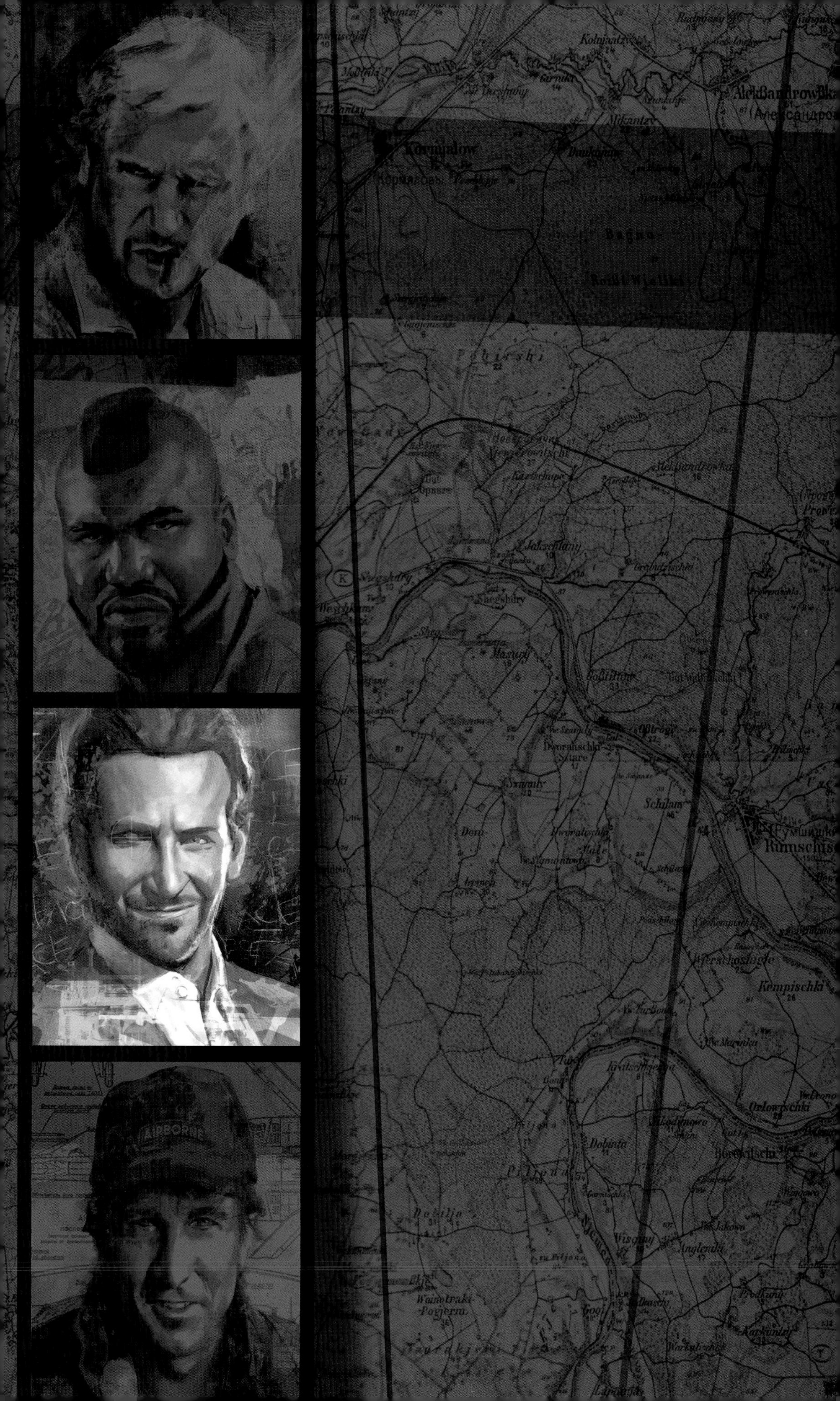
AIRBORNE
Kornjalow
Kempischki
Orlowschki

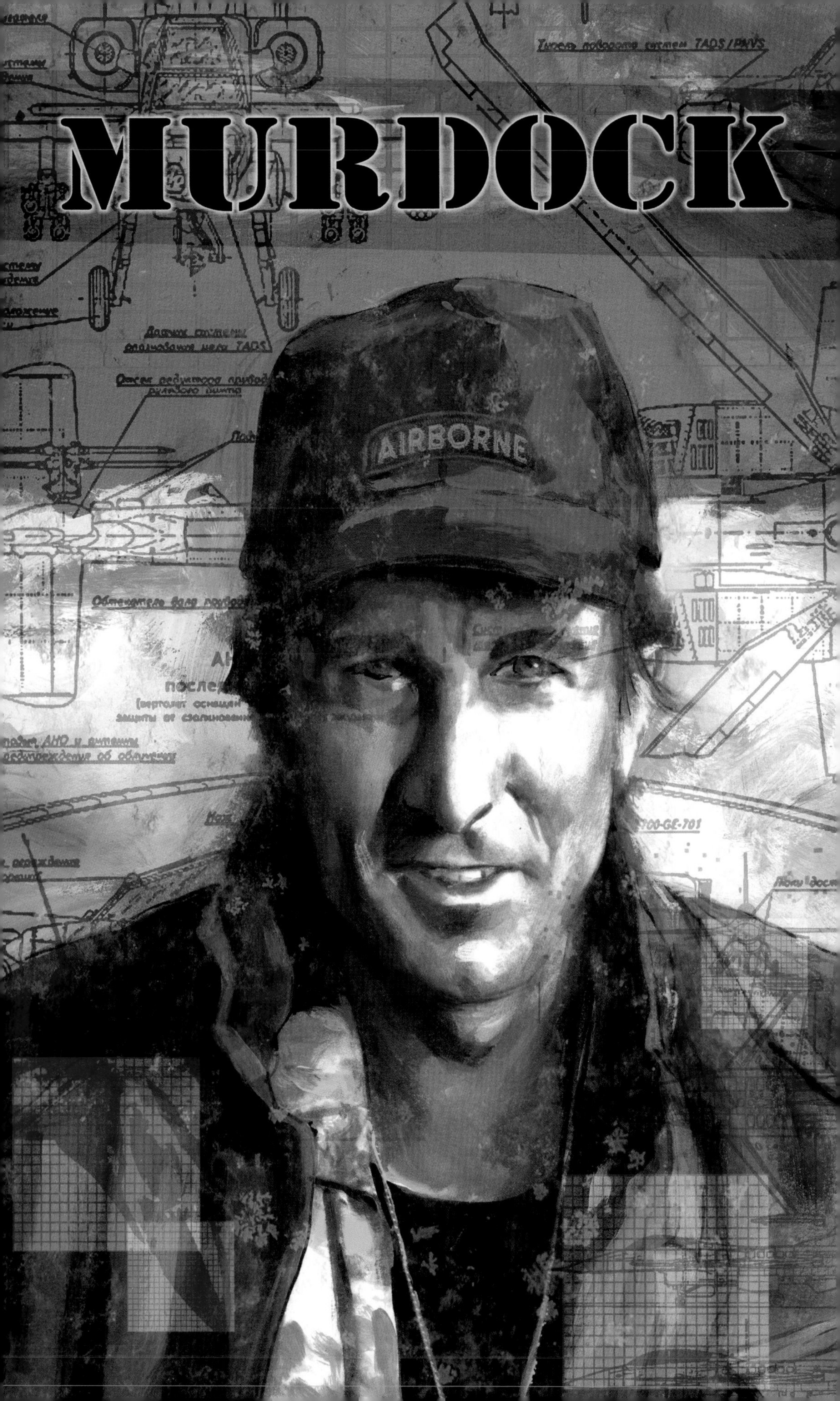
MURDOCK
AIRBORNE

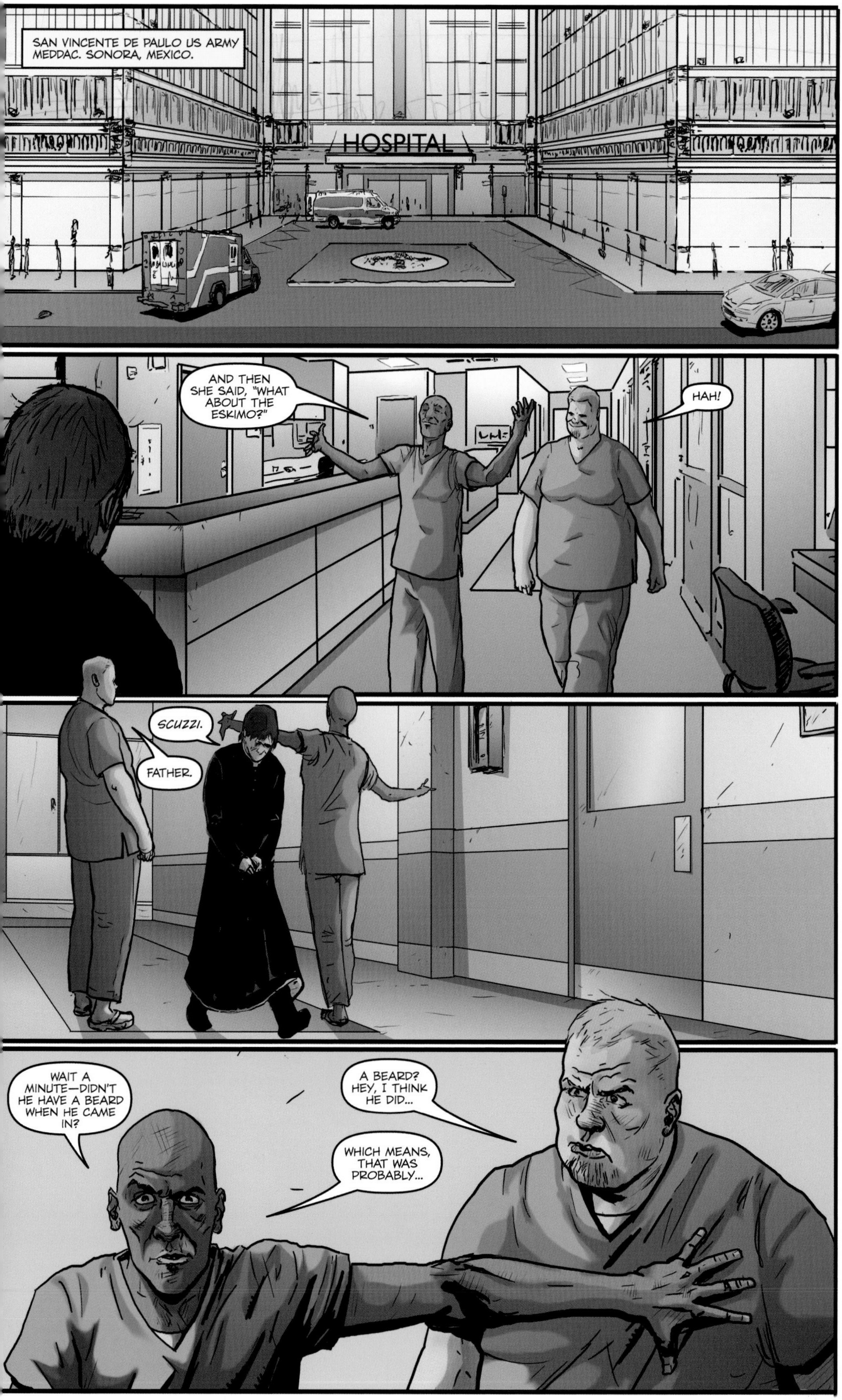
SAN VINCENTE DE PAULO US ARMY MEDDAC. SONORA, MEXICO.
HOSPITAL
AND THEN SHE SAID, "WHAT ABOUT THE ESKIMO?"
HAH!
SCUZZI.
FATHER.
WAIT A MINUTE—DIDN'T HE HAVE A BEARD WHEN HE CAME IN?
A BEARD? HEY, I THINK HE DID...
WHICH MEANS, THAT WAS PROBABLY...

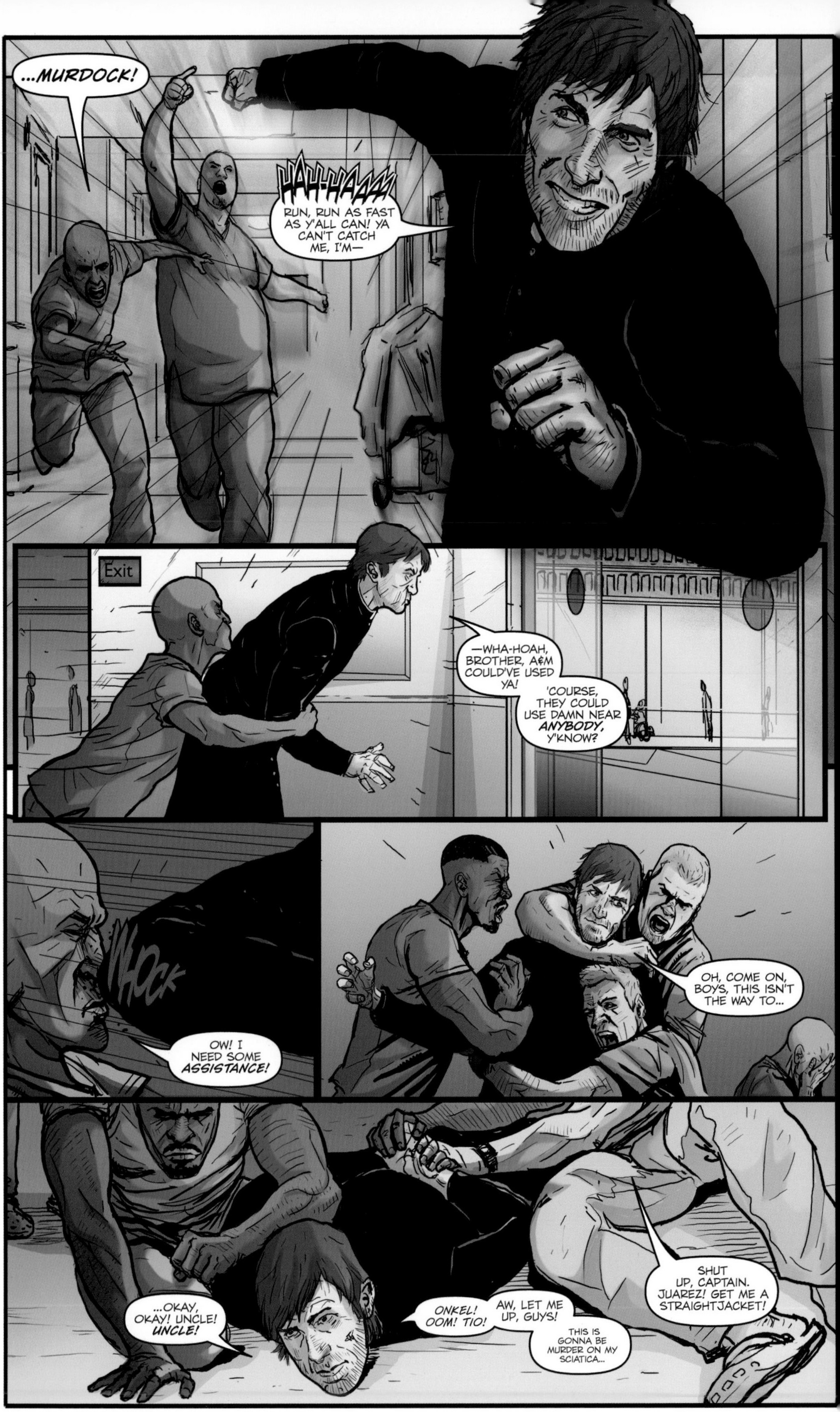
...MURDOCK!
HAH-HAAA!
RUN, RUN AS FAST AS Y'ALL CAN! YA CAN'T CATCH ME, I'M—
Exit
—WHA-HOAH, BROTHER, A&M COULD'VE USED YA!
'COURSE, THEY COULD USE DAMN NEAR ANYBODY, Y'KNOW?
WHOCK
OW! I NEED SOME ASSISTANCE!
OH, COME ON, BOYS, THIS ISN'T THE WAY TO...
...OKAY, OKAY! UNCLE! UNCLE!
ONKEL! OOM! TIO!
AW, LET ME UP, GUYS!
THIS IS GONNA BE MURDER ON MY SCIATICA...
SHUT UP, CAPTAIN. JUAREZ! GET ME A STRAIGHTJACKET!

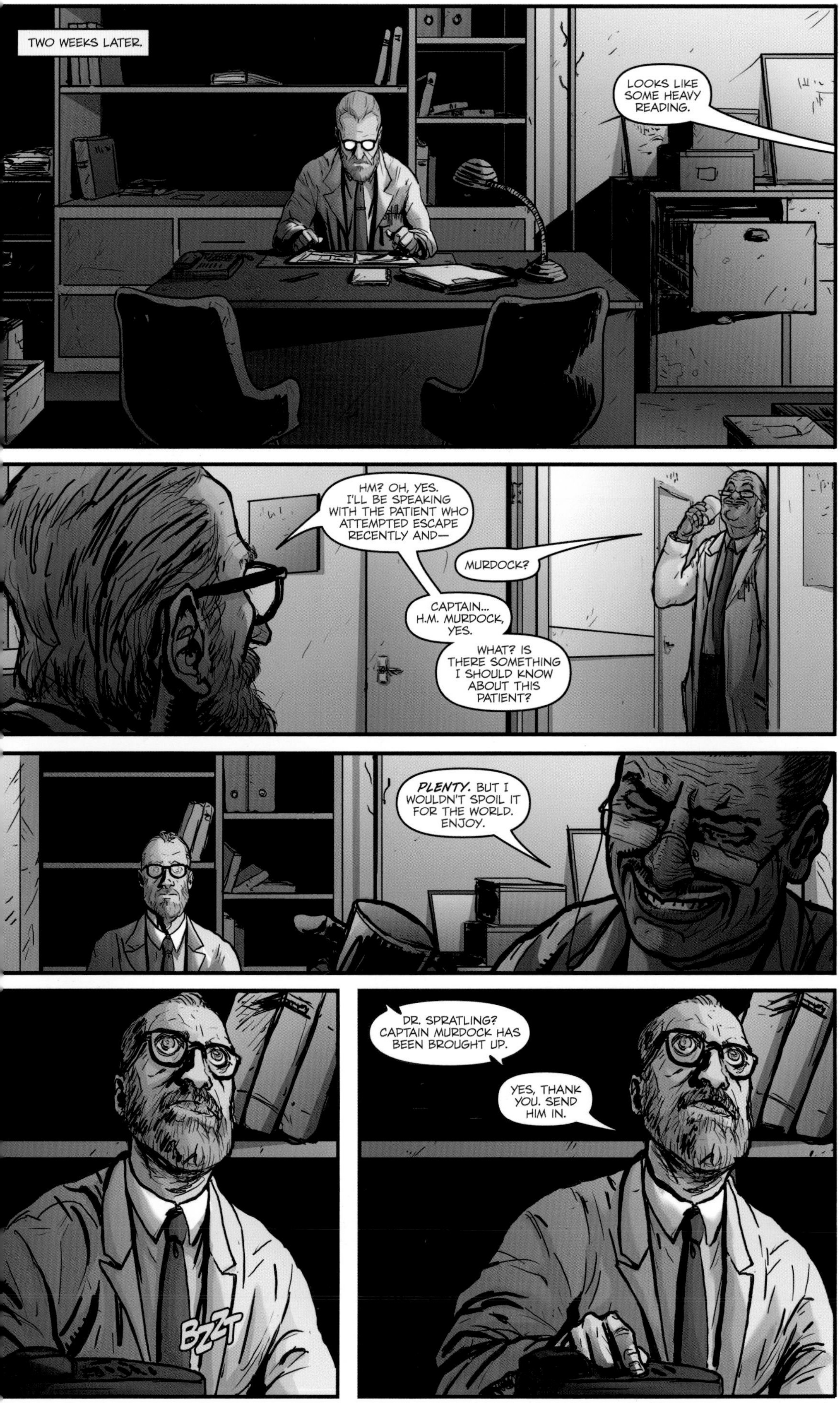
TWO WEEKS LATER.
LOOKS LIKE SOME HEAVY READING.
HM? OH, YES. I'LL BE SPEAKING WITH THE PATIENT WHO ATTEMPTED ESCAPE RECENTLY AND—
MURDOCK?
CAPTAIN... H.M. MURDOCK, YES.
WHAT? IS THERE SOMETHING I SHOULD KNOW ABOUT THIS PATIENT?
PLENTY. BUT I WOULDN'T SPOIL IT FOR THE WORLD. ENJOY.
BZZT
DR. SPRATLING? CAPTAIN MURDOCK HAS BEEN BROUGHT UP.
YES, THANK YOU. SEND HIM IN.

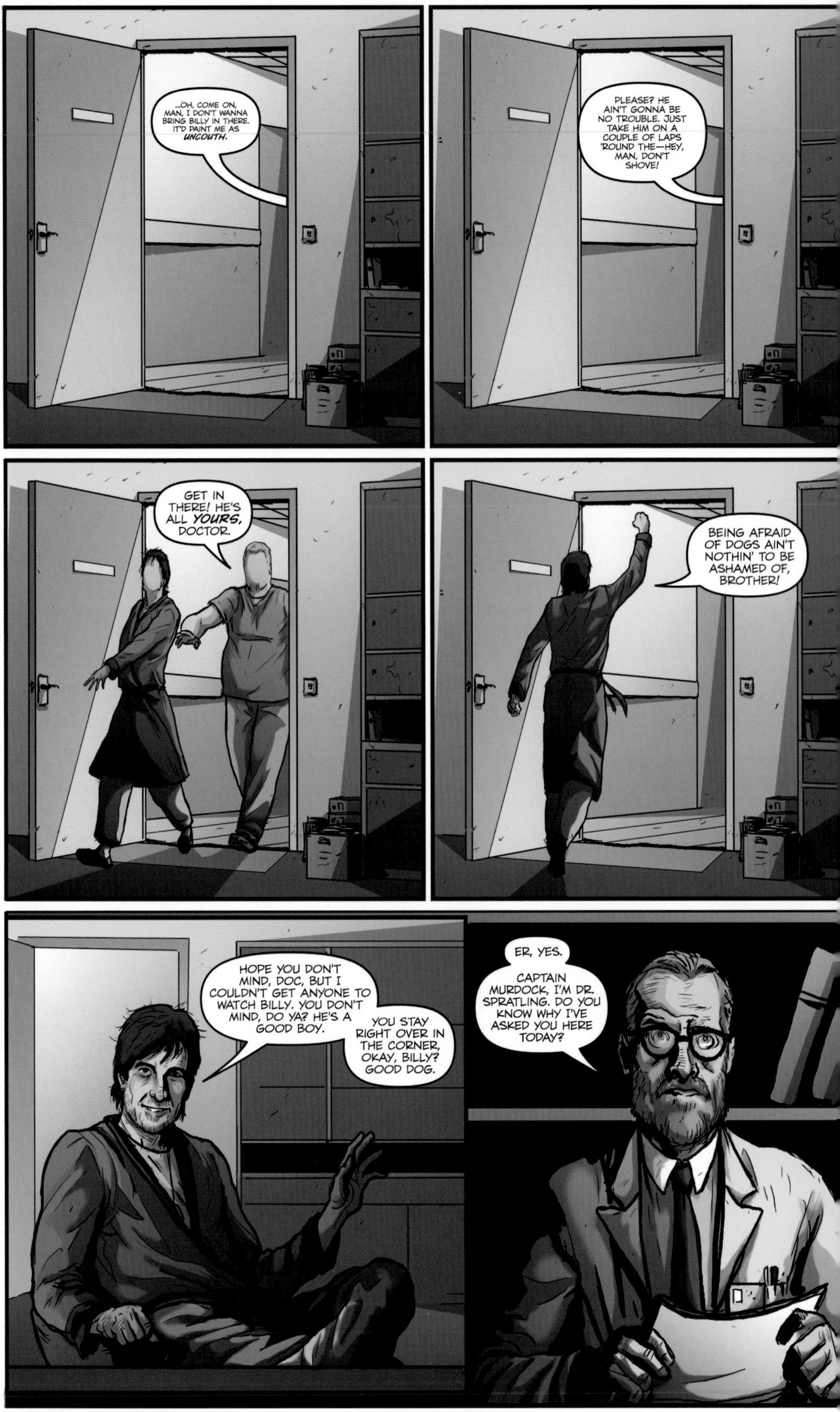
...OH, COME ON, MAN, I DON'T WANNA BRING BILLY IN THERE. IT'D PAINT ME AS *UNCOUTH.*
PLEASE? HE AIN'T GONNA BE NO TROUBLE. JUST TAKE HIM ON A COUPLE OF LAPS 'ROUND THE—HEY, MAN, DON'T SHOVE!
GET IN THERE! HE'S ALL *YOURS,* DOCTOR.
BEING AFRAID OF DOGS AIN'T NOTHIN' TO BE ASHAMED OF, BROTHER!
HOPE YOU DON'T MIND, DOC, BUT I COULDN'T GET ANYONE TO WATCH BILLY. YOU DON'T MIND, DO YA? HE'S A GOOD BOY.
YOU STAY RIGHT OVER IN THE CORNER, OKAY, BILLY? GOOD DOG.
ER, YES.
CAPTAIN MURDOCK, I'M DR. SPRATLING. DO YOU KNOW WHY I'VE ASKED YOU HERE TODAY?

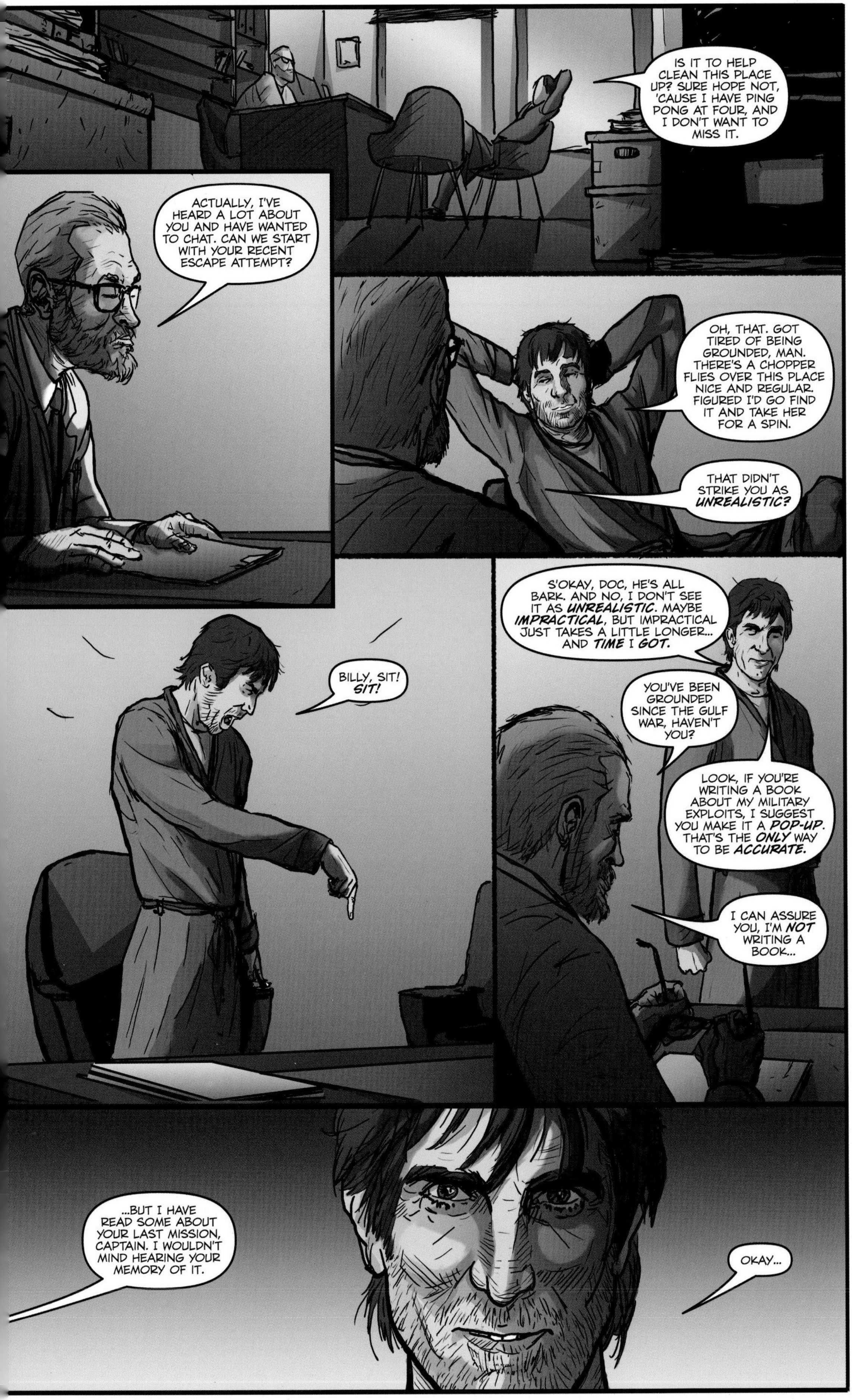
IS IT TO HELP CLEAN THIS PLACE UP? SURE HOPE NOT, 'CAUSE I HAVE PING PONG AT FOUR, AND I DON'T WANT TO MISS IT.
ACTUALLY, I'VE HEARD A LOT ABOUT YOU AND HAVE WANTED TO CHAT. CAN WE START WITH YOUR RECENT ESCAPE ATTEMPT?
OH, THAT. GOT TIRED OF BEING GROUNDED, MAN. THERE'S A CHOPPER FLIES OVER THIS PLACE NICE AND REGULAR. FIGURED I'D GO FIND IT AND TAKE HER FOR A SPIN.
THAT DIDN'T STRIKE YOU AS *UNREALISTIC?*
BILLY, SIT! *SIT!*
S'OKAY, DOC, HE'S ALL BARK. AND NO, I DON'T SEE IT AS *UNREALISTIC*. MAYBE *IMPRACTICAL*, BUT IMPRACTICAL JUST TAKES A LITTLE LONGER... AND *TIME* I *GOT*.
YOU'VE BEEN GROUNDED SINCE THE GULF WAR, HAVEN'T YOU?
LOOK, IF YOU'RE WRITING A BOOK ABOUT MY MILITARY EXPLOITS, I SUGGEST YOU MAKE IT A *POP-UP*. THAT'S THE *ONLY* WAY TO BE *ACCURATE*.
I CAN ASSURE YOU, I'M *NOT* WRITING A BOOK...
...BUT I HAVE READ SOME ABOUT YOUR LAST MISSION, CAPTAIN. I WOULDN'T MIND HEARING YOUR MEMORY OF IT.
OKAY...

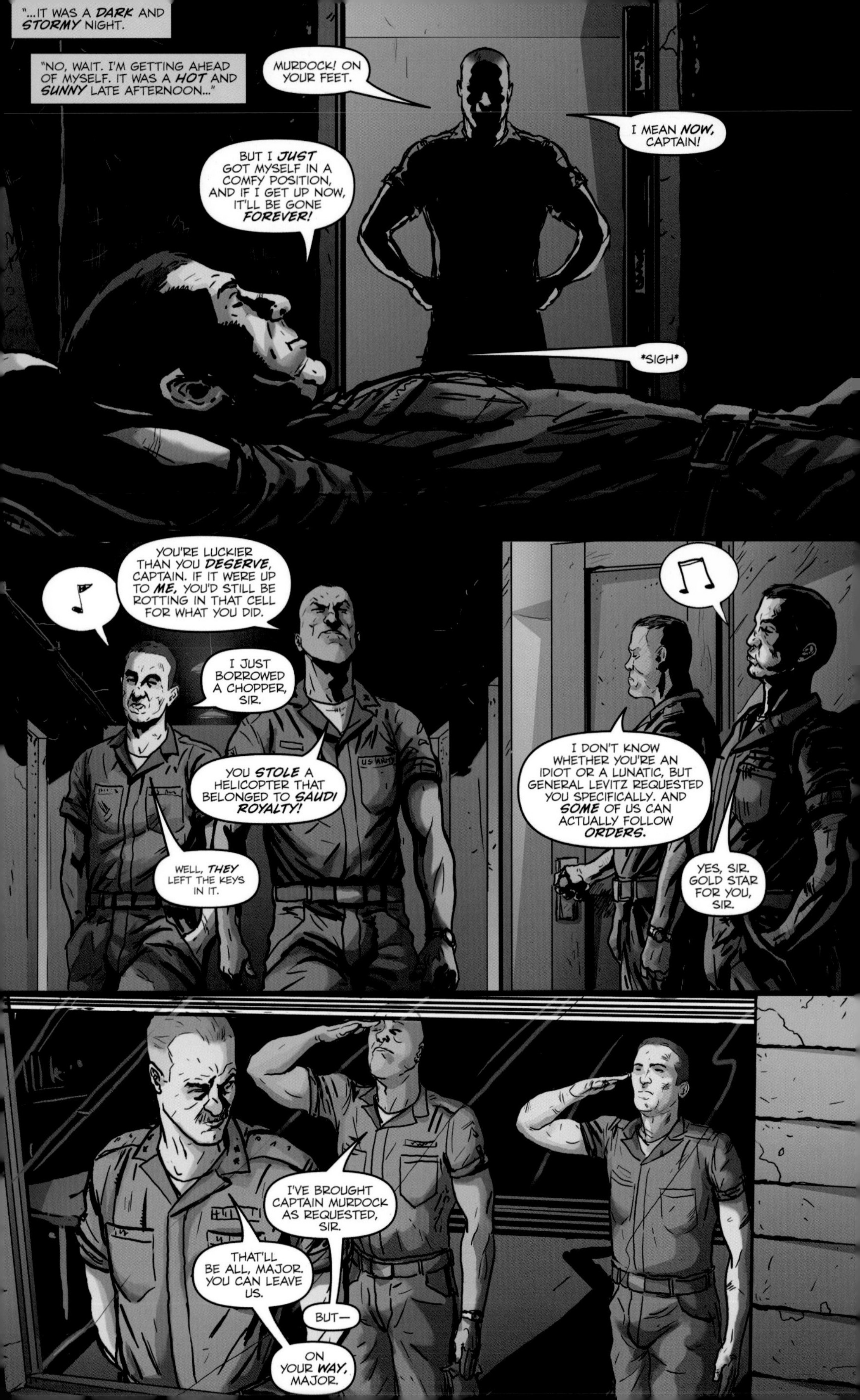
"...IT WAS A DARK AND STORMY NIGHT.
"NO, WAIT. I'M GETTING AHEAD OF MYSELF. IT WAS A HOT AND SUNNY LATE AFTERNOON..."
MURDOCK! ON YOUR FEET.
BUT I JUST GOT MYSELF IN A COMFY POSITION, AND IF I GET UP NOW, IT'LL BE GONE FOREVER!
I MEAN NOW, CAPTAIN!
SIGH
YOU'RE LUCKIER THAN YOU DESERVE, CAPTAIN. IF IT WERE UP TO ME, YOU'D STILL BE ROTTING IN THAT CELL FOR WHAT YOU DID.
I JUST BORROWED A CHOPPER, SIR.
YOU STOLE A HELICOPTER THAT BELONGED TO SAUDI ROYALTY!
WELL, THEY LEFT THE KEYS IN IT.
I DON'T KNOW WHETHER YOU'RE AN IDIOT OR A LUNATIC, BUT GENERAL LEVITZ REQUESTED YOU SPECIFICALLY. AND SOME OF US CAN ACTUALLY FOLLOW ORDERS.
YES, SIR. GOLD STAR FOR YOU, SIR.
I'VE BROUGHT CAPTAIN MURDOCK AS REQUESTED, SIR.
THAT'LL BE ALL, MAJOR. YOU CAN LEAVE US.
BUT—
ON YOUR WAY, MAJOR.

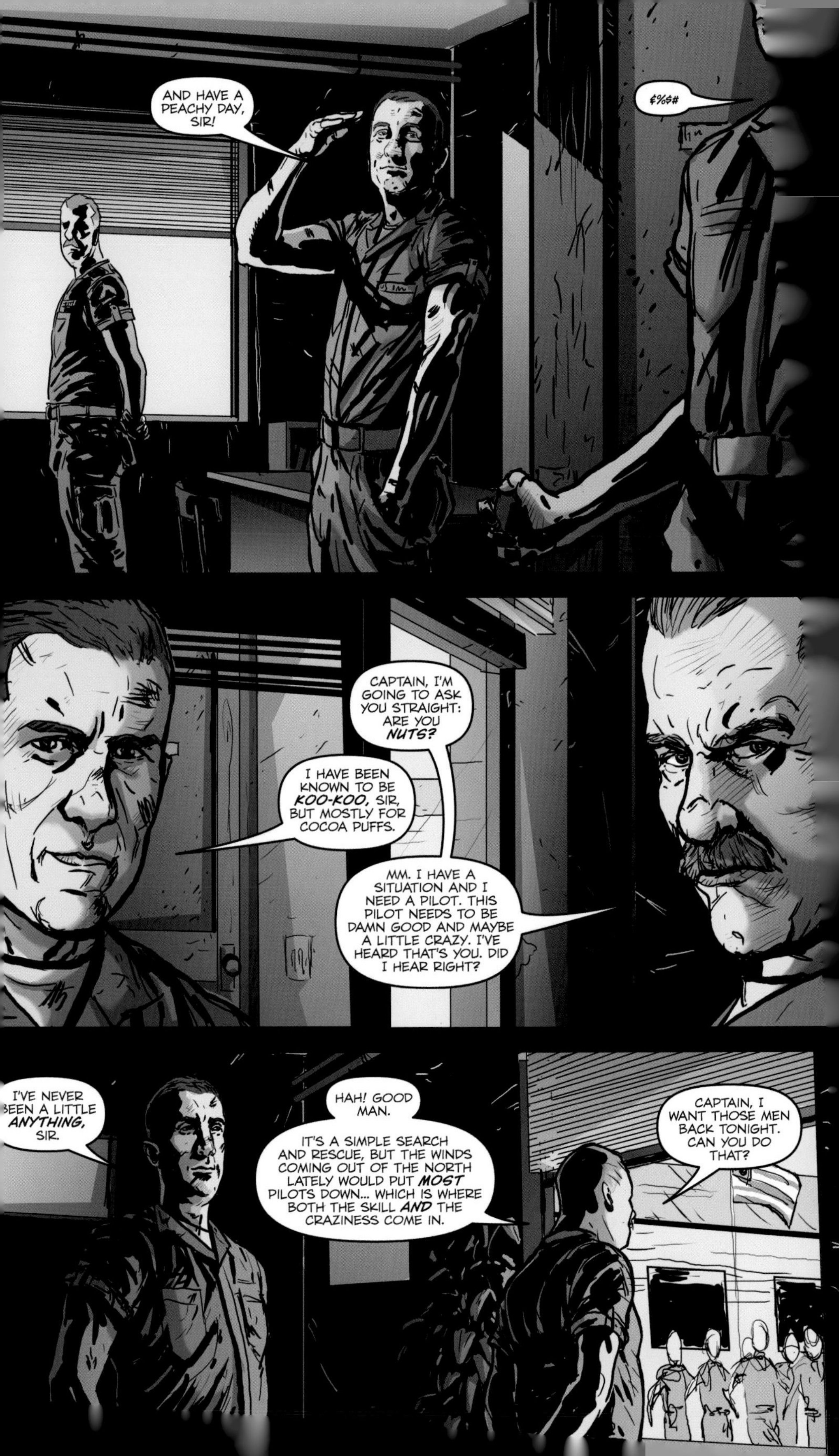
AND HAVE A PEACHY DAY, SIR!
$%$#
CAPTAIN, I'M GOING TO ASK YOU STRAIGHT: ARE YOU *NUTS?*
I HAVE BEEN KNOWN TO BE *KOO-KOO,* SIR, BUT MOSTLY FOR COCOA PUFFS.
MM. I HAVE A SITUATION AND I NEED A PILOT. THIS PILOT NEEDS TO BE DAMN GOOD AND MAYBE A LITTLE CRAZY. I'VE HEARD THAT'S YOU. DID I HEAR RIGHT?
I'VE NEVER BEEN A LITTLE *ANYTHING,* SIR.
HAH! GOOD MAN.
IT'S A SIMPLE SEARCH AND RESCUE, BUT THE WINDS COMING OUT OF THE NORTH LATELY WOULD PUT *MOST* PILOTS DOWN... WHICH IS WHERE BOTH THE SKILL *AND* THE CRAZINESS COME IN.
CAPTAIN, I WANT THOSE MEN BACK TONIGHT. CAN YOU DO THAT?

"I JUST NEED A *WHERE* AND *WHEN,* SIR."

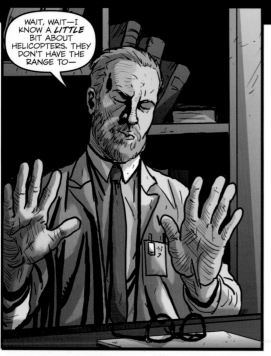

WAIT, WAIT—I KNOW A *LITTLE* BIT ABOUT HELICOPTERS. THEY DON'T HAVE THE RANGE TO—

DOWN, BILLY! HE DON'T MEAN NO HARM! *DOWN, BOY!*

I'M SORRY, DOC—BILLY DON'T COTTON TO INTERRUPTIONS. BUT, TO ANSWER, I FLEW OUT FROM A CARRIER, WITH EXTRA FUEL. AND GOD AS MY CO-PILOT.

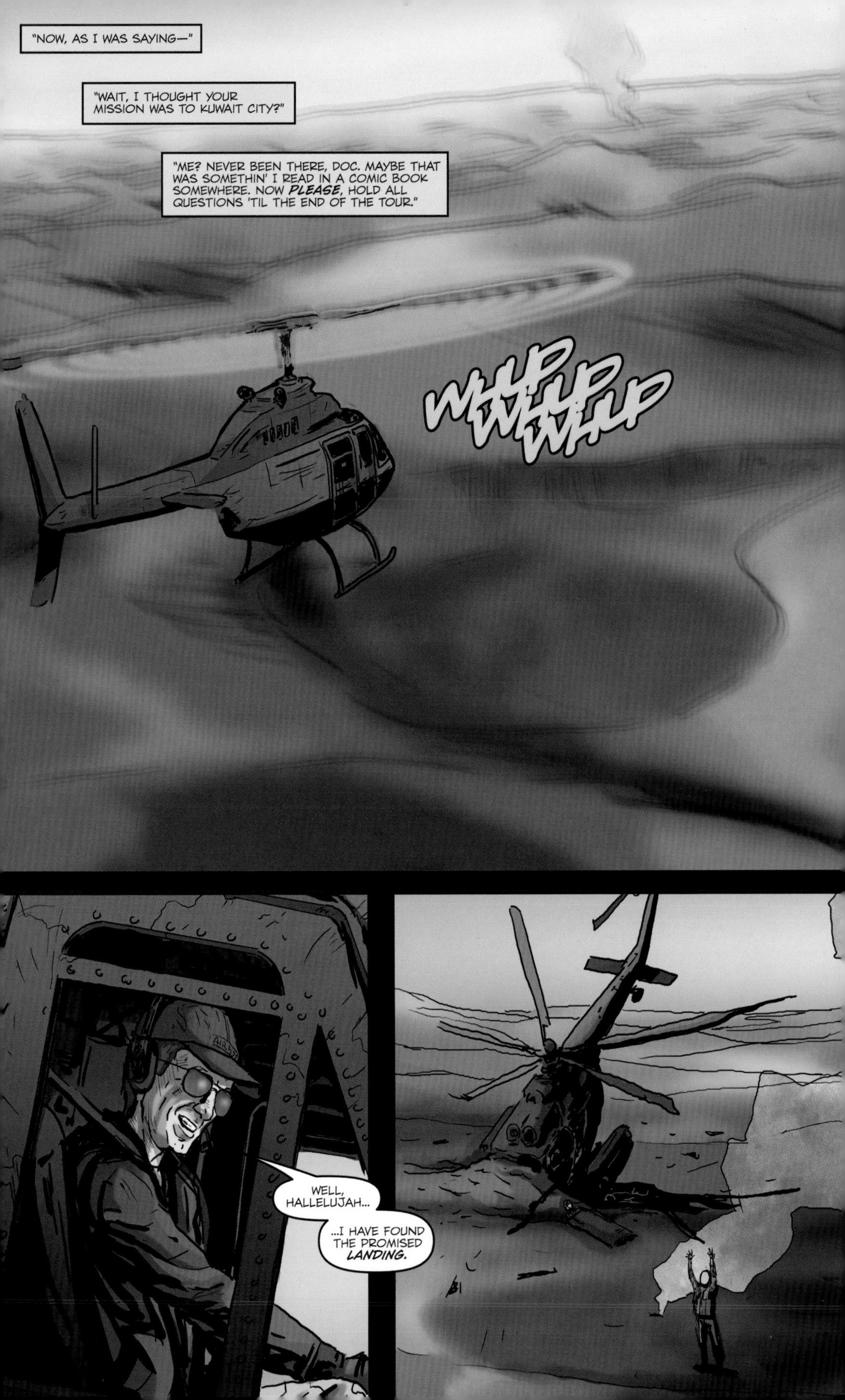
"NOW, AS I WAS SAYING—"
"WAIT, I THOUGHT YOUR MISSION WAS TO KUWAIT CITY?"
"ME? NEVER BEEN THERE, DOC. MAYBE THAT WAS SOMETHIN' I READ IN A COMIC BOOK SOMEWHERE. NOW *PLEASE*, HOLD ALL QUESTIONS 'TIL THE END OF THE TOUR."
WHUP WHUP WHUP
WELL, HALLELUJAH...
...I HAVE FOUND THE PROMISED *LANDING.*

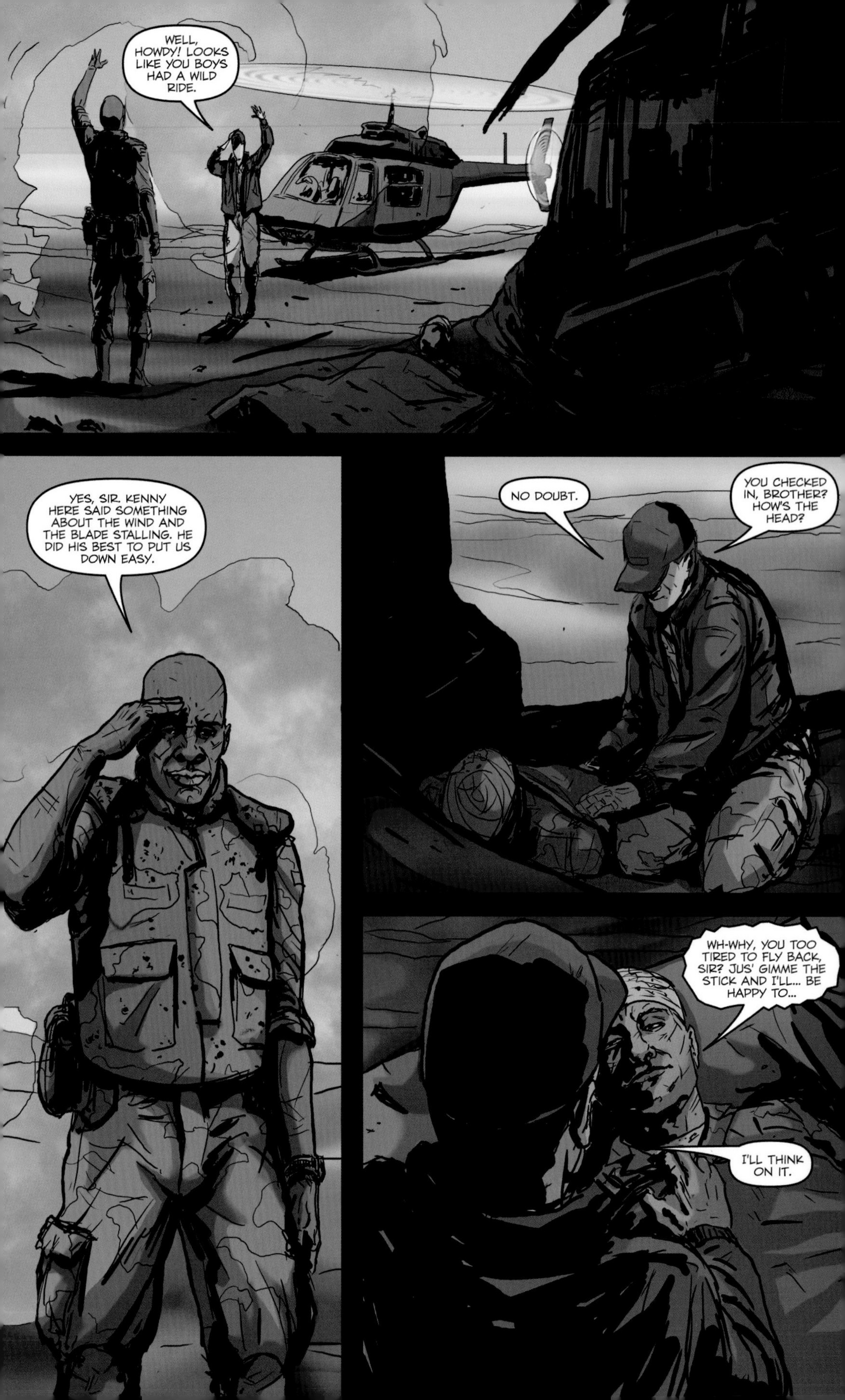
WELL, HOWDY! LOOKS LIKE YOU BOYS HAD A WILD RIDE.
YES, SIR. KENNY HERE SAID SOMETHING ABOUT THE WIND AND THE BLADE STALLING. HE DID HIS BEST TO PUT US DOWN EASY.
NO DOUBT.
YOU CHECKED IN, BROTHER? HOW'S THE HEAD?
WH-WHY, YOU TOO TIRED TO FLY BACK, SIR? JUS' GIMME THE STICK AND I'LL... BE HAPPY TO...
I'LL THINK ON IT.

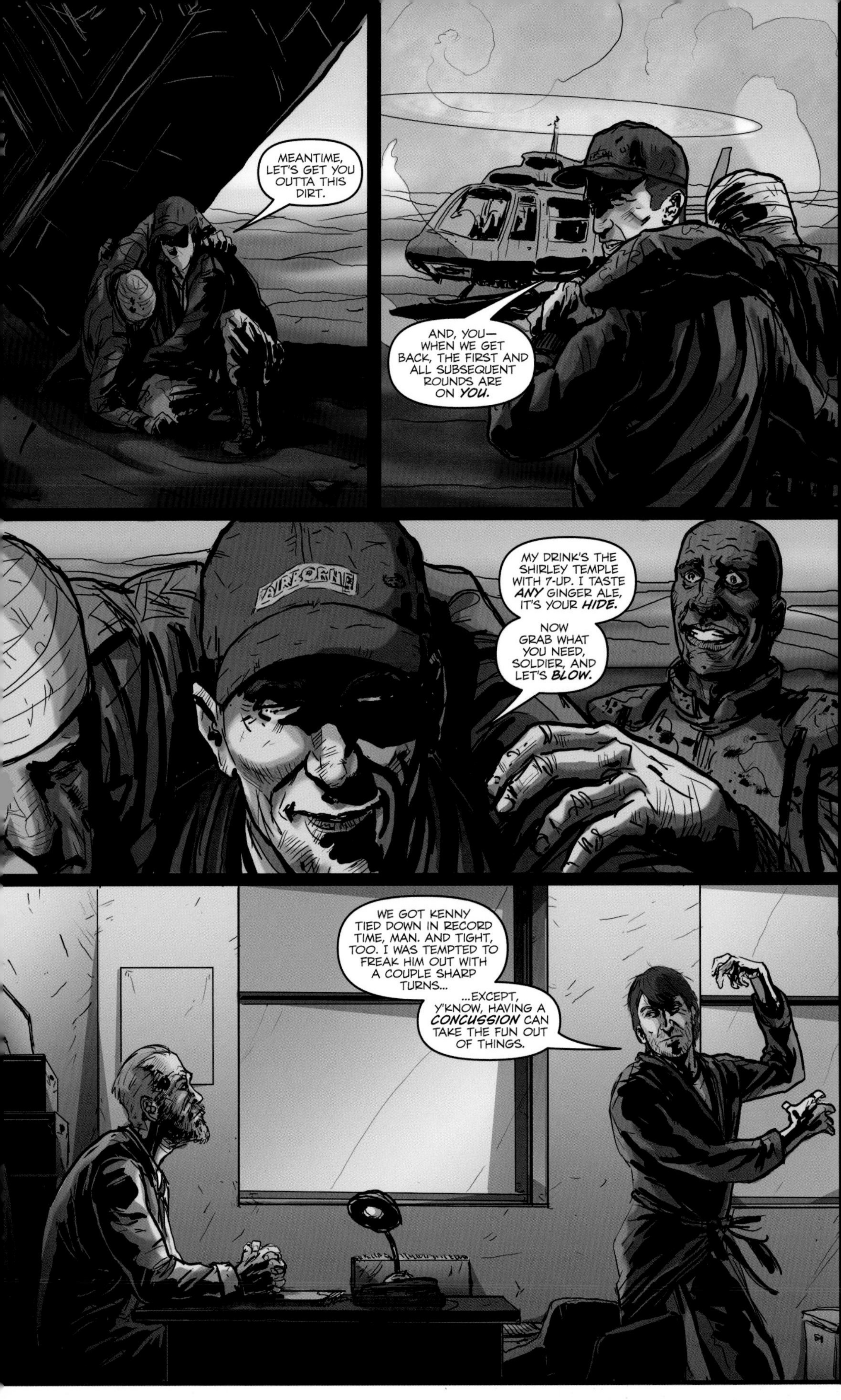
MEANTIME, LET'S GET YOU OUTTA THIS DIRT.
AND, YOU— WHEN WE GET BACK, THE FIRST AND ALL SUBSEQUENT ROUNDS ARE ON *YOU.*
AIRBORNE
MY DRINK'S THE SHIRLEY TEMPLE WITH 7-UP. I TASTE *ANY* GINGER ALE, IT'S YOUR *HIDE.*
NOW GRAB WHAT YOU NEED, SOLDIER, AND LET'S *BLOW.*
WE GOT KENNY TIED DOWN IN RECORD TIME, MAN. AND TIGHT, TOO. I WAS TEMPTED TO FREAK HIM OUT WITH A COUPLE SHARP TURNS...
...EXCEPT, Y'KNOW, HAVING A *CONCUSSION* CAN TAKE THE FUN OUT OF THINGS.

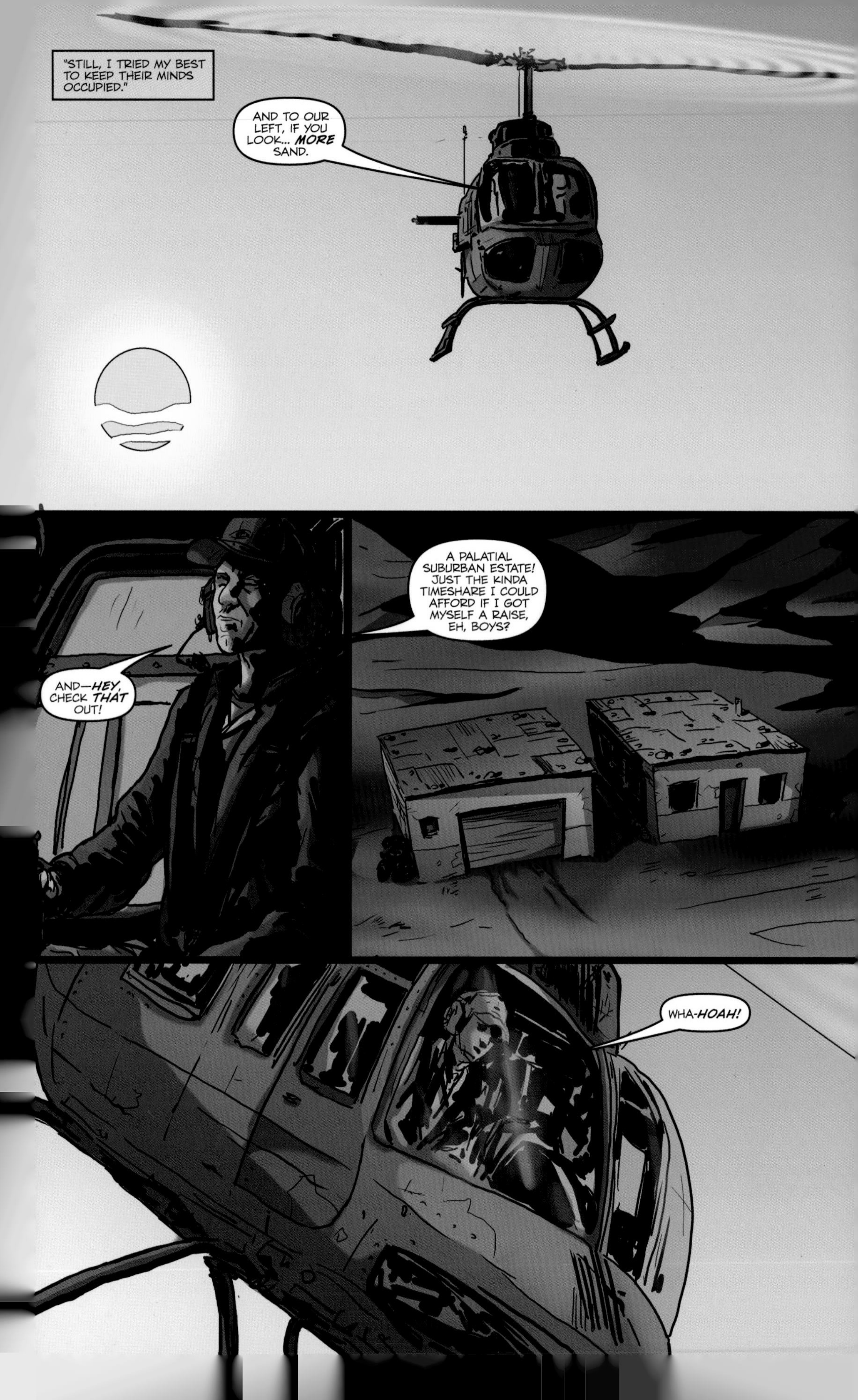
"STILL, I TRIED MY BEST TO KEEP THEIR MINDS OCCUPIED."
AND TO OUR LEFT, IF YOU LOOK... MORE SAND.
AND—HEY, CHECK THAT OUT!
A PALATIAL SUBURBAN ESTATE! JUST THE KINDA TIMESHARE I COULD AFFORD IF I GOT MYSELF A RAISE, EH, BOYS?
WHA-HOAH!

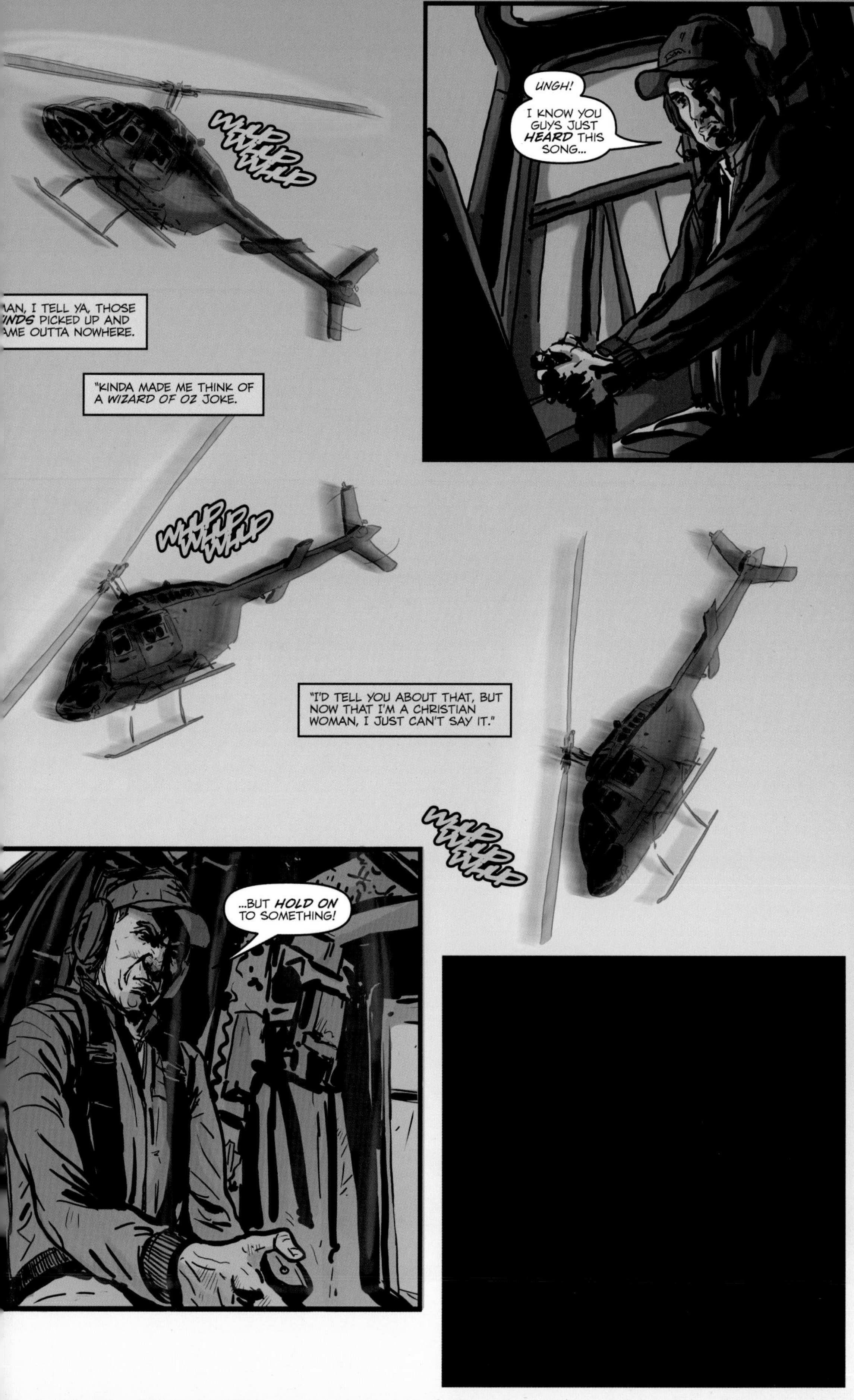

WHUP WHUP WHUP
UNGH!
I KNOW YOU GUYS JUST **HEARD** THIS SONG...
AN, I TELL YA, THOSE ***INDS*** PICKED UP AND AME OUTTA NOWHERE.
"KINDA MADE ME THINK OF A *WIZARD OF OZ* JOKE.
WHUP WHUP
"I'D TELL YOU ABOUT THAT, BUT NOW THAT I'M A CHRISTIAN WOMAN, I JUST CAN'T SAY IT."
WHUP WHUP WHUP
...BUT ***HOLD ON*** TO SOMETHING!

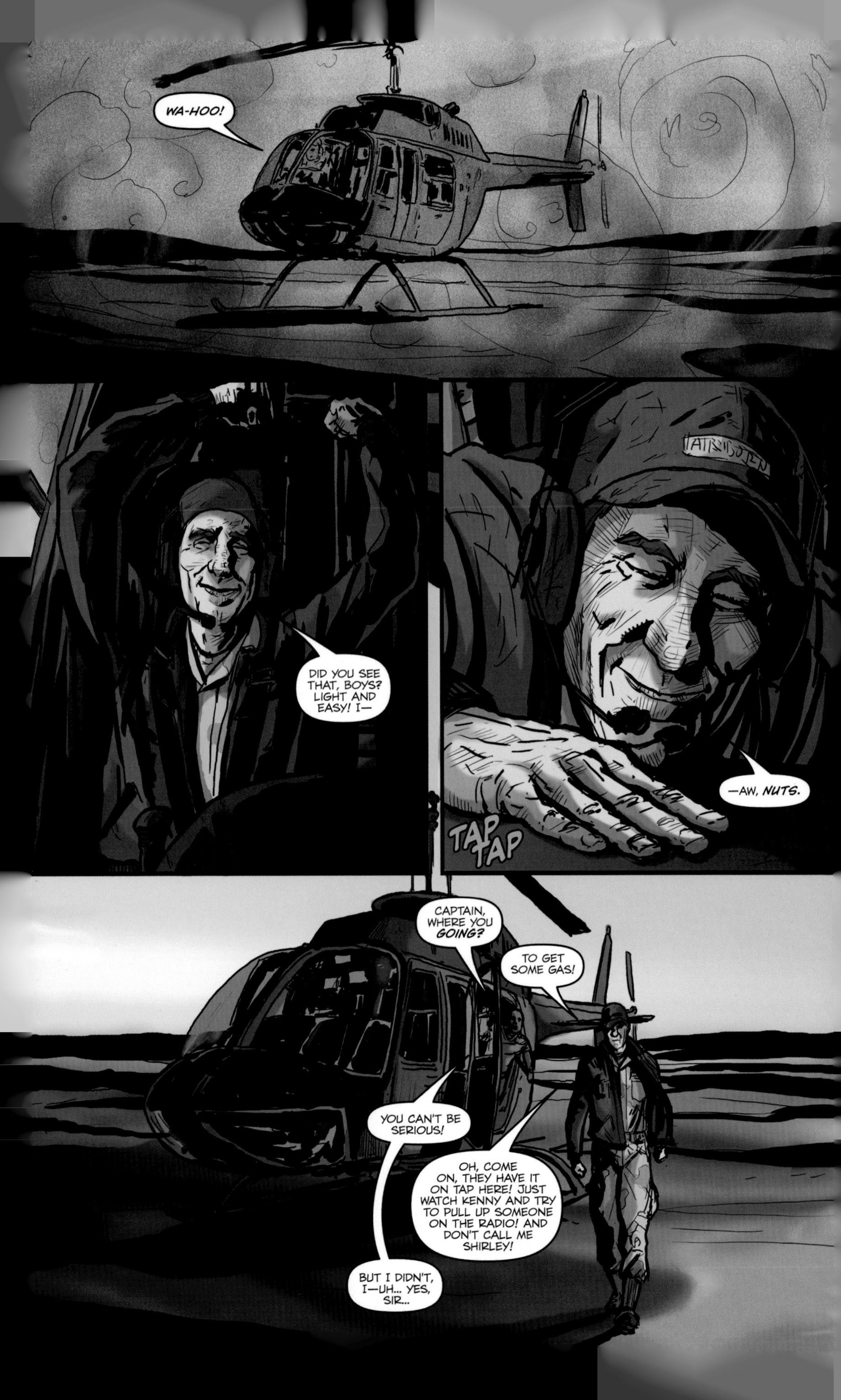
WA-HOO!
DID YOU SEE THAT, BOYS? LIGHT AND EASY! I—
—AW, NUTS.
TAP TAP
CAPTAIN, WHERE YOU GOING?
TO GET SOME GAS!
YOU CAN'T BE SERIOUS!
OH, COME ON, THEY HAVE IT ON TAP HERE! JUST WATCH KENNY AND TRY TO PULL UP SOMEONE ON THE RADIO! AND DON'T CALL ME SHIRLEY!
BUT I DIDN'T, I—UH... YES, SIR...

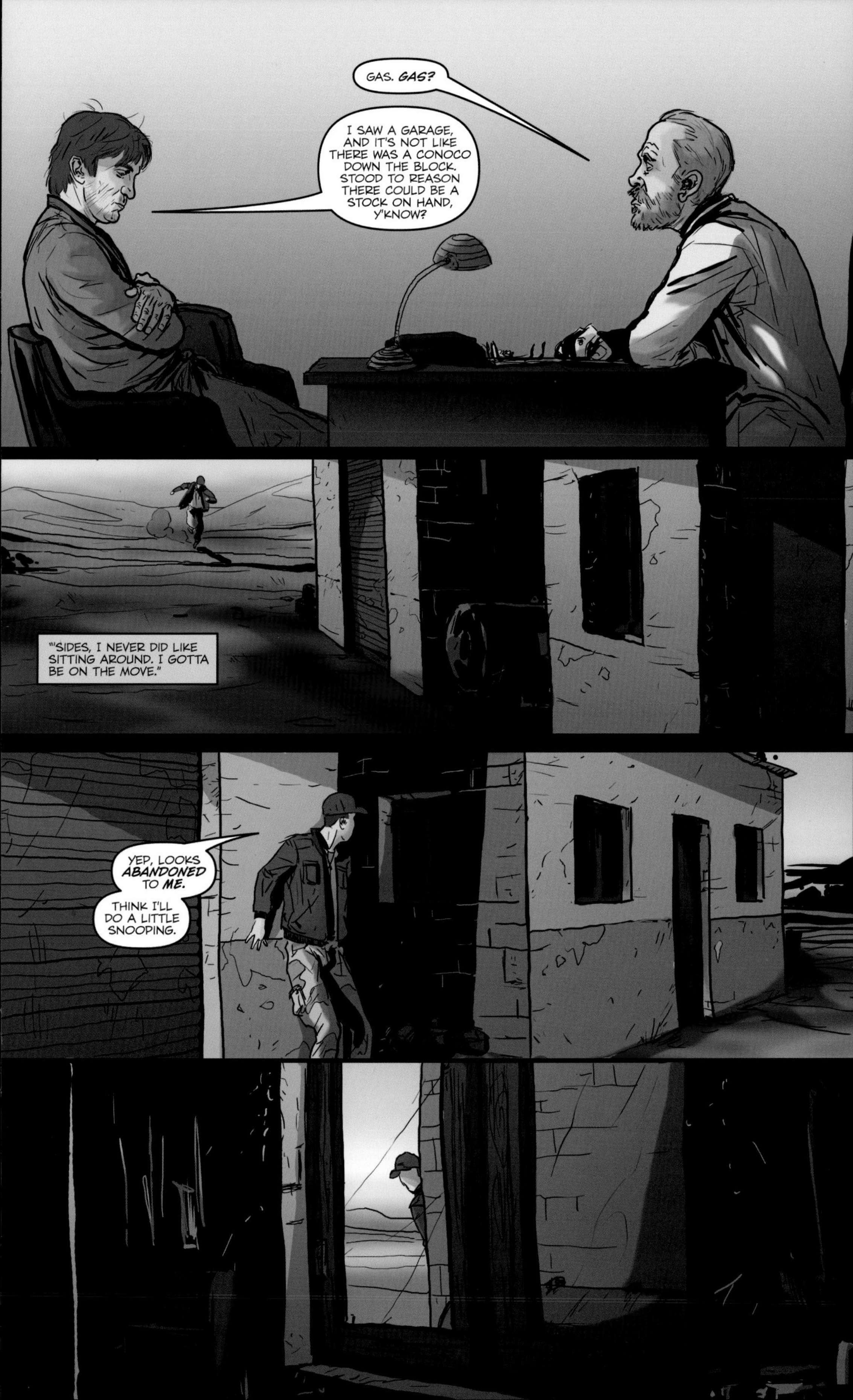
GAS. GAS?
I SAW A GARAGE, AND IT'S NOT LIKE THERE WAS A CONOCO DOWN THE BLOCK. STOOD TO REASON THERE COULD BE A STOCK ON HAND, Y'KNOW?
"'SIDES, I NEVER DID LIKE SITTING AROUND. I GOTTA BE ON THE MOVE."
YEP, LOOKS ABANDONED TO ME.
THINK I'LL DO A LITTLE SNOOPING.

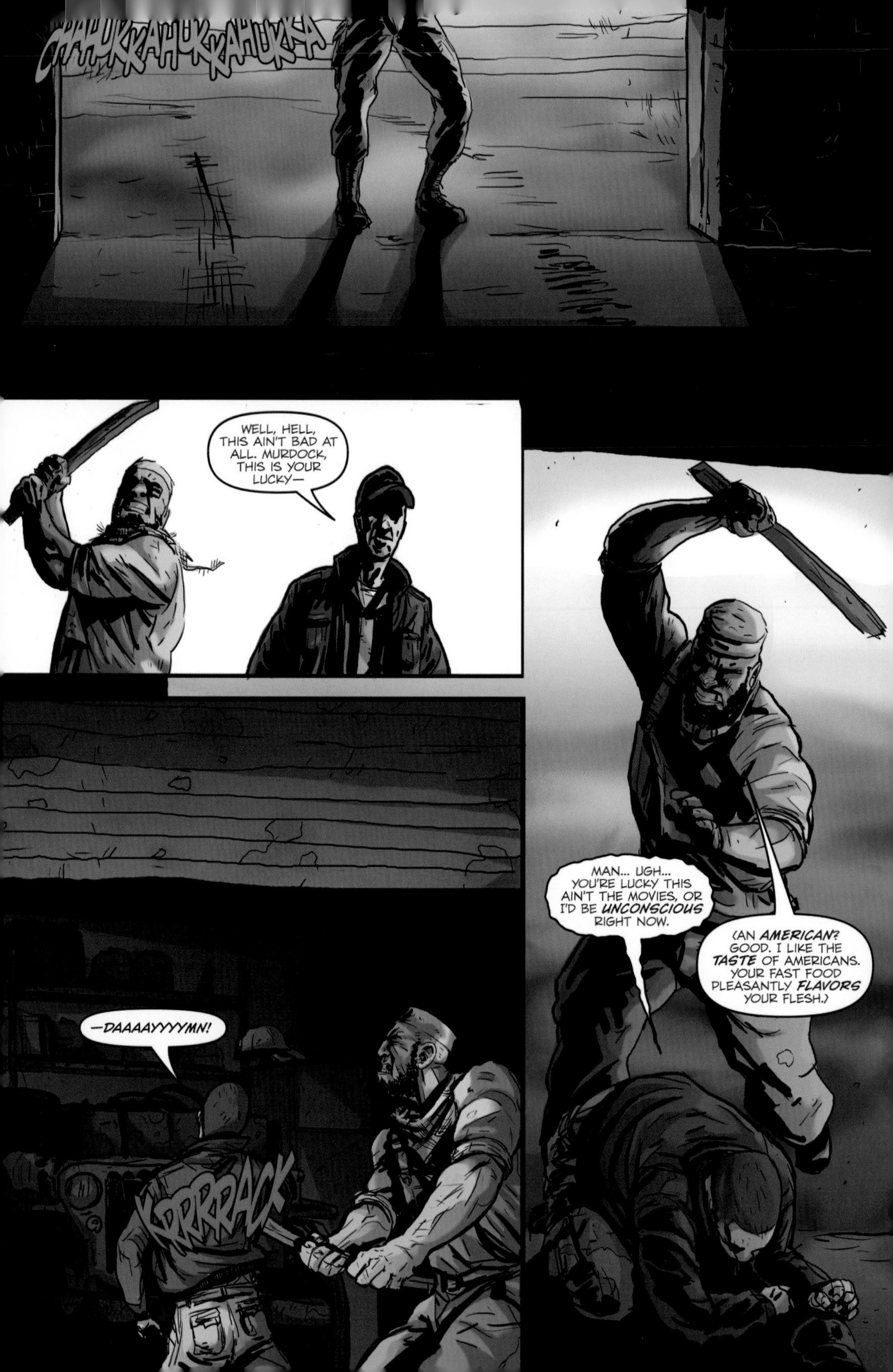
CHAHUKKAHUKKAHUKKA
WELL, HELL, THIS AIN'T BAD AT ALL. MURDOCK, THIS IS YOUR LUCKY—
—DAAAAYYYYMN!
KRRRACK
MAN... UGH... YOU'RE LUCKY THIS AIN'T THE MOVIES, OR I'D BE UNCONSCIOUS RIGHT NOW.
(AN AMERICAN? GOOD. I LIKE THE TASTE OF AMERICANS. YOUR FAST FOOD PLEASANTLY FLAVORS YOUR FLESH.)

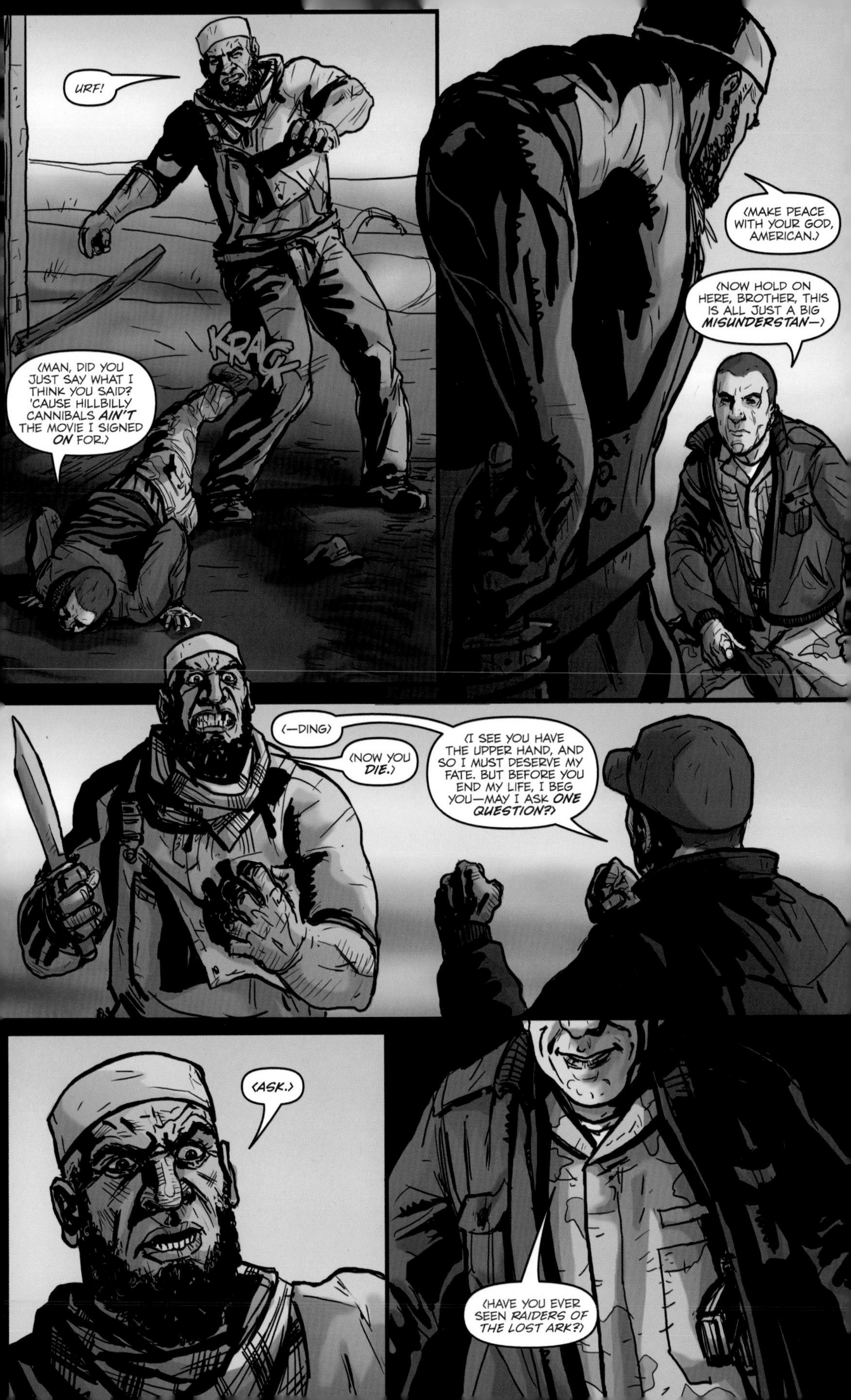
URF!
KRACK
(MAN, DID YOU JUST SAY WHAT I THINK YOU SAID? 'CAUSE HILLBILLY CANNIBALS AIN'T THE MOVIE I SIGNED ON FOR.)
(MAKE PEACE WITH YOUR GOD, AMERICAN.)
(NOW HOLD ON HERE, BROTHER, THIS IS ALL JUST A BIG MISUNDERSTAN—)
(—DING)
(NOW YOU DIE.)
(I SEE YOU HAVE THE UPPER HAND, AND SO I MUST DESERVE MY FATE. BUT BEFORE YOU END MY LIFE, I BEG YOU—MAY I ASK ONE QUESTION?)
(ASK.)
(HAVE YOU EVER SEEN RAIDERS OF THE LOST ARK?)

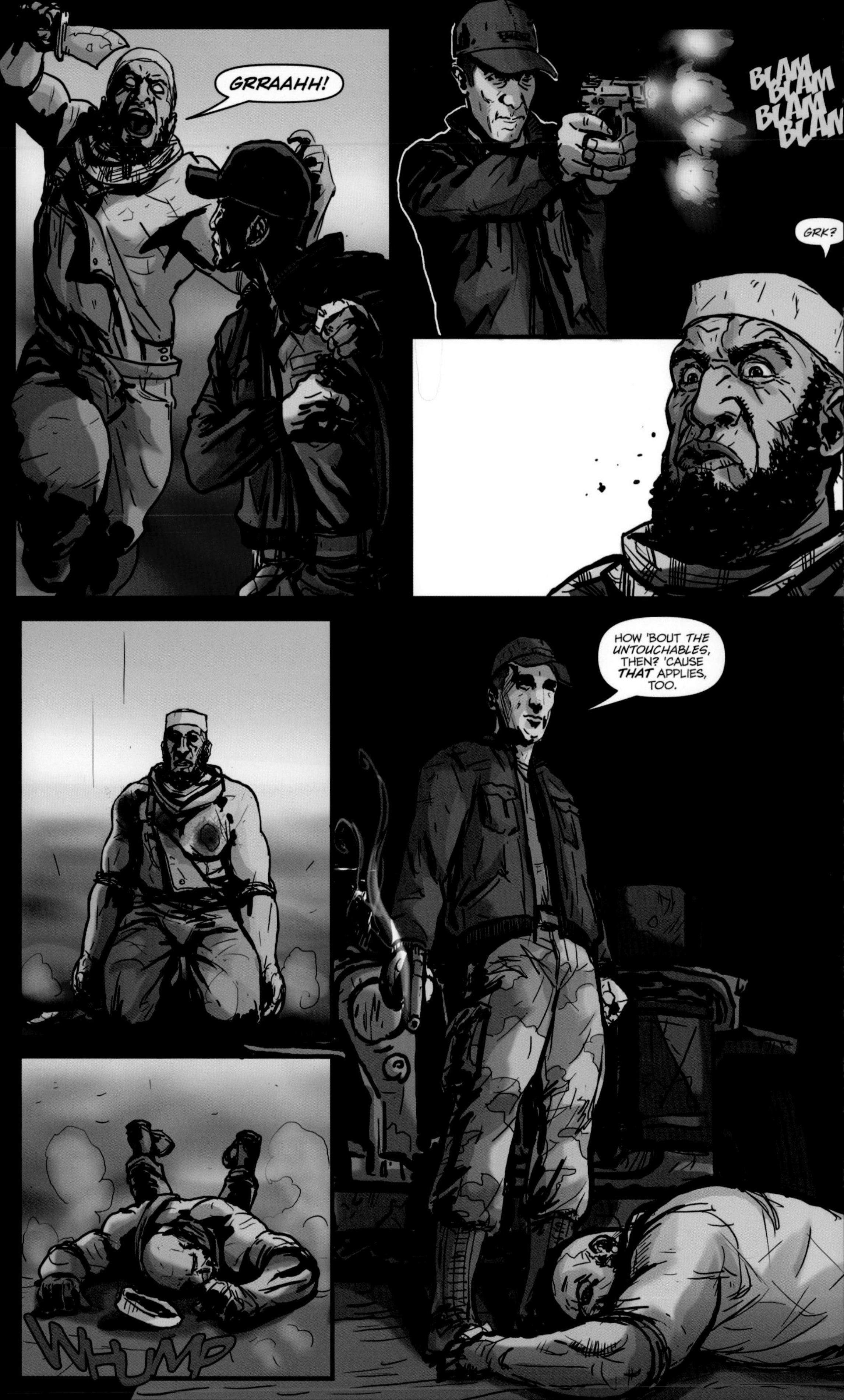
GRRAAHH!
BLAM BLAM BLAM BLAM
GRK?
HOW 'BOUT THE UNTOUCHABLES, THEN? 'CAUSE THAT APPLIES, TOO.
WHUMP

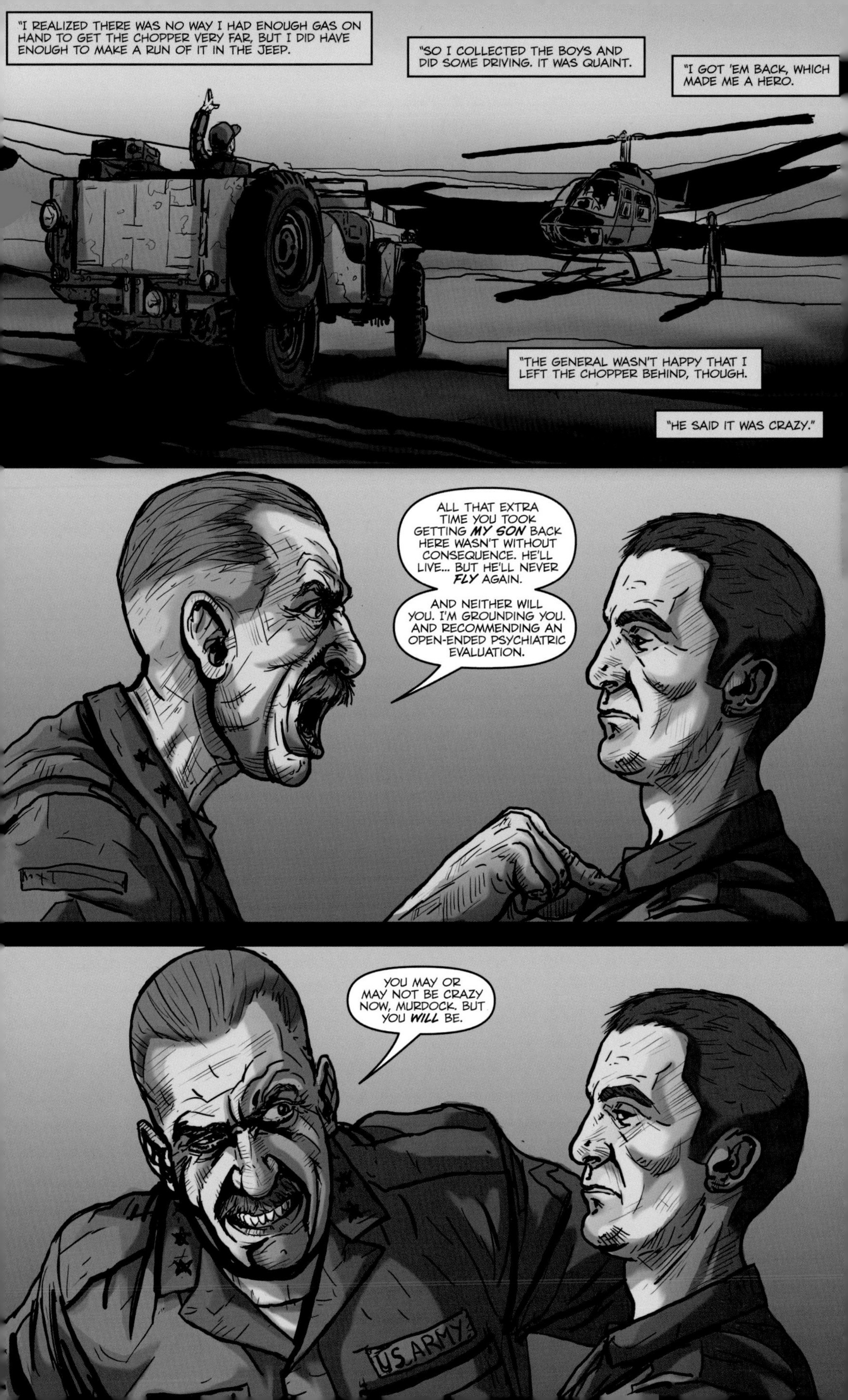
"I REALIZED THERE WAS NO WAY I HAD ENOUGH GAS ON HAND TO GET THE CHOPPER VERY FAR, BUT I DID HAVE ENOUGH TO MAKE A RUN OF IT IN THE JEEP.
"SO I COLLECTED THE BOYS AND DID SOME DRIVING. IT WAS QUAINT.
"I GOT 'EM BACK, WHICH MADE ME A HERO.
"THE GENERAL WASN'T HAPPY THAT I LEFT THE CHOPPER BEHIND, THOUGH.
"HE SAID IT WAS CRAZY."
ALL THAT EXTRA TIME YOU TOOK GETTING ***MY SON*** BACK HERE WASN'T WITHOUT CONSEQUENCE. HE'LL LIVE... BUT HE'LL NEVER ***FLY*** AGAIN.
AND NEITHER WILL YOU. I'M GROUNDING YOU. AND RECOMMENDING AN OPEN-ENDED PSYCHIATRIC EVALUATION.
YOU MAY OR MAY NOT BE CRAZY NOW, MURDOCK. BUT YOU ***WILL*** BE.
U.S. ARMY

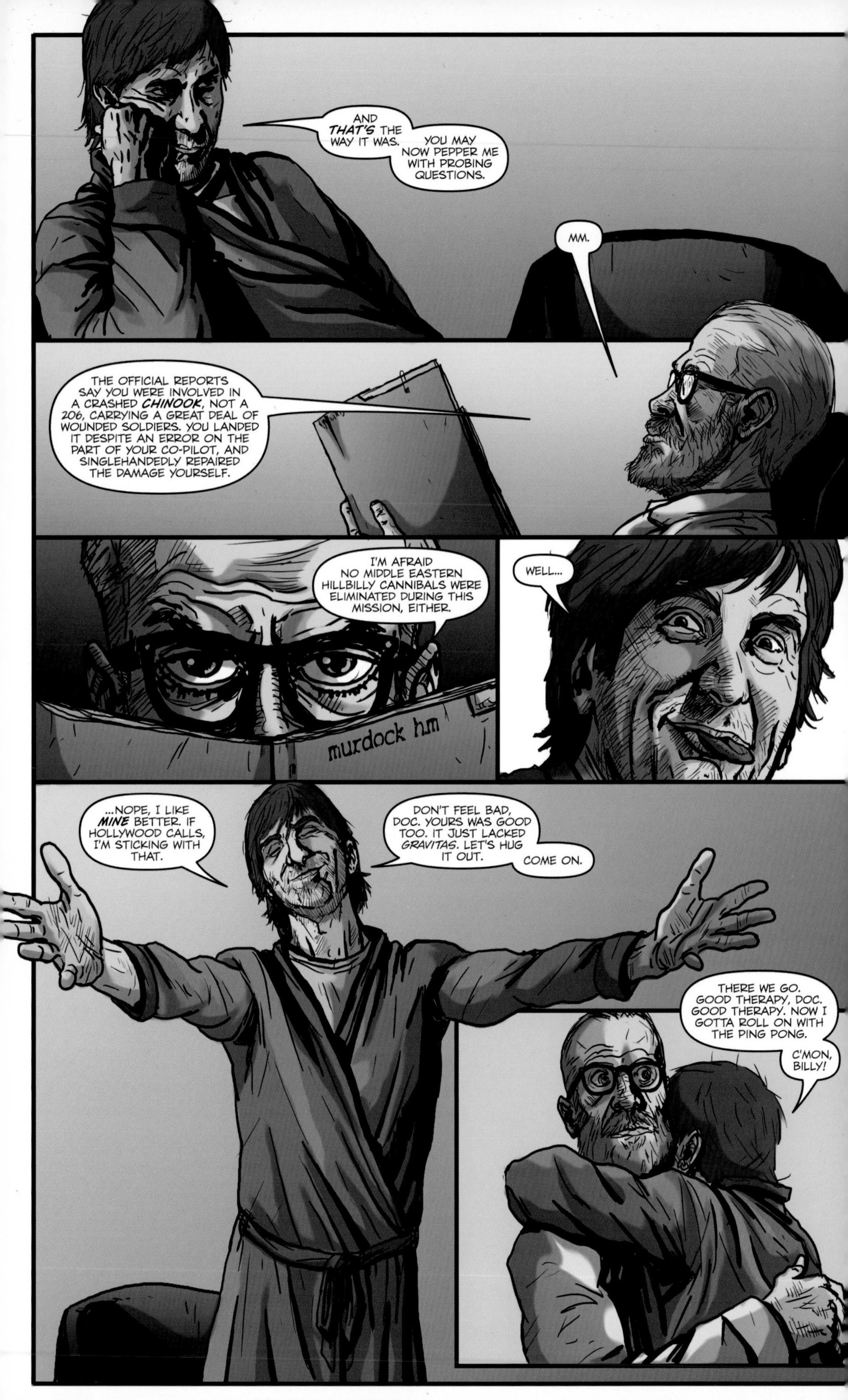

AND THAT'S THE WAY IT WAS.
YOU MAY NOW PEPPER ME WITH PROBING QUESTIONS.
MM.
THE OFFICIAL REPORTS SAY YOU WERE INVOLVED IN A CRASHED CHINOOK, NOT A 206, CARRYING A GREAT DEAL OF WOUNDED SOLDIERS. YOU LANDED IT DESPITE AN ERROR ON THE PART OF YOUR CO-PILOT, AND SINGLEHANDEDLY REPAIRED THE DAMAGE YOURSELF.
I'M AFRAID NO MIDDLE EASTERN HILLBILLY CANNIBALS WERE ELIMINATED DURING THIS MISSION, EITHER.
murdock h.m
WELL...
...NOPE, I LIKE MINE BETTER. IF HOLLYWOOD CALLS, I'M STICKING WITH THAT.
DON'T FEEL BAD, DOC. YOURS WAS GOOD TOO. IT JUST LACKED GRAVITAS. LET'S HUG IT OUT.
COME ON.
THERE WE GO. GOOD THERAPY, DOC. GOOD THERAPY. NOW I GOTTA ROLL ON WITH THE PING PONG.
C'MON, BILLY!

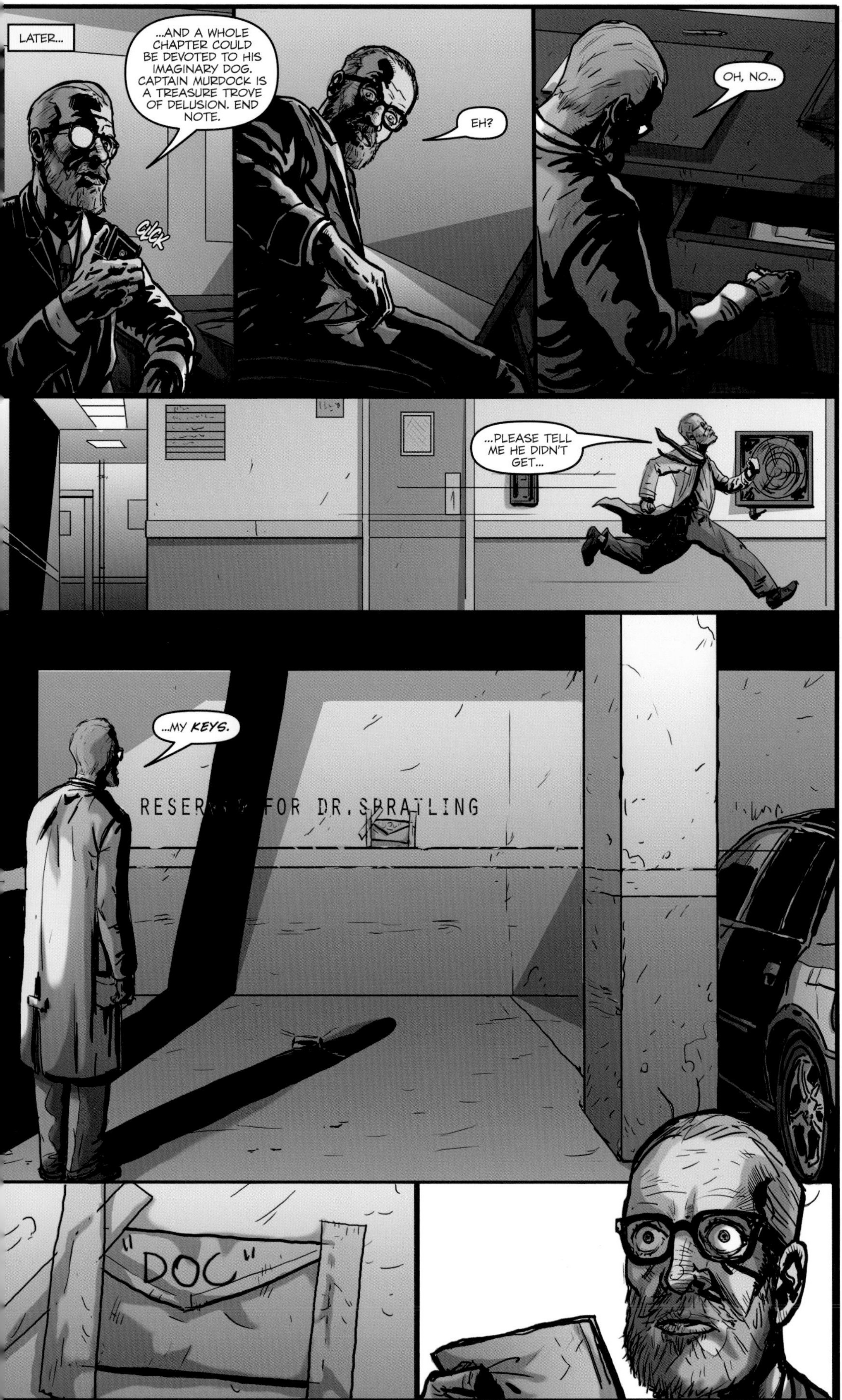
LATER...
...AND A WHOLE CHAPTER COULD BE DEVOTED TO HIS IMAGINARY DOG. CAPTAIN MURDOCK IS A TREASURE TROVE OF DELUSION. END NOTE.
CLICK
EH?
OH, NO...
...PLEASE TELL ME HE DIDN'T GET...
...MY KEYS.
FOR DR. SPRATLING
"DOC"

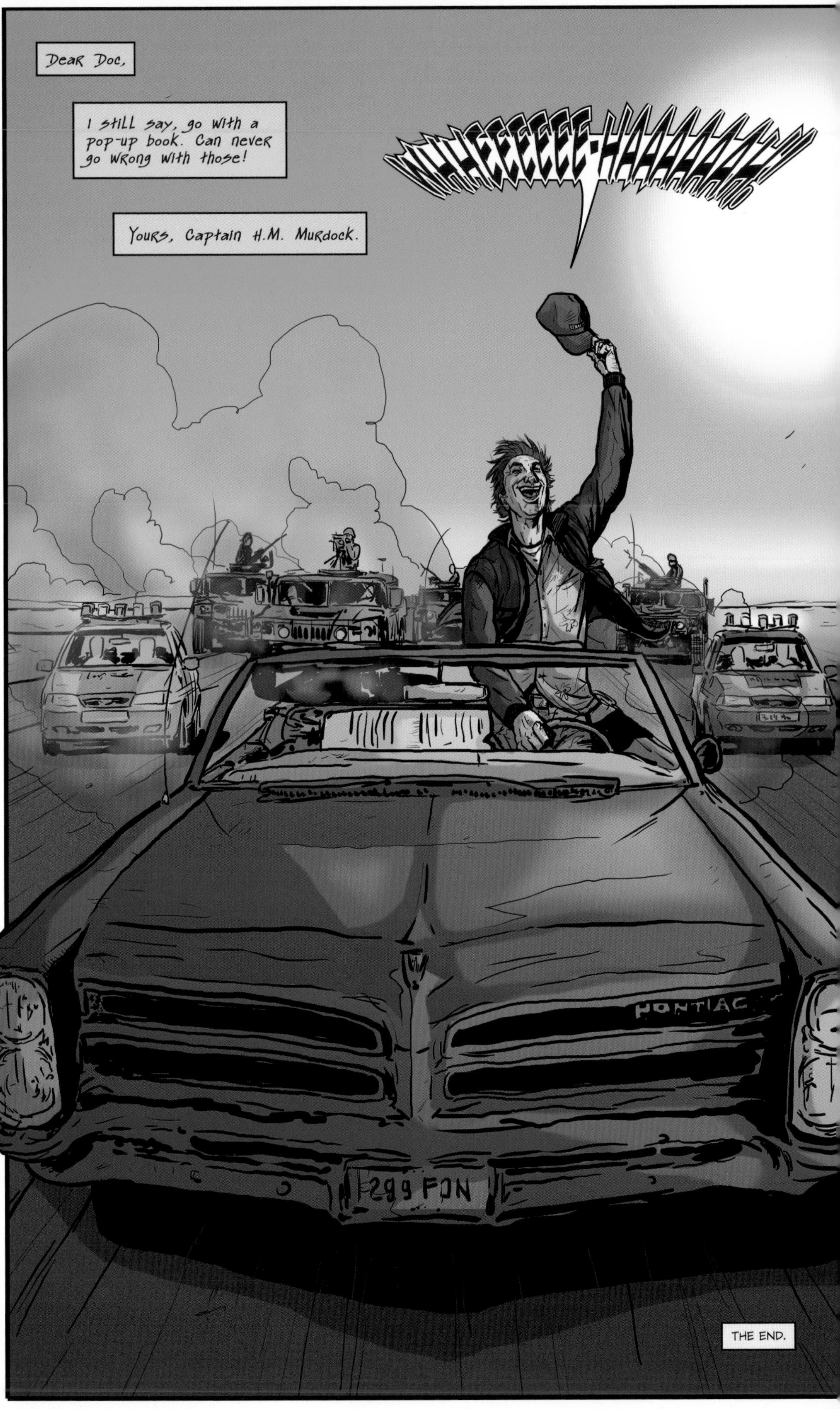

Dear Doc,
I still say, go with a pop-up book. Can never go wrong with those!
Yours, Captain H.M. Murdock.
WHEEEEEEE-HAAAAAAH!!
PONTIAC
299 FDN
THE END.

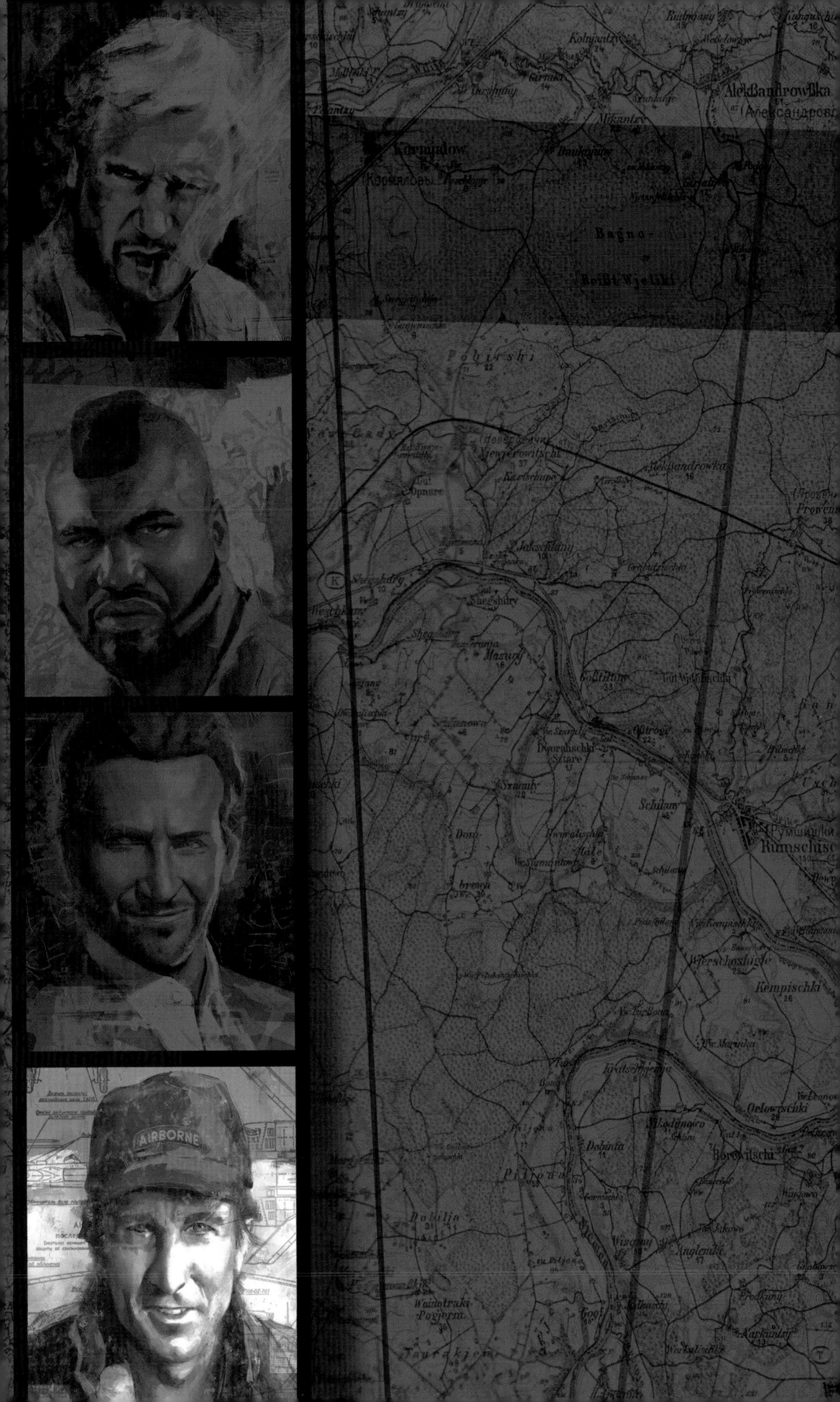
AIRBORNE
Bagno
Kempischki
Orlowischki
Borowitschi
Schilany
Masury
Dobinia

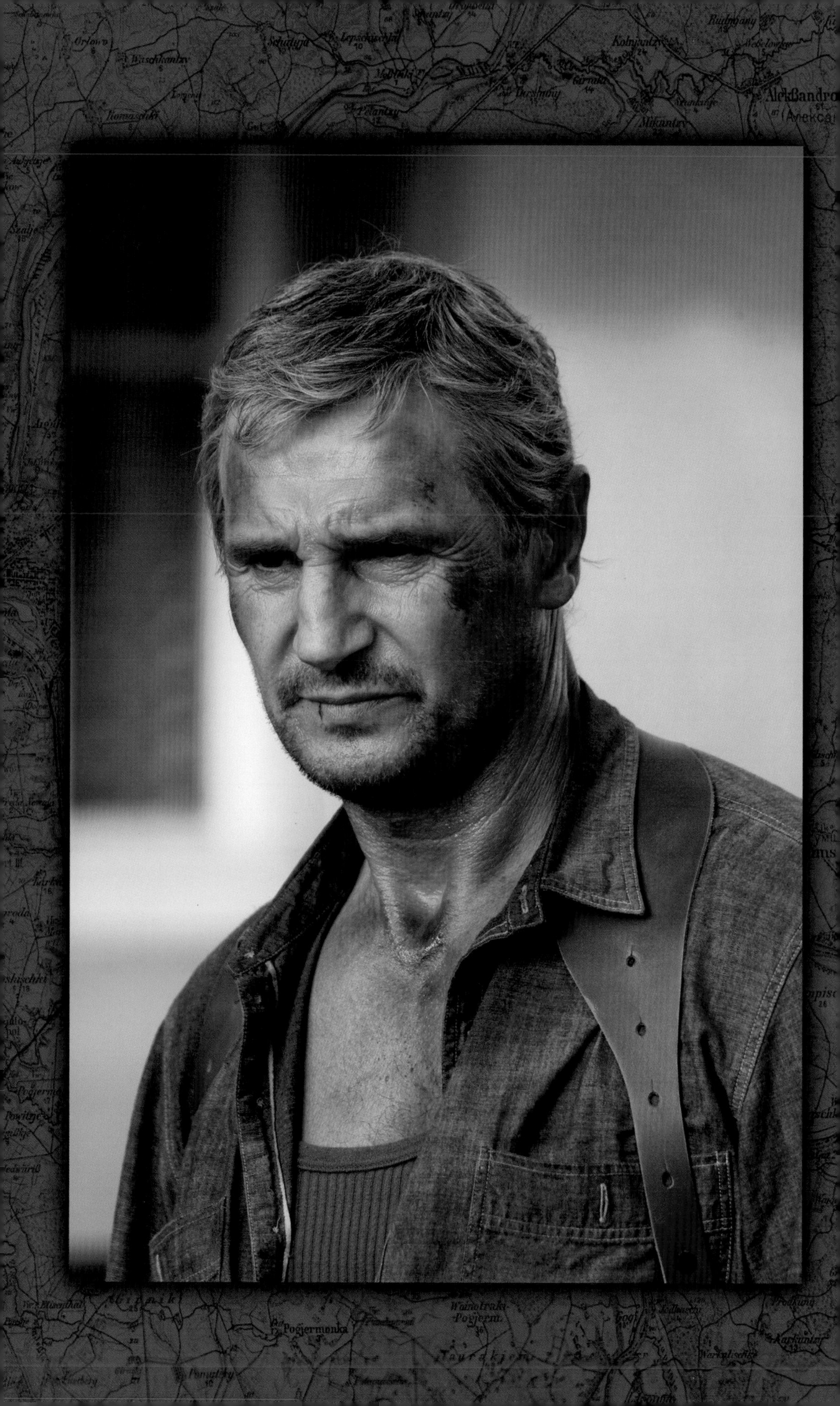

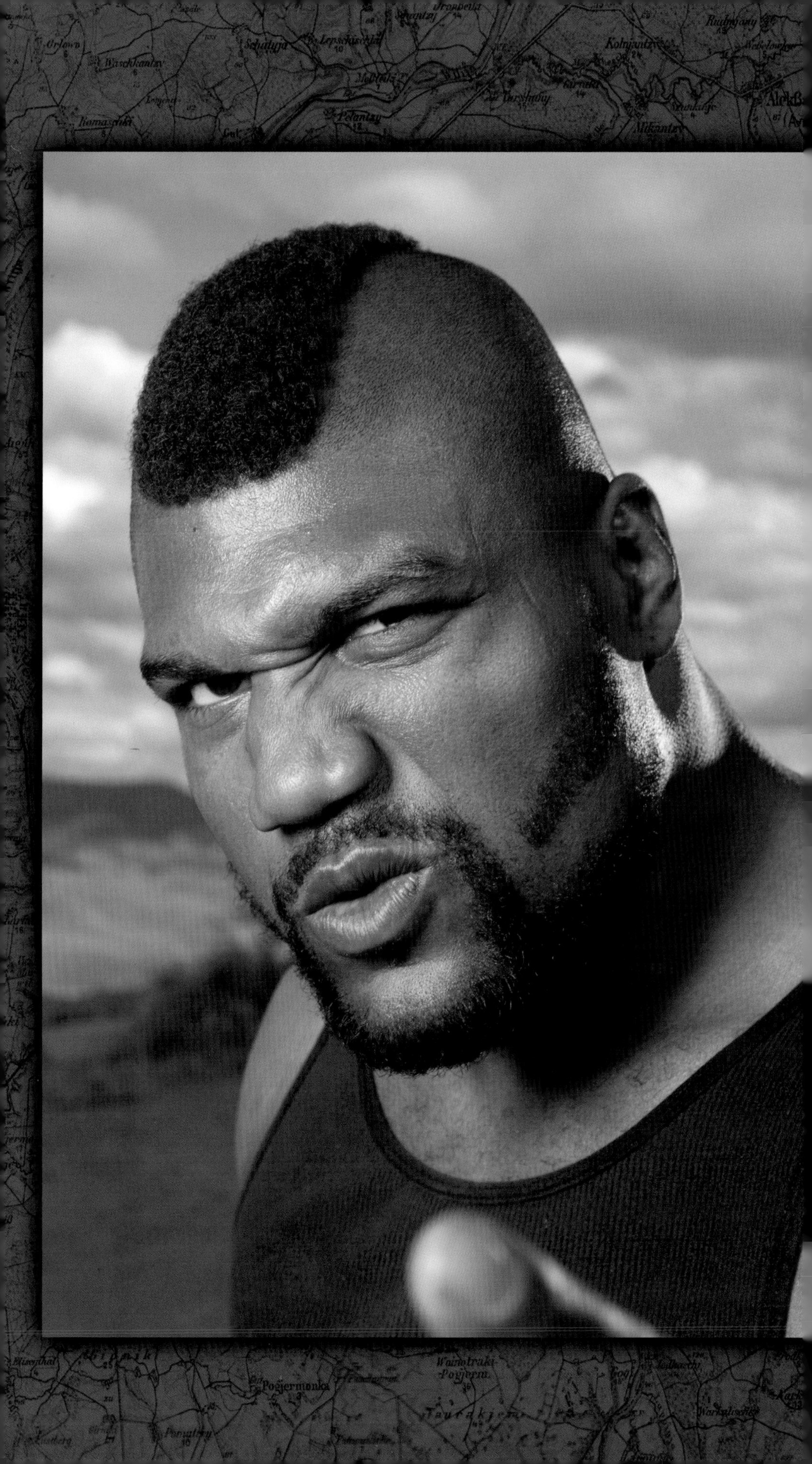

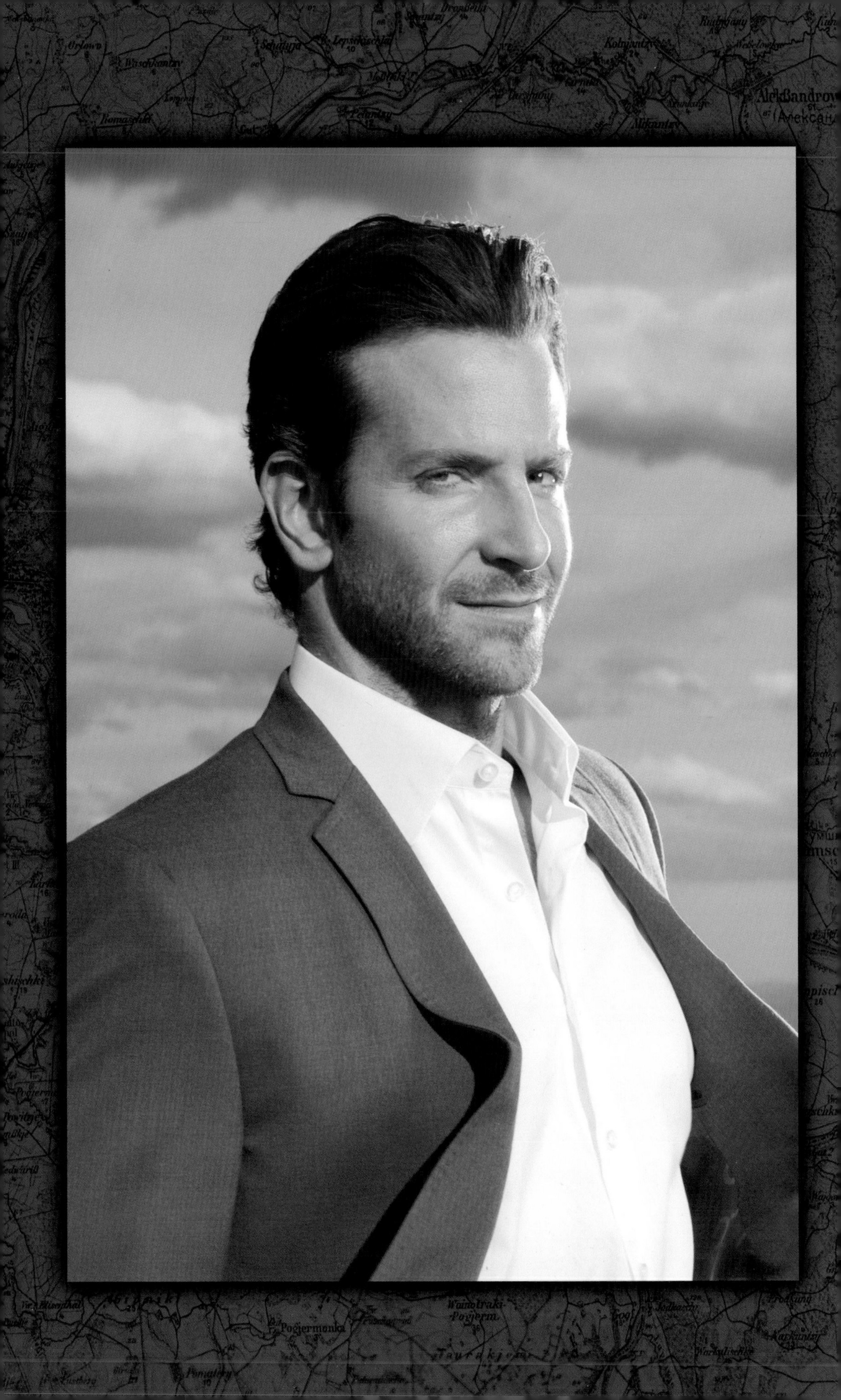

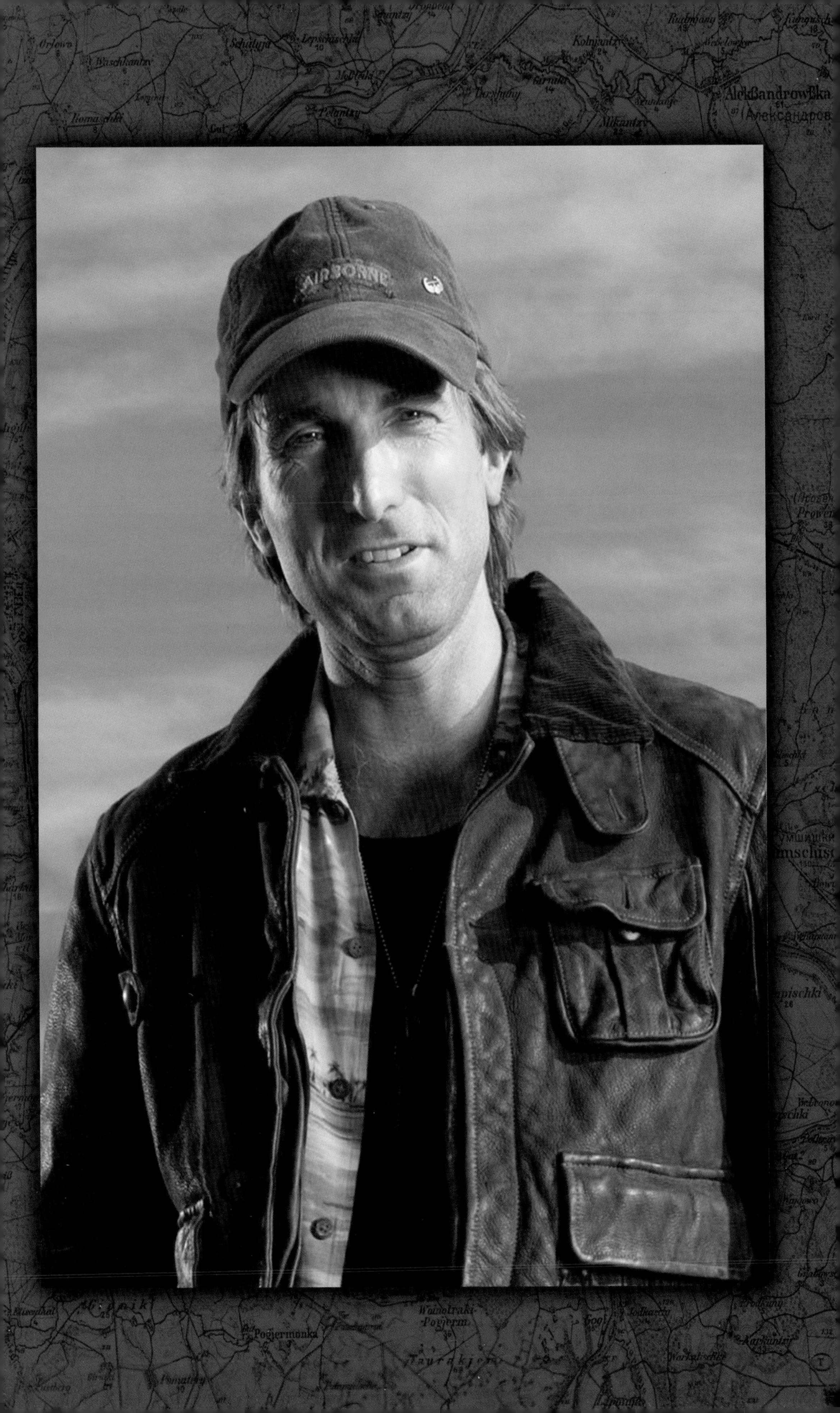
AIRBORNE

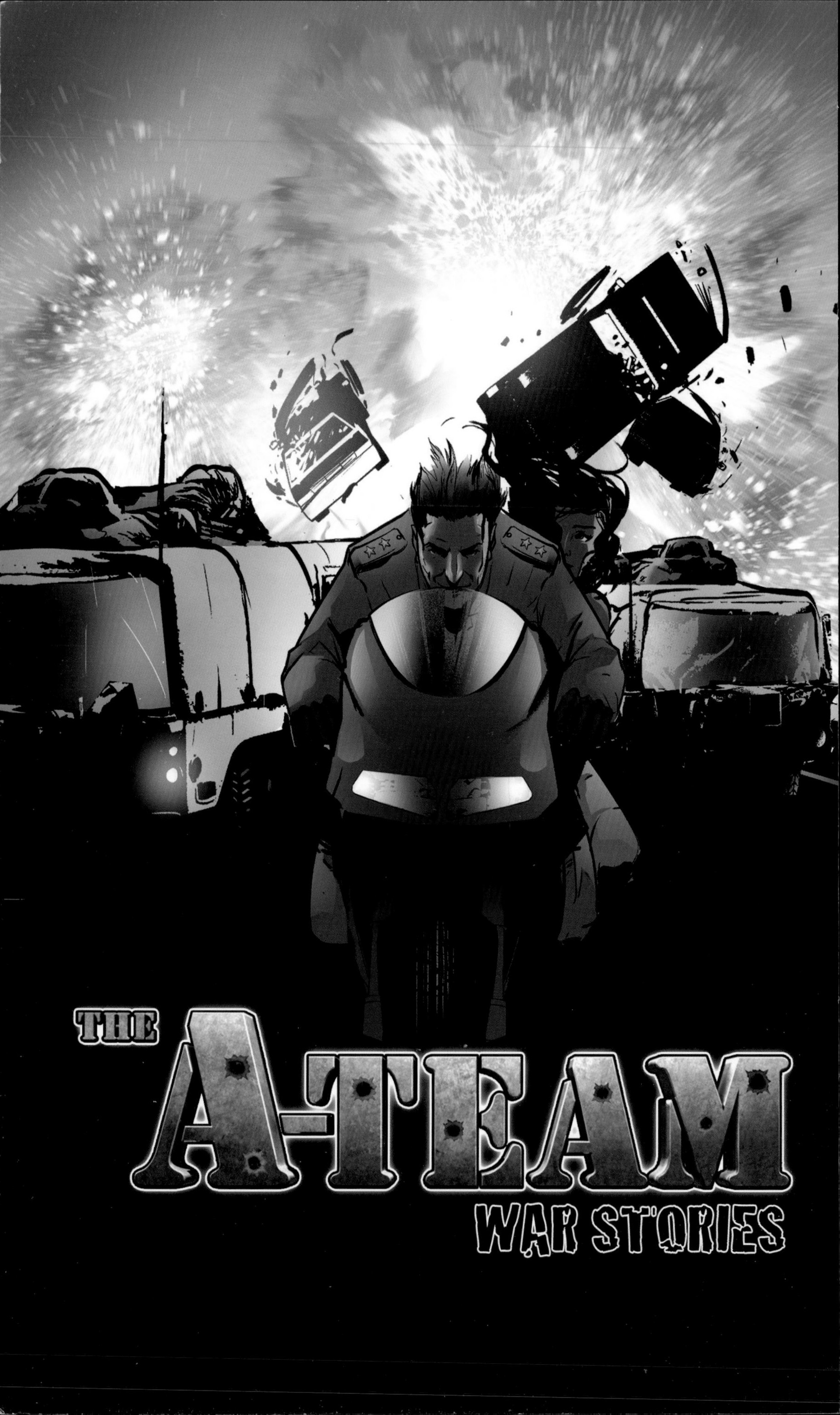
THE
A-TEAM
WAR STORIES